WRITING, PRODUCING, AND SELLING YOUR PLAY

PRENTICE-HALL INTERNATIONAL, INC., London
PRENTICE-HALL OF AUSTRALIA PTY. LIMITED, Sydney
PRENTICE-HALL CANADA INC., Toronto
PRENTICE-HALL OF INDIA PRIVATE LIMITED, New Delhi
PRENTICE-HALL OF JAPAN, INC., Tokyo
PRENTICE-HALL OF SOUTHEAST ASIA PTE. LTD., Singapore
WHITEHALL BOOKS LIMITED, Wellington, New Zealand
EDITORA PRENTICE-HALL DO BRASIL LTDA., Rio de Janeiro

WRITING, PRODUCING AND SELLING YOUR PLAY

Louis E. Catron

A SPECTRUM BOOK

Prentice-Hall, Inc., Englewood Cliffs, New Jersey 07632

Library of Congress Cataloging in Publication Data

Catron, Louis E.
  Writing, producing, and selling your play.

  "A Spectrum Book."
  Includes index.
  1. Playwriting.   I. Title.
PN1661.C37 1984   808.2   83-26923
ISBN 0-13-971995-4
ISBN 0-13-971987-3 (pbk.)

This book is dedicated with
respect and fondness to

Chris Moe, who introduced me and so
many others to the arts and crafts of playwriting . . .

The hundreds of students who made playwriting
classes the bright spots of my week and who
collectively and individually made teaching fun . . .

And most especially to my wife, Joy, for her
inexhaustible patience, warmth, and support.

---

1 2 3 4 5 6 7 8 9 10

ISBN 0-13-971995-4

ISBN 0-13-971987-3 {PBK.}

Editorial/production supervision by William P. O'Hearn
Manufacturing buyer: Pat Mahoney

This book is available at a special discount when ordered in
bulk quantities. Contact Prentice-Hall, Inc., General
Publishing Division, Special Sales, Englewood Cliffs, N.J. 07632.

Contents

Foreword

by Karen Hall

In the five years that I have been a professional writer, I have read approximately three hundred unsolicited manuscripts, most of them plays and television scripts. Of those three hundred, perhaps ten showed the slightest glimmer of potential. Not one was what I would call a good script. Many times, after reading a disappointing script in which some struggling writer had invested a great deal of time and possibly a lifetime of hope, I would think to myself, "If only this person could spend a few years in Lou Catron's playwriting class." I was lucky enough to have had that opportunity, and my own success is based in large part upon that fact. For obvious reasons, I can't write back to every new writer and say, "Please go to William and Mary and enroll in Dr. Catron's playwriting program." I can, and I will, write back to them and say, "Please go and buy a copy of Catron's *Writing, Producing, and Selling Your Play*."

Although this book contains valuable information on how to see a play through to production level, for the purposes of this foreword attention will be focused on the information that the book offers on the actual writing of the play. After all, an in-depth knowledge of how to sell a play isn't going to do the reader any good until he or she has a play to sell. Also, while this book concentrates on playwriting (and is by far the best book I have ever encountered on that subject), I feel it would be inadequate to limit discussion of the book to its purported topic. This is a book that will benefit *anyone* who is or has ever wanted to be a writer of *any* fictional medium. My own experience is a case in point, as I have enjoyed a successful career in television writing that emerged almost entirely from my knowledge of the information the reader will find in this book.

My position gives me the dubious privilege of watching fledgling writers make a wide variety of mistakes. The people who call themselves writers divide themselves into several categories, depending on the mistakes they happen to make. The first and most heavily populated group is composed of people who often refer to themselves as "potential writers." They file ideas on shelves and daydream at great length about the plays and novels that they are going to write as soon as they have the time, the energy, the inclination, or a word processor. They corner professional writers at cocktail parties and bore them for hours on end with stories of the Great American Whatever that they will someday write. These people expend a considerable amount of energy in the pursuit of a writing career. The problem is that they never *write*. As Eudora Welty once phrased it, "There is no such thing as a potential writer." A writer writes, and a writer writes because he or she cannot keep from writing. Read what Catron says about "wanting to *be* a writer" versus "wanting to write."

None of which is to say that a "potential writer" cannot become a "writer." I believe that the reason these people do not write has to do with little other than the fear that the thought of writing inspires in them. There are very few serious writers who do not experience this fear, and I do not know a single professional writer who does not grapple with it daily. The difference between a "potential writer" and a "writer" is that the latter has learned to overcome this fear.

Writing, Producing, and Selling Your Play will go a long way toward helping these people to break through the fear barriers. Catron manages to accomplish the massive task of breaking the intimidating art of playwriting down into component parts that can be readily grasped by the reader. The exercises at the end of each chapter will be of particular benefit to "potential writers." While they may find themselves chocked with fear at the thought of tackling a play, they will probably be less intimidated by the thought of writing a few pages of dialogue or character analysis. If they then follow the exercises step by step, they will find themselves well on the way to having *written*, rather than having *wanted to write*.

The second category of writers is very different from the "potential writers." These people write constantly and can back their aspirations with closets full of short stories, plays, or television scripts. Unfortunately for them, quantity does not compensate for poor quality, and the latter is almost always the case with these writers. The problem is that these people confuse the *mechanics* of writing with the *art* of writing. Most people learn how to write—how to form letters, words, and sentences—at an early age. As time goes on, what they fail to realize is that the fact that one is able to fill up a page does not mean that one is a writer.

I received a phone call one day from a psychologist who had decided to try his hand at writing scripts and wanted my advice as to how he should proceed. I started to rattle off books he should read and then suggested that he check into playwriting courses at area colleges. There followed a moment of silence, after which he stammered, "You mean I'll have to study to be able to do this?" I wondered how he would have felt had I called him seeking advice on breaking into the field of psychology and asked him the same question. Likewise, few people would think of climbing into the cockpit of a 747 and attempting to fly it across the country, yet they think nothing of writing a script without knowing the first thing about how to do it.

The first step in helping these people to overcome their problem is to make them realize how very much there is to learn about the craft of writing. This book will make them aware of aspects they may have never dreamed existed, such as how to write dialogue (so that it doesn't sound like two people on a party line), how to create characters who have depth and dimension, and, most importantly, how to structure a story. No amount of natural talent can make up for not knowing how to do these things.

The third category of writers is the group I feel will benefit most from this book. These people understand the craft of writing. They can push all the right buttons. To look at their work, it is difficult to tell what is wrong. Still, something is missing. These writers are not *grounded.* They cannot isolate (and, therefore, cannot communicate) what it is that they want to say. These writers desperately need to read Catron's chapter on the Credo.

I spent three years in Catron's classes, ignoring his advice on writing a Credo. His insistence upon the Credo seemed like a waste of time, and I was more intent on writing the Great American Play. While I accumulated a lot of valuable knowledge during those years, I never came within a hundred miles of writing the Great American anything. I graduated, and although I found work as a professional writer almost immediately, I could not shake the feeling that something was blocking me—that I could be doing work of far greater quality, if only I could find the key. Then came a three-month WGA (Writers Guild of America) strike. Finding myself with nothing better to do, I finally sat down and wrote the dreaded Credo. I can honestly say that the experience made a drastic and permanent change in the quality of my writing. For the first time in my life, I realized that I did indeed have a foundation from which to write. I realized that my love for John Steinbeck's novels, Bruce Springsteen's albums, and Ansel Adams' photography were deeply connected, and that every opinion I held could be traced to my feelings on a couple of key issues. From all of this, I realized what it was that I wanted to write about, and all the floundering that I had sensed for years found direction and focus. The truth is that everyone possesses such a foundation, but understanding and being able to utilize it does not come easily. I feel confident that anyone who writes an honest and detailed Credo, as Catron suggests, will find that foundation. If the reader takes from this book nothing other than the importance of starting with a Credo, he or she will have acquired something of infinite value.

The final category of writers are those who give the craft the dedication it both requires and deserves. They take the time to learn, they write, and they search their souls to discover what it is that they want to tell the world through their writing. These people become professional writers. I can speak from experience in saying that even professional writers get weary and uninspired, and for them this book will serve as a refresher course for years to come. A writer needs to know not only where to start, but also where to go from there. It is a question that any serious writer can never stop asking. This book not only blazes a trail, it also puts up road signs that, if followed, will bring the traveler closer and closer to the goal: a knowledge of writing that is as deep and as complex as the art itself.

Shortly after graduation from the College of William and Mary, Karen Hall began a television writing career that took her as story editor to Eight Is Enough *and then to* M*A*S*H; *at the time of this writing, she is executive story editor of* Hill Street Blues. *She has been nominated for two Emmy Awards.*

Preface:
You Can Learn
Quality Playwriting

The basic premise of this book can be stated simply: *You can learn to write a stageworthy play, regardless of your previous writing experience or knowledge. If you now are writing plays, you can learn to improve the quality of your work.*

In this book you will find details of play construction. Guidelines will help you work through the writing process, from original idea to final revision and into production. Concrete examples illustrate concepts. Whether you are writer, actor, director, or audience member wishing to understand more clearly what makes a play work, the following chapters will give you insight into the pieces that form the structure of drama.

You find here no promise that quality playwriting is easily accomplished. And certainly you should not expect overnight success. Playwriting demands dedicated apprenticeship and disciplined effort. You will find a number of concrete steps designed to lead you toward the creation of a play that will give you justifiable pride in your accomplishment.

A second premise governs this book: *Plays are constructed.* Throughout the chapters you will notice emphasis on *structure*. A playwright builds a play, an imaginative process remarkably similar to the physical construction of a home or skyscraper. There must be a master plan—a scenario for the writer, a blueprint for the architect—and a foundation strong enough to hold all that will be placed on its top. The pieces of the play are crafted together as are the joists and beams of the home. Just as there can be a variety of homes—ranch, split level, colonial, brick, wood—so also are there many play styles. The freedom of choice is exciting. Regardless of the play's style, however, it must be well constructed. *The playwright is a craftsman as well as an artist.*

I do not expect everyone to agree with all the stands I take in this book. Indeed, there may be materials here that will provoke sharp disagreements leading to enlightened new perceptions.

Acknowledgment is made to the following for the granting of permission to reprint passages from their publications:

The quotation on page 69 is from Anton Chekhov's *The Cherry Orchard*, translated by Constant Garrett. Used by permission of Simon and Schuster.

The quotation on page 71 is taken from *A Raisin in the Sun*, by Lorraine Hansberry. Copyright © 1958, 1959 by Robert Nemiroff as executor of the estate of Lorraine Hansberry. Reprinted by permission of Random House, Inc.

The passages that appear on pages 134 through 149 are from *The Desperate Hours* by Joseph Hayes. Copyright © 1955 by Joseph Hayes. Reprinted by permission of Random House, Inc.

The excerpts from *The Glass Menagerie*, by Tennessee Williams, that appear on pages 178, 210–211, 214, and 216 are reprinted with the permission of Random House, Inc., and International Creative Management.

The quotation on page 198 is taken from *Winterset*, by Maxwell Anderson. It is used by permission of Anderson House Publishers. This play is fully copyrighted. All rights reserved.

The passages that appear on pages 199 and 200 are from *Cyrano de Bergerac*, by Edmond Rostand. Translated by Brain Hooker. Copyright © 1923 by Henry Holt and Co.; copyright © 1951 by Doris C. Hooker. Reprinted by permission of Holt, Rinehart and Winston, CBS College Publishing.

The lines from *Marty*, by Paddy Chayefsky, that appear on pages 201 through 203 are used by permission of Simon and Schuster.

The excerpts from *Who's Afraid of Virginia Woolf*, by Edward Albee, that appear on pages 204 through 206 are reprinted by permission of Atheneum Publishers and the William Morris Agency. Copyright © 1962 by Edward Albee.

The quotation on pages 207 and 208 is taken from *The Bald Soprano*, by Eugene Ionesco. Translated by Donald M. Allen. Used by permission of Grove Press.

The lines from the *Dumb Waiter*, by Harold Pinter, that appear on pages 208 and 209 are used by permission of Grove Press.

The quotation from *Ghosts*, by Henrik Ibsen, that appears on page 213 is reprinted from *Six Plays*, by Henrik Ibsen. Translated by Eva Le Gallienne. Copyright © 1951 by Eva Le Gallienne. Used by permission of Random House, Inc.

The excerpt from *The Iceman Cometh*, by Eugene O'Neill, that appears on page 215 is used by permission of Random House, Inc. Copyright © 1946 by Eugene O'Neill.

*We write because we have to say
what we believe.*

*We discover what we believe
because we write.*

*All else of writing is but a searching
for a form, a style, a technique, to show those
beliefs in an acceptable artistic manner. When
we succeed, our hearts are on the stage to touch
the hearts and minds of the audiences. It is
an awesome process.*

Introduction:
This Book's "Audiences"

In a sense, there are several hundred coauthors of the chapters in this book. I owe much to the students who have taken my playwriting courses, to my colleagues who teach playwriting and fiction writing, to the professional writers who have given so freely of their time and talents toward helping their colleagues, and to the performers who have worked with me in over a hundred plays. It is appropriate here to describe briefly those various contributions that together create audiences for whom this book is designed.

First. Pieces of many chapters originated as handouts for playwriting classes and for participants in writing workshops. The handouts were modified in response to writers' comments. *This book therefore speaks from a quantity of experience to beginning and advanced playwrights, amateur or professional.*

Second. All of us who are continual students of theatre can discover a great deal about the essences of drama from productions of original plays. One quickly sees how the construction devices fit into the whole and how a play's structure can be improved and its meaning therefore enhanced. Original productions can also show us the importance of clear communication from author to audience, the need for a recognizable sharp beginning of the plot (the "point of attack") relatively early in the play, character dimensions, plot movement, proper revision techniques, and effective working relationships between playwright and director. Contributing directly to this book are hundreds of new plays I have overseen as they have been put into production. Working with new plays is amazingly educational as well as theatrically exciting. *This manual uses a large amount of production experience with new plays to emphasize the importance of writing stageworthy scripts that directors and performers can bring to life in an artistic communication to the audience.*

Third. Playwrights will learn theory from practical writing experience, but the reverse does not hold true: One cannot learn how to write a play, nor how to improve one's writing Quality, from studies of theory. Of even less value are the convoluted theories that pour unabated from people who have neither written plays nor participated in production of original scripts. The working playwright demands less theory and more details and specifics. *This book's overall approach therefore has a distinctly pragmatic tone, and discussions of abstract theory have been minimized to the extent possible.* The book has a "how to" thrust that students so often have demanded.

Fourth. Over the years a number of poets and novelists have gravitated to the playwriting courses. As a result, new ingredients have been added to help the fiction writer better understand the significant differences between writing fiction and writing for the stage. *This book addresses people with little practical experience in theatre as well as those with more detailed knowledge.*

Fifth. Adult education programs bring older writers into playwriting classes, and special workshops take playwriting to people with incomplete education. Often playwriting begins with explosive talents in high schools. Work with all groups shows it is possible to design effective playwriting approaches for people in many different environments and age groups. *This book reflects that broad definition of "the playwright," and it is designed for those not enrolled in writing classes as well as for those who take playwriting courses within an educational system or privately.* Whether it is learned in a class or alone, playwriting is a solitary, do-it-yourself activity; equally, *this book addresses those who use it in connection with a class or as a home study guide.*

Sixth. Many difficulties face playwrights and directors as they work together toward a production. Misunderstandings are all too possible, and in the highly-charged emotional atmosphere of rehearsals the misunderstandings can become fatal to the production. The playwright needs to know how to revise for production during rehearsals. Guidelines for working with directors and performers are necessary. *This book addresses the playwright who will have a nonprofessional theatrical production. There will be suggestions regarding revising the play during rehearsals.*

Seventh. Taking one's work seriously does not demand that one must take oneself seriously. Playwriting should be fun. If it is approached with an optimistic attitude, it can be. Laughter is a vital part of the creative process, and the ability to laugh at one's mistakes will help the writer come back from the inevitable downturns which are a normal part of writing.

Attitude is important. The playwright ought to experience the heady excitement of the downhill skier, the grace of the balloonist, the oneness with nature of the sailor. In playwriting lies the opportunity to sit at the desk, quite alone, while at the same time filling the room with people of your own creation.

They can be drawn from memory or totally imaginary. They can be full of happiness or despair. They may be in love with life or grimly destructive, winners or losers, people you like or people you want to change. Your room sparks with their lives. You select, shape, interpret, and arrange the lives of your characters.

When the script is finished, it goes into the hands of vitally alive and talented performers who will give freely of their talents in order to bring the play to life. When it is performed, hundreds of people will sit in one auditorium, pulled to the stimuli you created and concentrating their energies as if hypnotized. All of the combined focus comes to a point on the stage where your creation lives. You are reaching out to touch the hearts and souls and minds of those members of the audience.

What other creative activity can offer you so much? It is a rare event, flowing with the magic of creation. *Playwriting is exciting and fun as long as the playwright seeks to create Quality. The achievement of Quality is in itself a more than adequate reward.*

The Maker
of Plays

Defining the Self

The writer's definition of the self will dictate the results of the work; as the writer develops a feeling of himself or herself, so will the written work be created. There are two views of the writer's self. One has to do with the writer's concept of *what a writer does and what a playwright actually is.* We discuss that in Part One. You will conclude with an awareness of why the playwright is "a maker of plays." The other view of the writer's self focuses upon *what the writer feels and what his or her personal beliefs and ideals are.* We will discuss that later in Chapter 4, "The Credo."

Chapter One

Why Playwriting?

Why do you want to study playwriting?

Reasons for wanting to be a playwright abound. For each individual, there is a private motivation. There are those of a literary bent, who have a deep respect for writers. They seek to become part of that elite society, that world where people talk of literature and create works for others to discuss.

Some persons who enter playwriting have already tried poetry or fiction. They hope that playwriting will be a more effective medium to express concepts about the world, that it will be easier because of their previous writing experiences. Playwriting, they hope, will in turn increase their ability to write poems and novels.

Many enter playwriting because they have an ability to see and hear characters in action and they want to bring them to life, much as a sculptor envisions a shape hidden inside a block of stone and works to let that shape fly free. In both cases a mental image begins the creative process, and technique will bring the image to final form.

There are those who enter playwriting because they are loners, people who are shy or awkward in social situations. For them, playwriting is a way to bring humans together in a world that they can control. The solitary writing hours are a natural way of life; being alone is, for such people, a necessary recharging of internal batteries.

Others, the romantics, have already practiced their acceptance speeches. They have spent hours preparing to stand on the stage to acknowledge the cheers of the crowd. If asked, they will admit that the odds of succeeding in playwriting may be discouraging, but there is always that conviction that the odds apply only to other people—"Someone has to succeed, so why can't that be me?"

The mercenaries have heard of the huge amounts of money paid for Broadway hits. They know enough about screenwriting and television writing to realize that residuals accumulate and that the successful writers need good tax lawyers. For them, the road to riches comes from playwriting.

Frequently, the beginning playwright's previous theatrical experience will prompt a desire to write for the stage. Performers and directors, in particular, are well aware that the art of the playwright is the fountainhead for all theatre. Without the playwright, there can be no theatre.

Playwrights often are the people who like to entertain others. One finds them at the campfire telling ghost stories to young campers and bringing a delicious sense of fear to the audience. They are the writers who need to make people laugh and cry.

Some persons who enter playwriting are aware of the impact the playwright has upon society. Plays are often intellectual challenges, asking questions about our relationships: with other humans, with other countries, with the gods, and with fate. Some plays have sought to correct society with laughter; others have been frankly didactic. Others pose questions but leave answers for the audience. For the writer with a social awareness, playwriting offers many opportunities to communicate with the group.

All playwrights are motivated by a pure desire to create, to give of themselves in the construction of a new entity that did not exist before they gave it form and breath. The playwright finishes a play with a deep sense of achievement and justifiable pride in the accomplishment. Even if no one knows of that accomplishment, it will provide enough satisfaction by just having been written.

To explain his reasons for wanting to write plays, one former student returned years after he had graduated from our playwriting classes. He sat in with the new writers and told them of an Emerson quotation that guided him: "The ax is always cutting down the forest. Thank God it can't cut down the clouds."

The writer told the beginning playwrights that he had found too many fallen "trees"; everywhere he went he seemed to see a person cutting off the possibilities of a richer life, much as a guard with an ax would cut off the slightest sprig wherever it might attempt to grow. Playwriting gave him a feeling of being able to escape to the free clouds.

Whatever brings you to want to write plays, let us hope that your motivations are strong. You face frustrations and difficulties. Playwriting is not learned quickly. Often you will feel that your new play is worse than all the ones that you wrote when learning. Playwriting is not learned easily. The art and craft of writing is full of mysteries. You must be strongly motivated to persevere.

The complexities of playwriting are well known. Many writers think of playwriting as the most difficult type of writing. Thornton Wilder, author of novels such as *The Bridge of San Luis Rey* and plays such as *Our Town* and *The Skin of Our Teeth,* has said he found playwriting significantly more difficult than writing novels, and James Kirkwood, author of *A Chorus Line, P.S. Your Cat is Dead,* and *There Must Be a Pony,* has reported the same thing.

If you genuinely wish to become a playwright, you will need the self-discipline of the person training for the Olympics. The playwright must match the dedication of the weight lifter and the cross-country runner who believe in "no pain, no gain." The playwright, like the long-distance runner, must find a number of breakthroughs to new plateaus through discipline; the "second wind" the runner experiences will also come to the playwright who works daily to improve ability.

The discipline of the writer is difficult to learn because it is a solitary art; in contrast, those who work within a group may derive comfort and encouragement from the group. In theatre, for example, rehearsals build morale for all participants. If one person is mentally or emotionally unenthusiastic about the task, the spirit of the group will bring that individual into higher accomplishments through a more positive outlook. The playwright, on the other hand, may feel left out and alone when writing; there is no group support. Thus, a writing class may often be valuable for the writer's emotional needs.

Sometimes playwrights may feel that the writing process is just too demanding. Often frustrations accumulate, and there is a severe test of faith. At such times, the playwright needs to remember that at the end of the process may come *production,* a heady wine that enriches the spirit and soul. The playwright may then pity fellow writers because the novelist and the poet will never have that rich experience. When you have your first production, and your fiftieth, you will be storing golden pieces in your memory to sustain you for long periods thereafter. For many playwrights, the answer to "Why should I bother with playwriting?" is "For the excitement of public production." To sit in the midst of that psychic energy focused upon the stage is awesome. "Those are my words, my people up there," the playwright thinks. "I'm watching these audience members laugh or cry, think or rebel, because of something I created."

Why do you want to write plays?

One hopes it is because you have *emotions* you need to express, *ideas* you are driving to present, and *actions* you know are meaningful expressions of aspects of humanity. You want to *entertain,* in the largest sense of that word.

What follows are discussions of ways to set your ideas into a form, methodologies of writing, suggestions about appropriate approaches to writing, and opinionated views about the nature of drama. My goal here is to help you experience the remarkable freedom of being up in the clouds, away from that ax that haunts so much of our day-to-day existence.

Chapter Two

Prelude
to Playwriting

Wanting to Be a Writer
and Wanting to Write

The beginning playwright must sooner or later make the transition from "wanting to be a writer" to "wanting to write." The difference is significant. In the writer's life the transition ranks in importance with the change from childhood to one's full maturity.

"Wanting to be a writer" evokes romantic images of the slim writer oh-so-palely languishing at a Queen Anne desk on which sits a crystal vase containing a solitary, but of course perfect, fresh white rose. Or perhaps the image is of a dark room with a single harsh light over a messy desk on which is an overflowing ash tray in which a number of cigarettes still burn, next to an unkempt and stringy-haired soul who squints through the smoke at an antique Remington while sipping cold coffee or warm gin. Either way, "wanting to be a writer" involves much waiting for The Visit From The Muse. If nothing gets written, who is to blame? The Muse, of course. There are many sighs. It is all very much like a 1930s movie.

"Wanting to write," in contrast, is hard-nosed and serious work. One *writes*, not languishes; one does not talk about writing but instead gets to it. "Wanting to write" means an ability to spend long solitary hours writing, discarding, revising, selecting, and rewriting, over and over, until the piece finally takes proper shape. There is no one to blame for the lack of writing product; there is no Muse; there is only the often-heard statement that writing is 99 percent perspiration and only 1 percent inspiration.

11

"Wanting to write" demands maintaining a *daily* writing schedule. The writer writes, seven days a week, without fail or excuses, and nothing is permitted to take priority over the writing. The writer's goal will be either working a set number of hours each day or else working until a prespecified number of pages have been completed daily.

The person who "wants to *be* a writer" somehow feels above all writing rules, even before she or he learns what the rules are. For such a person, rules are tiresome roadblocks that stifle the oh-so-creative spirit; a wasteful amount of creativity is expended in trying to circumvent even the most basic concepts. Often, too, there are unfortunate tendencies: One may hear such a person claiming earnestly that his or her "best work" comes with quantities of drugs or alcohol. There will be impulsive attempts to write at 3:00 A.M. following a night of parties.

In truth, there is but one way to be a writer and that, simply, is to write. One writes neither in little bits nor in explosive spurts but in sustained and concentrated effort bent toward creating a whole piece. No sham, no act, no old movie treatment will substitute for honest writing that comes from the mind, heart, and soul. Writing creates writing; the more one actually writes, the more one thinks to say and wants to communicate. With practice, playwriting grows satisfying, often easier, and more rewarding. Practice and experience bring accomplishments that bring pride.

The writer can take lessons from the concert pianist, the painter, or other artists. The dancer, for example, knows well the importance of daily workouts: after only seventy-two idle hours, the unworked body is losing muscle tone and flexibility, which means that the dancer must schedule daily life around the all-important regular exercise period. So, too, must the writer hold tightly to a daily rhythm of writing. Each day without writing makes a sharp loss in output and, worse, a decrease in the writing's muscle tone and flexibility. The playwright, no less than brain surgeon or concert pianist or gymnast, must consciously develop effective work habits which will sustain a life career. Any less is mere playfulness with the art. You owe yourself more.

The Playwright as Storyteller

The playwright, before anything else, is a master storyteller. In the playwright's veins runs the blood of long-ago ancestors who gathered around a fire that held off the night and the jungle's fears. In that ragged and often bewildered group would be a master storyteller who was able to thrust back the night and bring light into souls searching for unknown directions. The storyteller might sing of the great fight that shook their jungle, a battle to the death between the tribe's legendary hero and the wild saber-toothed tiger. No doubt everyone knew the story, but familiarity is comforting; and at any rate, the storyteller would have new techniques to bring the story freshly alive, new ways of creating suspense, new insights into the characters. At proper moments, the storyteller would put on the skin of the beast—a mystic and almost religious act—and jump about as the tiger, showing the creature's command of the jungle. Then, putting aside the costume, the storyteller would become the man, showing him walking unconcerned through the jungle, unaware of the dangers. Then, with horrible sounds, the battle between man and tiger would be enacted around the fire until its plausible conclusion had been played out. The evil tiger's treachery and the man's ignorant but brave heart would have been shown. The tribe, now richer and wiser, would prepare to sleep. A mystery had been illuminated, which is the goal of all great drama.

Let us not overlook the fact that *the master storyteller's first task is to entertain.* The word "entertain" should not be taken in a small sense; it means "to divert consciousness from present concerns." The storyteller must artfully pull the audience's full concentration from its world of reality into the world the storyteller is creating. No matter how important the story may be, the listeners will pay little attention unless the storyteller works magic to transport each member of the audience into the creative image.

The storyteller will use techniques and craftsmanship to grasp the audience's full attention. Action is essential, and the craft of storytelling demands holding attention with foreshadowing and complications, twists and reversals, successes and failures, all leading inexorably to the final climax. Here is no story for the teller's own amusement—no tight little "art for art's sake"—but instead a work designed to communicate to the audience. If the storyteller assumes the posture of preacher or professor, forcing the audience to sit through a didactic sermon because it will be "good for them," art and craft will become corrupted and worthless.

The playwright today is a combination of many people. For students of psychology, the playwright is a psychologist, creating characters worthy of psychological investigation, even giving names to mental disorders (Oedipus, Electra). For those who study government, the playwright is a political scientist, showing in plays such as *Macbeth* how absolute power will corrupt absolutely and turn the world topsy-turvy. Philosophy students, when examining plays such as *No Exit,* see the playwright as a philosopher. For observers of society, the playwright is a world commentator—*The American Dream, Death of a Salesman, A Raisin in the Sun.* Antiwar proponents have their voice in *The Trojan Women, Lysistrata, Viet Rock,* and *Streamers.* The playwright's works are magnificently suitable for study in these and other areas.

But it is as a storyteller that the playwright works first. The playwright aims to captivate, woo, enchant, enlighten, shock, and awaken the audience. The playwright must speak to contemporary sensitivities, designing plays for today's people who are perhaps no less confused than were those cavemen of the past, and certainly no less hungry for a light to hold back the jungle.

Showing, Not Telling

A major secret of effective playwriting is too often overlooked by playwrights. The playwright must fashion a story that will *show* the basic idea of the play, not *tell* it. *Showing, instead of telling, is the artistic goal of all playwrights.*

A play's "message"—its intellectual concepts which we call *Thought*—is communicated to the audience by characters through a combination of their actions and reactions to many stimuli. The stimuli, most often complications and twists and reversals, are structured into action. That structure we call *Plot*. The interactions of plot and character combine in a gestalt sense—that is, the whole is more than the sum of its parts—to communicate the play's idea.

Showing, not telling, is a phrase to be fixed firmly in your mind. Novels tell. Essays are required to tell. But plays follow Hamlet's advice: "By indirections find directions out." Plays show the actions of humanity, either optimistically or pessimistically, instead of stating the author's particular viewpoint in direct words.

Finding a story to show concepts may be difficult, but you must not allow yourself to think that the task is impossible. You will need to translate abstract concepts into concrete human behavior patterns. Theatre, you need remember, deals with humans, not issues. The characters themselves face the issues.

Are there limits to what topics can be dramatized? Take for example the philosophy called existentialism: Is it possible for a play to demonstrate existentialistic concepts? Can that play show the essences of that complex philosophy? Or must the playwright resort to telling audiences what the philosophy means in a sort of verbalized essay?

The answer, of course, is that a play can indeed deal with such a lofty topic. Jean-Paul Sartre, the famous French philosopher, wrote many essays telling readers about existentialism. But he found a way to show how the philosophy is part of daily life: His play, *No Exit*, shows three people captured in a sharply existentialistic situation. The play communicates rich details and essences of that philosophy. Never once does Sartre *tell* his audiences about the philosophy—never does he have a character pause, look at the others on the stage, and start a two-page speech by saying, "You know, what we have here is an existentialist situation. I mean by that, the qualities of existentialism which are, as you may remember. . . ."

For the playwright the secret is first to believe that plays must show instead of tell and, second, to find the best situation filled with action and conflict that will influence characters to behave in a manner that shows the author's intellectual concept. For example, to show that man cannot win in a battle with the gods, Sophocles wrote *Oedipus the King*. To show that young love experiences wild extremes, Shakespeare wrote *Romeo and Juliet*. To show how one can lose sight of the right values and thereby lose one's world, Arthur Miller wrote *Death of a Salesman*. To show that man is to go on waiting for meaning, perhaps even eternally, Samuel Beckett wrote *Waiting for Godot*. To show that the American ideal must be reassessed, David Rabe wrote *Sticks and Bones*. All of the playwrights might have written essays to speak directly to these points, but they instead elected to write for the theatre. That decision meant *they wished to show, not tell, how humans live within the concepts*.

Actions show content. The playwright therefore has no need to tell audiences the play's meaning. *The art of drama is showing, not telling, what meaning lies within the actions*.

The Self-Censor

Imagine a most incredible computer. It is capable of the fastest possible decisions, able to store amazing quantities of information, and designed to make connective jumps between two apparently disassociated items. It stores easily, is nicely portable, and suffers few periods of downtime. It has a capacity quite beyond demand.

Perched inside that computer is a violent "off" switch which is part of a unit that examines all output critically. With amazing rapidity this switch is able to turn off potential output before it even surfaces: "Not of value," "Not useful," "Of inadequate quality." For all of its incredible power, this fantastic computer will become immobile if the "off" switch is operative.

Writers must learn to disconnect the self-censor portions of their brains. Such self-censor units will judge a rough idea and pronounce it worthless even before the writer has had time to work it over, to smooth off the edges. "No, don't bother writing that. It isn't worth the effort." "No, that's a stupid idea." "No, you can't do that."

The self-censor unit can become a major contributor to what is often called "writer's block." If the self-censor is allowed to dominate, the thing can freeze the creative process. Every idea is given critical scrutiny, and the slightest flaw calls for rejection of the whole. Writing becomes a joyless drudge. All laughter is gone. Instead of rejoicing that a new idea has come to the conscious mind, the self-censor will be dismayed that the idea is not perfect the moment it is born. As a result, the writer will reject perfectly viable concepts because they did not jump out, full-fledged and perfect, in one flash.

The writer works best by ignoring those signals which evaluate every small or large idea, or phrase, or even words. The best technique for the writer is speed writing, writing as quickly as possible, overpowering the self-censor by sheer output and fire. When the project is finally completed, the critical portion of the brain can be called in.

A major portion of writing is a spontaneous outpouring. The self-censor, on the other hand, will prevent that flow. The writer must let the writing move along as quickly as possible, even though filled with mistakes, in order to get material on paper. Later revisions can correct errors, but first there must be the writing.

Originality: The False Goddess

The playwright who wants to be somehow "new and different" will expend great quantities of energy and creativity chasing the Goddess of Originality. The chase almost always will end in a cul-de-sac and the writer will have very few rewards for the effort. Even if the playwright manages to capture the goddess, there is no promise that she will turn the play into fine art. All too often the pursuit costs the loss of far more valuable parts of the drama.

Where did this effort to be "new and different" originate? For many centuries artists sought to improve the quality of art, but few ever thought about trying to be new or different. Never did the artists value originality over a perfection of the art. If their art turned out to be a step out of the ordinary and thereby proved to be a way to advance art into new dimensions, that was fine. But if their art stayed within already established boundaries, that too was fine. The unspoken motto was, "Let us create Art." Never would they have said, "Let us be different and that will create Art."

The advent of the twentieth century brought with it a concept that it did not matter if the art achieved Quality as long as it was, somehow, different. Art became self-conscious. Art studied itself and looked for ways to give itself something more to study. Being Original was, for some, an acceptable alternative to creating Quality. Today's playwrights have been influenced by that concept, and many tend toward the belief that more than anything else they must create unique works.

If that's your concept, throw away the idea now. The truth is that any plot and set of characters will be different according to the author. True originality consists of the playwright letting his or her own voice be heard. The playwright must write about what is important to his or her private soul, heart, and mind. No doubt that play will remind others of previously written plays, but there also is no doubt that the play will have its own uniqueness.

Do not worry about being original, but do worry about being true to yourself. Do not search for something "new and different," but search yourself to find what is most important to you. Do not depend upon the Goddess of Originality; she will fail you. Instead of chasing her wherever she may lead, demand that you write Quality.

The Law of Conflict: The Prime Directive

Conflict is the essential ingredient of dramatic action. Without conflict, dramatic tensions and plot movements are lost; without plot movements, characters are flat and dull. An effective play, comedy or tragedy, will contain conflict which can be sustained throughout the play. The conflict must be of a size appropriate to the play's character and thought. If the conflict is too small, the play will become draggy and talky. If it is too large, the play will lack plausibility.

Conflict provides the structure of action. It takes many forms. It may set individual against individual, individual against group, or group against group. It can be internal (one thinks of a *Hamlet*, *Macbeth*, or *After The Fall*), but external conflicts are necessary to show the internal. Spouse against spouse, child against parents, individual against employers, or person against institutions—conflict provides the play with the richness of action that illustrates the playwright's basic theme.

Conflict will be discussed in detail later. For now, learn to think in terms of conflict in the plays you seek to write. Whatever ideas come to you, examine them for conflict content. If there can be no conflict in the play you are considering, you would be wise to discard that germinal idea and start afresh with a more viable dramatic concept.

Quality: Trust Your Instincts

You have noted that the word "Quality" seems a part of this prelude. It is not a difficult word. You know instinctively the difference between "bad" and "good" art. You have within you the knowledge to differentiate between genuine Quality versus the trendy and tricky trash. Trust your instincts.

It is possible for us to confuse ourselves by seeking middle ground. We can set up situations in which the presence or absence of Quality may be difficult to judge. But such exercises waste energy. Instead, we must trust our instincts to tell us when we are creating Quality and when we are making junk. We can hone those instinctive responses by ensuring we accept only Quality from others; instead of living with junk music, junk painting, inferior books, or inferior entertainment, we should seek to feed our souls with the best. We deserve no less, and we can control the input. The choice is a very private one: You can surround yourself with low-grade materials, or you can invest in yourself by accepting only Quality in all aspects of life.

As a writer, you will face many sensitive decisions. You will have to decide what to do with your play when you receive criticism from audiences, friends, performers, directors, and those lofty souls who write for newspapers and magazines. You cannot listen to them all. Nor should you disregard all criticism. You must develop the ability to recognize Quality in your own writings as well as in the criticisms of it. Believe in yourself.

Chapter Three

"A Maker of Plays"

The Correct Title

Theatre practitioners who are properly attuned to the nuances of the art will make a point of emphasizing the correct spelling of the title for one who creates plays. The word is play*wright*. Neither a pomposity nor an accident of spelling that became conventional, this careful word "playwright" is remarkably precise. We mean "one who makes plays." The alternative—"playwrite"—is simply incorrect because it does not accurately describe the way a play is created.

The "Wright," Not "Write"

A "wright" is a skilled worker. The word carries an implication of superior craft, a pride in one's work, and a respect for one's materials and equipment. We mean construction. There are nice images in such words as "shipwright" and "wheelwright"; one senses a preoccupation with Quality. There is an old-world feel to "wright."

"Wright" suggests ideas about years of apprenticeship, careful work techniques, a concern that the project be completed correctly regardless of personal sacrifices. There is no clock-watching for a "wright," and certainly there is never an attempt to pass off shoddy work.

The same images are found in the playwright. The playwright creates, fashions, builds, and remodels; he or she also works within physical parameters and lays a foundation upon which pieces are interwoven and raised to a higher plane.

The Playwright Compared with Other Writers

Comparisons and Contrasts. We can better explore the dimensions of the playwright by making comparisons and contrasts with the novelist, the essayist, and the poet. Each of the writers can be briefly described by their goals:

- The novelist *records* Life.
- The essayist seeks to *correct* Life.
- The poet *responds* to Life.
- The playwright constructs a work which *imitates* Life. The work therefore appears to *be* Life.

Similarities can be listed. All are respected members of the literary community. All share a dedicated respect for the written word and a love for precise use of language. All are excited by the magnificent turn of a phrase, the sweep of a sentence. All share immense self-discipline, and all must have strength to endure those solitary hours. All take pride in independent work. They share a dependency upon the powers of creative concentration and flights of pure fantasy.

All writers are philosophers, and their works are studied for intellectual content. All are psychologists, often inclined to study humankind as it is, or should be, with a critical eye suggesting improvements. All willingly spend two years of full-time, all-out labor to create a work which then is placed upon a sacrificial altar for a self-appointed high priest to criticize and accept or dismiss in the comparatively easy process of writing a "review."

The playwright must be more than these things, however. True, the playwright combines the art of the poet with the art of the essayist and the novelist, but the process of making plays is not the same as the working process of other writers. The maker of plays has special concerns.

Past, Present, and Future Tense. The novelist's work is forever past tense. It is written in the past tense. Although a small percentage of novelists may change tense to the present, the reader experiences a story already over and done with.

The playwright's work lives in a perpetual present tense. In a play, events this very moment are even *now* happening in front of auditors. So important is this that the producing team—actors, directors, and technicians—constantly strive to achieve an "aura of spontaneity," attempting to make the audience believe that *the action on stage is taking place for the first time.*

In a novel, the action can be frozen in place while the auditor leaves for hours or even days. The auditor can look at past chapters to refresh memory or clarify action. In a play, it is patently impossible to back up to explain what happened while the audience's attention was distracted. If the novelist's reader is pulled away to the telephone, it is possible for the reader to return to the novel and reread enough to recapture the mood and story line. If the playwright's auditors are unable to hear lines because of a coughing fit or the commotion of late arrivals, the information is forever lost, perhaps even to the detriment of a basic part of the story.

The novelist is permitted to digress from the main line. The playwright finds that digressions are fatal to the focused attention of the auditors.

The novelist, the poet, and the essayist speak one-to-one: writer to reader. The playwright speaks to a large audience: writer-through-interpreters-to-group. The former types of writers use the printed word; the latter, the spoken word. The former communicate only through words; the latter primarily through actions and events.

The novelist, the poet, and the essayist may moralize. In their works one is not surprised to find passages which have godlike insight into humanity's plight. For these writers, there can be conclusions about right and wrong, or life and death.

The playwright avoids moralizing. A play's "message" should be implied, never stated. The reason the playwright is limited to *showing, instead of telling,* has to do with the nature of the stage versus the novel. The playwright must have actors speak the godlike moralizing passages, and mere flesh-and-blood is ill-equipped for the task. The novelist does not have to rely upon characters to speak the moral passages.

The playwright, as noted earlier, deals with the present tense. But that is not enough. *The sense of the present must be charged with a feeling of the rush of a forthcoming future.* For a comedy, that coming future will echo fortune; for a tragedy, the future will be fate. In either, *it is the sense of future which creates drama.* These events, happening now, take on greater significance because the auditors recognize their implications in the coming future. If the events do not suggest a future, they then will be meaningless digressions; if the events suggest a future but nothing comes of them, they will be viewed as irritating smoke screens and the play will appear to lack unification.

"Flashbacks" are so dangerous to a play because of this matter of the sense of future. There is a limit as to how often a play can look backwards instead of moving to its future. The past can haunt the current action and influence a motion toward the future. If, however, too much of that past enters the present, the play tends to become emasculated. If the past is so important, then one begins to suspect that the playwright would have been wiser to set the action in its past. Even a play such as Henrik Ibsen's *Ghosts*, very heavily influenced by a complex past that haunts the present, remains focused upon its present action and upon the future of Oswald and Mrs. Alving. For the playwright, that sense of future is highly important. The play's dramatic impact stems from the action's movement from past to present. The novelist, the essayist, or the poet may safely ignore the stress upon present and future, but the playwright constructs plot and characters so that they move to that future. The play's basic meaning is expressed in the manner in which plot and characters combine in the movement toward the future.

A Sense of Urgency.   Plays are not constructed of a series of random events that are only mildly connected. Instead, the playwright will carefully select a highly significant moment of the story. The play will start there. The playwright will magnify the action from that moment.

To be effective, a play must happen *now*. It cannot take place tomorrow or yesterday. The events are of special importance *now*, and from this "sense of urgency" can spring a number of plot devices and character responses.

Words and Sentences.   The poet's focus is upon word choice. Finding the precise word is, for her or him, a task to warrant the expenditure of hours and days. The novelist, too, to paraphrase Ernest Hemingway, is locked in a perpetual battle to create the perfect sentence. For the essayist, the exact word and phrase will ring clearly, a clarion call to action. The novelist delights in being told that sentences are beautiful, and the poet expects nothing less.

The playwright, however, finds that specific words or sentences are much less important. True, the playwright will rework speeches until they are right, and of course the playwright examines word choice carefully. But the efforts bring few dividends of true value. The playwright cannot afford to distract audiences, and if a given speech calls attention to itself the playwright may conclude it must be deleted. The playwright knows the truth of the cliché that actions speak louder than words; he will fashion characters and actions into forward moving dramatic scenes to rise to a final climax.

Actors and directors often are not aware that the playwright pays little attention to this or that particular phrase or sentence. The mistake of the performer is to draw sweeping conclusions about a character, or even the entire play, from a scattered sampling of speeches. That error happens far too often: Directors and actors will come to twisted concepts of a play, based upon some sort of thread of sentences. No playwright can depend upon communicating with some words here or sentences there. The stage-wise author knows all will be lost if a performer bobbles a line or if members of the audience suffer coughing fits. Instead of words, you seek to communicate with well-structured actions and characters who are alive and responsive.

Some playwrights may fall into the same errors as actors or directors: The writer may insert a line, heavily laden with crucial meaning, and expect that to give the play clarity. It will not. The playwright will argue that of course the play's subject and theme cannot be missed: Look at this speech in scene one and that phrase in scene six! But audiences will not draw conclusions from *words*. The play's *actions* communicate far more clearly.

Does this mean that the playwright should ignore word selection and sentence structure? Of course not. Speeches must be constructed to fit the character, and ideally each character should have a special way of speaking. The playwright will avoid repetitions and "literary" speeches. The writer will attempt to create artistic interpretations of the way people speak in "real" life. More details are found in a later chapter on diction.

Instant Clarity. The novelist's readers are permitted to leaf backwards for pages or even chapters to reread passages to clarify confusing points. The poet's readers are expected to return continually to taste individual words and groupings. The essayist will be delighted if readers pour over concepts.

In contrast, the playwright has but one chance to communicate. There can be no turning back. Plays, we must never forget, are designed to be performed, not read. If a haziness murks up the playwright's meanings, no audience can stop the play and return to previous scenes. An inexorable forward motion is inherent in the whole of the play.

But "instant clarity" has nothing to do with simple-mindedness. A play must have a basic clarity so the audience will know the name of the game, a clarity of essentials and circumstances, actions and motivations. "Instant clarity" means something other than gross simplification; we mean here that the audience must be able to perceive the basics. Even the ambiguities which so often are found in great drama, in plays such as *Waiting for Godot,* exist within a framework of clean communications. No one can ever be confused about the basic concepts of a *Godot*—those are written clearly. That clarity allows audiences to encounter the sharply put questions about the meaning of life.

Form. The making of a play requires attention to form and structure. The process depends a great deal upon intuitive evaluations which can be enhanced by careful studying and training. Old-time shipwrights had a "feel" for the lines of a sailing vessel and could lay out a ship on the floor of a loft, adjusting her hull's curves according to eyeball measurements. The ship's seakindliness was a result of the shipwright's concept of a rightness of form. So, too, the playwright must respect the form of drama in order to develop an intuitive grasp of correct proportions.

In drama, as in all art, specific measurements and set rules are difficult to state. But a play with no regard to form is likely to be misshapen and ugly. Certain guidelines can be expressed to help the playwright. These will be discussed more in later chapters under the heading "The Six Elements of Drama," but some significant areas will be mentioned here briefly.

Beginning, Middle, and End.   According to Aristotle, there must be three parts to every play—a beginning, a middle, and an end. The principle is sound. Do not allow yourself to be deceived by its apparent simplicity. Consider plays you have seen or read. Undoubtedly you can think of one which seemed full of unfilled promises, indicative of a script with a rich beginning but a skimpy middle. Or perhaps you can recall a play which seemed to dwindle to a stop instead of actually concluding with necessary strength. The playwright must be sure the play contains each of the three parts.

Further, each part must be constructed so it will be a meaningful part of the whole. Each must be crafted to the others so the seams are not visible to the audience. Each is dependent upon the others; often a play with problems within its end actually has structural problems within the beginning or middle. Each must be a correct size in relation to the others. For example, which of the three should be the largest? Of course you know the answer to that: The middle portion of a play is the most significant, and therefore it needs to be substantially larger than either the beginning or the end.

The Six Elements.   A second part of a play's form is influenced by the playwright's conscious or unconscious decision to emphasize various dramatic elements. There are six elements of drama, according to Aristotle—plot, character, thought, diction, music, and spectacle. A play seldom seeks to use equal parts of all six. Instead, a play more often will emphasize perhaps two of the first three.

The play must be appropriately shaped by whichever of the elements are most significant to the playwright. To return to the shipwright analogy for a moment, it is clear that the sailing vessel's form will depend upon her mission. If she is built to race other ships, she will be formed in one manner; if she will carry cargo, she will necessarily have a quite different form; and so on.

The playwright will decide the play's form according to its mission. If the author is most interested in human psychology and interactions, quite likely the play will have a relatively insignificant plot and thought but instead will accent character. If the playwright wishes to build suspense and fear, the play will stress plot but carry much less thought and character.

Most often a playwright will have a germinal idea that stresses one of the first three dramatic elements—that is, the idea is primarily concerned with character, plot, or thought. No matter which element begins the idea, the playwright will attempt to construct the play with definite use of the other two.

Length.   A third consideration of the play's form is its length. In full-length plays, the two-act and three-act form have become standard. The four- or five-act structures are less common. In the three-act play, the final act will be shorter in playing time than the second. If the last act is equal in length to or longer than the other two, the entire play will seem long and it will wear on the tiring audience.

Playing time is conventionalized. The full-length play today will be about two and a half hours, including intermissions. The script is typed according to standard typographical format, which makes it between 90 and 110 pages. The one-act play may be quite short or very long, but the average one appears to be forty-five minutes long.

The Building-Block Concept.   Plays are constructed of "building blocks," climbing one atop the other, higher, until the play reaches its ultimate height. This concept is based upon the theory that drama consists of ever-rising actions. A play consists of units, often called beats or scenes, which continually combine to increase tensions and thereby contribute to overall rising action. The opposite of this would be a play which is at its peak when it begins and thereafter contains falling actions. Clearly, such a play would be nondramatic.

The playwright constructs rising action with carefully planned sections of actions, new angles brought in by complications and reversals, character development for movement, perhaps even machine-gun dialogue. The rising action cannot be continuous, of course. There will be moments when the play might pause, almost as if catching its breath before attacking the next mountain top. Those pauses cannot be serene valleys; the decline likely would cause the audience to lose concentration.

Genres.   Finally, the form of the play will be determined by its genre. Comedy, tragedy, comi-tragedy, drama, realism, expressionism, symbolism, neo-romanticism, neo-poetic, naturalism, absurdism, neo-absurdism—only modern drama could create such an impressive variety of styles and genres. Today many will be mixed together—we call the blend eclecticism—to permit the playwright an individualized approach to the play's subject. In modern drama one finds a tight wedding of form and content, with one interwoven into the other and influencing and influenced by the other. The playwright has many choices to make deliberately or instinctively.

Entertainment.   Once the play begins there must be an instant communication. The novelist's readers may lose focus and put aside the book for an hour or week, but the playwright must reach out to grasp audience attention for the entire playing time of the play. Therefore the writer builds a piece that *entertains*.

The concept here does not imply some sort of lightweight song and dance routine, nor does it suggest pandering to the lower interests of a crowd. *Entertainment* means diverting the audience's attention from mundane daily concerns to the mysteries that the play seeks to illuminate. Entertainment can be *Guys and Dolls* or *King Lear*.

The playwright must design and construct scenes and actions that will continually hold audience attention. There have to be fresh moments to awaken

emotions and intellect, to fashion the growing blocks of suspense, and to stimulate the growth of characters.

A *play must have conflict for it to have forward motion.* The conflicts must be
adequately sustained, and the characters will have to be made logical portions of
the actions.

A *play must be full of surprises to draw the audience's attention.* These are not
shockingly incongruous qualities but are instead fresh insights into people and
situations.

Possible, Plausible, and Probable.   Dramatic action and characters must be
probable and plausible. It is not good enough to say events are "possible." We
live in an era of fantastic happenings—mass genocide, space travel, organ trans-
plants, computerized robot slaves—and so we are trained to think that all things
may well be possible. But the fictional creations of life upon the stage cannot
violate the audience's beliefs of what can be plausible and probable. The universe of the play must be true to itself. We know that audiences will accept
illogic if presented logically: Audiences accept the premise of fairies who can
make people fly (*Peter Pan*) or of a magical six-foot rabbit seen by only a few
(*Harvey*). A man's dead wife can haunt his new marriage (*Blithe Spirit*) and a
protagonist can speak to a friend who is invisible (Willy to Ben in *Death of a
Salesman*). Within the context of the plays, these events are totally plausible.
Why? Because the playwrights have crafted situations, events, and characters
which make acceptable the implausible. The writer's careful craft is necessary;
one cannot expect the audience to simply accept implausibilities or impro-
babilities. It is true, certainly, that audiences will bring to the theatre what
Samuel Taylor Coleridge so neatly called "a willing suspension of disbelief for
the moment" in his *Biographica Literaria,* but that "poetic faith" cannot survive
an onslaught of implausibilities. The playwright must craft the work to be easily
plausible to be both probable and necessary, so no extraneous movements will
disrupt the spectators' acceptance of the play's truths.

Conclusion

A portion of the playwright's task has been suggested here. We emphasize the
concept of the playwright as a writer, and more. Starting with the necessary
conflicts in the action, and building with moving action that stimulates human
responses in the characters, the playwright constructs the play with ever-rising
suspense. The playwright seeks to entertain the audience, holding attention
with the skills of the master storyteller.

Many of these aspects are examined in detail later in the book. Here you
want to perceive the broad objectives of the playwright, the maker of plays.

Preparing
to Write

The First Steps

The following chapters focus upon the first steps you take in preparing to write. You are urged to take these steps in the order presented and, further, to pay special attention to the instructions or exercises along the way. These first steps are designed to help you approach playwriting in an orderly way, not only for your first play but for years of playwriting.

Establishing Habits Now

Is it possible for you to write a play without going through the various steps mentioned here? Yes, of course you can. Why, then, is there so much stress upon these steps? First, this approach will make you feel more comfortable about writing. Secondly, and much more important, we are here establishing habits which will govern your entire future life as a playwright. As psychologist Will James once observed, if one only knew that habits started when beginning will be the habits one has the rest of one's life, one would choose those habits with greater care. If you are to benefit from playwriting, you will want to ensure a strong foundation that will support your future efforts.

Yes, you certainly can write plays without first writing a credo. Yes, you certainly can write the one-act play without a scenario (but you will not succeed with the full-length play without a scenario, so why not learn now how to design one?). All of these you can do with the flush of first excitement. But when that excitement falters, you will need to have a strong steady pace to help you write in the years to come. Rather than start the marathon with a dash, why not get yourself properly prepared? The materials that follow will help you establish working habits which, in turn, will help you create a professional approach for a life in playwriting.

Chapter Four

The Credo

Introduction

Beginning writers often are uneasy when asked to write a personal "credo" before starting the first play. To them the credo is unattractive labor and they distrust the idea. Students' questions seem prompted by a desire to procrastinate until the credo no longer exists: "But we can't write *everything* we believe, can we?" "Well, how long does it have to be?" "Do we have to turn it in? If not, who reads it, and why bother?" Their reactions suggest the credo somehow is threatening. Nonetheless I persist: "You should write a credo before you write your first play or before you continue writing."

What is a Credo?

A credo is, simply, a personal statement of convictions. A credo is the writer's beliefs concerning topics he or she feels are highly important. It is focused most especially upon those portions of life that concern the writer most. It addresses topics about which the author has a deep emotional attitude—a burning anger, a scorn, an affection. It is, then, "This I believe . . ." It is uniquely your own.

What Are the Topics?

"This I believe . . ." can touch any number of areas: Religion; religious hypocrites; inner peace; religion and the state; politics; the nature of serving one's country; leadership; the nature of death; love; family; children; relationships; old age; the decline of morality in America; crime; and anger. Writers tend to look at topics that affect their future, such as peace, justice, war, and disarmament. Or they may select topics that have more personal concepts of future, such as choices, professions, marriage, and materialism. The credo may touch all of the above topics or none of them. There is no assigned quality, no maximums or minimums. Writers may decide upon only a relative few—perhaps under a half dozen—or many.

Often the credo reflects the individual's environment. Perhaps a mother's credo will focus upon family structure, discipline within the family, love, freedom to balance career and family, and women's rights. A businessman's credo may examine honesty, loyalty, the work ethic, people's rights, product quality, profits. A student's credo might look at drugs, friendships, studies, pressure, finding goals, sex, cheating, the nature of pressure. Such reflections of surroundings are expected. Indeed, the more the credo touches the individual's actual life, the more likely it will deal with areas the writer believes are significant.

What Is the Ideal Length for a Credo?

The credo may be any length. Serious writers report that a credo grows to be quite long. They say they start with a credo perhaps fifteen pages long and within a week they have doubled it. Other writers seem to find ten pages satisfactory. I dislike specifying the number of pages, but when pressed I suggest a first credo ought be eight pages for a start.

The Basic Requirement for the Credo. "This I believe . . ." must deal with the writer's *strong* beliefs. The credo will be important to the writer only if it tackles significant topics with a deadly honesty. A credo full of materials given light treatment, as if simply trying to complete an assignment, will have less value to the writer.

Values of the Credo to the Writer

The playwrights who have written credos will report that they find they contribute meaning and concepts to their work. Their plays have a greater depth and insight. Advanced playwrights urge beginners to work on a credo in order to develop personal concepts. These writers say the credo is a direct assistance not only to playwriting, but also to many other activities, and it makes better understanding of what one believes. Some of the values of the credo are suggested below:

- *Writing a credo gets the beginning playwright into writing.* The credo will not be seen by others and therefore it is a nonstressful writing project. No outsider will judge it "good" or "bad." The credo helps the writer move into personal writing. Further, the writer does the credo for personal reasons. There are no other rewards. The project will in this manner help the writer become more aware that writing in many ways is its own reward.

- *The credo suggests to the writer the values of "self as source."* For the beginning playwright, the idea that self is source may be disturbing. More experienced writers, however, understand that no better source for drama can be found than the writer's inner self. What the writer must do is free himself or herself from inhibitions that prevent digging into the self. Writing the credo is, in this sense, preparing resource materials for future use.

- *The act of writing forces deeper thinking of one's values.* It is possible to talk at length about one's attitudes regarding this or that topic. Indeed, many of us participate in bull sessions from time to time, testing our ideas against concepts held by others. But talking does not test our ideas very deeply. Writing does. Writing is thinking: *To write what one believes is to be forced to think more deeply about the topics.* The result is rich understanding of the concepts the writer finds significant. One knows better what one thinks.

- *For some writers, the credo is an introduction of self to self.* The very idea of the credo is threatening to some writers because they recognize it will make them examine their inner beliefs. The writers reluctant to participate in any meaningful self-examination will find that the credo helps them overcome their hesitation.

- *The credo may show the writer conflicting convictions.* It is possible for a writer to feel extremely strongly about two areas which cannot co-exist. I know one writer who was quite surprised to discover he felt positively in favor of total religious freedom, but yet when writing on another topic he had shown he was unable to accept one particular religion's existence. Until he wrote the credo, that conflict had not surfaced. Once conscious of the discrepancy, he then understood some illogical positions he had earlier taken. That insight into oneself is an exciting aspect of the credo.

- *The credo provides the playwright with materials for plays.* The playwright's credo will be seen in the thought of plays written. Indeed, my advice to playwrights who say they've written themselves out and cannot find anything to write about is simple: "Let's talk about your credo and see what is most important to you, then find a way to bring those concepts into human form for a play." The credo is a resource bank from which the playwright draws materials for plays. Whatever a playwright considers to be highly important, as shown in the credo, ought be visible in the plays.

- *Finally, and significantly, the process of writing the credo will help the playwright remember that a major part of a play is its intellectual value—its thought.* For some playwrights, thought is the single most important aspect of the play. There are many plays written primarily to communicate the authors' concepts, an absorption-in-art of the credo. For all playwrights, attention to moral, spiritual, and intellectual concerns—the ingredients of the credo—cannot be ignored. Writing the credo, working over personal convictions, is a highly effective way of ensuring that the playwright will remember that plays communicate the writer's beliefs.

The Credo and the Writer's Journal

The writer's journal, described elsewhere, contains materials that are stored for future use. The credo fits into that category, and therefore the journal is an appropriate receptacle for it. The credo should be in the journal where it can be revised frequently. The writer will expect to make additions and changes to the credo.

Summation

The credo is important to the writer both for personal growth and for the plays which will reflect the author's inner convictions. Plays written without reference to the credo may be simply exercises, full of sound and fury but signifying nothing, to steal a concept from Shakespeare. The credo gives the playwright direction, a compass for a long ocean voyage. The playwright's credo contributes shape, a hull for the sailing vessel. And the credo gives meaning and a reason. It will sustain the playwright during the solitary passage.

Exercises

1. Some plays appear to be developed from the playwright's personal credo. One thinks of Sartre's *No Exit* and Miller's *The Crucible* as examples. Construct a list of plays that share that quality. Briefly describe the basic similarities in tone you perceive in all the plays.

2. If you were to write a credo, list the topics it would contain. How many topics? The number depends upon the writer, but I'd guess that six is too sketchy and twenty is too many. Think of this list of topics as a table of contents. A word or a phrase for each topic will suffice.

3. If you have a table of contents, it needs to be organized. Divide the topics into several basic parts. Part One will contain the most important concepts, Part Two will be the second most important, and so on. In this manner you will revise your list into order of importance to you.

4. Take your most important topic. Write a short essay, perhaps six pages or so, regarding your conviction about that topic.

5. Develop a scenario from the topic you examined for the preceding exercise. Find a protagonist who cares deeply about the topic. Make the topic concrete and specific. Describe the protagonist's efforts to achieve a goal which relates to that topic. Create an antagonist who will stand in the protagonist's path, putting obstacles in the way of the protagonist's direction. The play's

subject and theme will relate to the topic, bringing it to life and making it affect humanity. Is a play being born?

6.   Write your own credo. You will be prepared to add to it during the years, and of course it will change as your values change. Start a credo now, perhaps beginning with a dozen pages.

Chapter Five

The Writer's Journal

Introduction

The well-maintained writer's journal is the writer's constant companion, confidant, receptacle for ideas, storehouse of projects, and stimulus for further writing. For writers, the journal becomes an indispensable file system. The journal also contributes to the writer's psychological well-being, providing an essential support system of reassurance and comfort, because it makes no demand upon the writer. Despite its many benefits, the journal costs surprisingly little in time or money.

Serious writers sooner or later will learn to keep a journal, although sometimes they first will use all other illogical systems first. Usually the nonjournal writer seems destined to try the messy process of jotting hasty notes on any available napkin, envelope, or shopping list. Several months later these notes will surface from the mysterious limbo that manages to capture such materials, and the writer will look at the notes in blank confusion while trying to recapture the flash of insight that prompted the hurried squibbles.

After enough precious ideas have been squandered, the writer becomes determined to be less of a wastrel. "Next week we have to get organized," the writer mutters tiredly, "and this time I really mean it." The writer finally begins a formal system for keeping notes and communications with the inner self. A journal begins.

One wonders why writers must first wantonly throw away those golden thoughts and visions. After all, the journal is often recommended to writers.

Professional writers often attest to the values that the journal plays in their writing. Biographers of authors find riches in the journals. Some journals permit an amazing view into the mind of the creators. A good illustrative case is Eugene O'Neill's notes about masks and Greek Tragedy, written during many years while he was also putting other ideas in his journals and writing other plays. The playwright had not quite found out he was thinking of *Mourning Becomes Electra*, the great tragedy which was to grow from those notes. Clearly, O'Neill's subconscious was mulling over the idea for several years before he became consciously aware of the play. The journal held those notes, storing them for him until he was ready to put them into one whole; the journal saved the notes so they would not be lost; the *act of writing encouraged his subconscious* to continue at work, feeding yet more ideas. If he had not been a conscientious journal keeper, one suspects the play would never have been written.

Journals have been kept by many other writers. Some journals, often in diary form, have become famous in their own right. *The Diary of Samuel Pepys*, written in a secret code that was unlocked in the Restoration period, brings to life the seventeenth-century world of Pepys. *The Diary of Anne Frank* is a play taken from *Anne Frank: The Diary of a Young Girl*. *The Journals of André Gide*, started when he was eighteen and determined to be a writer, are precisely designed for his future growth. *The Journal of Katherine Mansfield* collects the materials for her short stories. Henry Thoreau's journal attests to the values of the journal's encouragement of the communication of self to self.

Despite this evidence favoring use of a formal journal, writers will continue to use scraps of paper. They will persist in mourning loudly when they cannot find precious notes. They will squander ideas. Some of this is, no doubt, a product of image building: There is something deliciously bohemian to the feverish searches for key pieces of paper. The rakish disdain for organization is, for the image builder, further proof of genius: Chaos proves creativity.

Such showmanship is hardly worth the effort in the privacy of one's room while writing. You are urged to bypass the waste of time and energy involved in the napkin-note process. Instead, for the sake of efficiency and to help you enjoy being a writer, invest immediately in your journal. The cost is little, perhaps five or ten dollars, and the rewards will be many.

Physical Aspects of the Journal

What does a journal look like? What works best for the writer's needs? There are many choices. Some writers begin journal-keeping with a purchased diary, but those dated pages become grimly dictatorial in their insistence upon daily entries of a length that will fit into those arbitrary spaces. Other writers work with note cards, which are convenient to carry but awkward to keep in order and which usually get stuck in boxes where they tend to be ignored.

The writer's best two choices are either a very large (eight-inch by eleven-inch, or ten-inch by fourteen-inch) bound log such as the kind sold at office supply companies, or hardcover, three-ring, ubiquitous student notebook (approximately eleven-inch by ten-inch). The log, also often called a journal, usually has lined pages and it allows the writer all the space desired because it does not have blocks marked off by dates. The notebook also will contain lined pages on which the writer can put notes without limit.

The notebook is usually better for the writer's journal because of the three-ring binding system. The rings must open. This will allow the writer to move materials easily from one section to another. Notes can be relocated into areas newly discovered to be more appropriate. Add tab dividers to keep contents appropriately organized, and the journal is ready for the writer's scripts, ideas, fragments of pieces, character sketches, snatches of dialogue, mental doodles, plays in progress, news clippings, and glimpses into self.

The bound log or the spiral notebook that binds the paper in place lack the versatility of the three-ring notebook. I urge my playwriting students to begin with the notebook—one has to start somewhere—and if experience suggests a system better for the personal needs of the individual writer, then the change can be made easily.

Public or Private?

The writer must decide if the journal will be kept private or made available to others. That decision affects the nature of the journal and its contents. A journal intended for others' eyes will perhaps be sanitized; a private journal, on the other hand, can be more candid and expressive of the writer's moods.

The journal often is assigned in various adult education or college classes; in such cases the instructor may call for it. There are those who read the journals and grade them. I think this is a horrible invasion of privacy; the writer ought to feel free to express private concepts without intruding eyes. Worse, the idea of *grading* the journal suggests a sort of "right" or "wrong" nature to its contents, a silly idea and one that will inhibit the writer's feeling of freedom to use the journal to catch half-thought ideas.

The journal should be private. The writer ought not allow the journal to fall into others' hands—if a class requires a journal to be turned in to the instructor, I think the writer is in the wrong class—and it is a good idea to be sure relatives and friends know that they are not free to look at it.

Journal Contents

The writer's creative energies rumble through the journal pages. Here are not the final finished works for the public. Instead, in the journal are the more exciting private communications that are internal, from the self to the self. *Whispers, shouts, cries: The Journal is the creative boiling cauldron of secret efforts and thoughts.*

Certain ingredients seem essential to the journal. They will be listed briefly below. After the basic core, however, the journal can grow according to the individual's personal needs. Over the years I have noticed that journals of my playwriting students have ranged from the spare and precise to the cluttered and confusing, from prim to bawdy, from an ordered universe to a lumpy smorgasbord.

I know no evidence that good or bad writing is a product of the neat or confusing journals. But I have clear evidence that the writers most richly interested in writing are those who have the thickest journals, often scabbed and edge-worn but preserved closely like a favorite possession. Those who do not bother to start a journal are the one-shot writers; they have one play, an interesting first work, but they cannot sustain the effort because they are not replenishing the font with such processes as a journal.

Listed below are some of the contents one assumes will be in every playwright's journal. The italicized portion suggests a title for the tab dividers that organize the journal:

1. *In Progress #1.* Here is the script that is first on the "to do" list. An ample supply of blank pages is ready to use as inserts to correct or amend. Following the script are playwright's notes of "things of fix." Here, too, may be notes from critics who have read the script and made written suggestions. Some playwrights will keep here the early drafts of the script.

2. *In Progress #2.* For the writer there is something comforting about the knowledge there is another project underway; when the first one is finished, the next one will already have been started. There will be no long dull period while the writer anxiously wonders what to do next or if, indeed, any idea will come at all.

3. *Scenario and Notes for a New Script.* This section is self-explanatory. Note, however, this function of the journal: Indirectly it keeps the writer looking toward the future. Again there is that comforting reassurance for the playwright that ideas always will be ready for development. There also is the implication that the writer's ideas are valuable, worthy of saving. Psychologically, the journal is the writer's support.

4. *Character Sketches.* In this subdivision the journal holds the people the writer meets and imagines; perhaps snips of dialogue may be included. It may contain conjectures about how real people would behave under different circumstances: What would happen if this person who takes such pride in infallibility suddenly is faced with personal error? What if a quite lonely person has the opportunity to build a warm companionship but at the expense of a firm moral principle? This section may also contain other types of conjectures: How do people become liars? How do a husband and wife begin to break? The good people and the bad, what makes them behave the way they do? The people one likes and those one does not, how do they interact?

5. *Situations.* Here one is thinking of plots. What if a burglar gets into the wrong room of an expensive hotel and there he meets the inhabitants who con him into robbing some haughty friends? What if an inventor has a truth machine? What if a male and female, strangers, are taken hostage and locked in a room where they are held in dim light without knowing the passage of time? What if a politicial being enters an environment of trust and manages to begin an Iago-like process of sowing evil and distrust?

6. *News Clippings.* The people and events of our world, chronicled in the news magazines, provide material for entries here: The siege mentality in this or that country. The pains of unemployment. Hunger in America. A national concern about a dog whose dead owner decreed it be put to death. A man returning money he took years ago. Confidence games upon the old and poor. News clippings may be pasted into the journal where they may grow to be materials for a future play or support of a brief scene.

7. *Dialogue.* Often a playwright will "hear" dialogue. The speaker expresses an idea, an attitude, an emotion. The journal receives it. Usually the dialogue is an interesting phrase or a series of words which somehow perfectly encapsulate a whole personality. The playwright enters these speeches as they come. After a period of months the speeches may be drawing a complete character who has been sketched in character sketches; at some point the writer will suddenly see that all the pieces fit into one. A play may be born.

8. *Thoughts.* This section contains thematic concepts. For many playwrights, the angry message play is the most interesting to write. Here the journal receives entries about concepts: The invasion of privacy. The failure of the American family, or instead, the successes of the family and its reliance upon each member. Systems which persecute. Crime and punishment. War and peace. These ideas are written in the journal where one or more may be a magnet for future entries. A linkage with an entry in situations may bring out a concept for a new play.

9. The *credo*, described elsewhere, likely will fit in this division.

10. *Notes from Self to Self.* This division holds the diary. Here the writer enters thoughts, emotions, and attitudes—a series of entries about the way the self moves. They are self-examinations. The writer may address them to the diary or, perhaps, to an imaginary person. Anne Frank wrote her diary to "Kitty," a friendly auditor. Mary Shelley wrote to her dead husband. Virginia Woolf wrote to herself. The diary may take the form of daily entries, letters which will not be sent, free-form associations, lists of angers and peeves and major events and hopes, or dialogues between parts of the self. The notes should be uninhibited, and therefore this section should be guarded from unfriendly eyes.

The above lists the minimum elements needed to start one's journal. If the writer works on the journal constantly on a daily basis, the entries will change. New ones will come, older ones may die.

Some fascinating entries have popped up in the journals of my past playwriting students. *Character photographs* were in the journal of one writer who saw meaning in the faces of people and heard them telling their stories. *Cheerful illustrations* were in another student's journal, prompted by her concern that her playwriting should be as bright as the pictures of spring flowers and happy people. Other entries were *Quotations from other writers, Excerpts from books, To read*—play, novels, non-fiction, and *Today's thought.* One student attached to his journal a large envelope. In it were clippings, letters, and physical curiosities that he considered the flotsam and jetsam of a world he was determined to master.

Using the Journal: Mechanical and Psychological Advantages

The journal becomes a safe-deposit box, a receptacle for germinal ideas and concepts for play elements that may shape themselves toward a play in whole or in part. The journal holds the pieces in logical groupings; it stores them patiently. It is a noncritical bank. The three-ring book allows the writer to move notes from one division to another when they are melding into a coherent whole.

The materials may not have immediate use. Some may lie apparently dormant for a length of time. Then there can come that "Eureka!" moment when a brand new thought suddenly explodes into the creative mind. But that thought had only been dormant; it had glimmered into life in a different guise, gotten nudged from side to side, looked at only from the top, relegated to the subconscious which added other views and perspectives, and then it popped out in full-born splendor.

The journal's role in all of this may be major or minor, depending upon the individual writer's personal use of it, but no doubt it can help nudge the pieces, provide a place for them to be stored conveniently, and allow them to be studied by the conscious thereby feeding them to the subconscious for the final Eureka! During all of this, the journal's role is supportive; it is a warm friend, noncritical, who helps the writer put pieces together into a final whole.

Some writers refuse to carry the journal with them. "I'll remember those flashes of ideas when I get home," they say. "I'll enter the idea in the journal then." Most likely, however, they will not be able to remember the details of the idea. In any case, they will lose that spring of enthusiasm which came with the flash of idea. Most importantly, they are being nonreceptive; in effect they are telling the subconscious that new ideas are not encouraged except under the very restricted circumstances of being home. A door is being closed. The subconscious will try less.

Other playwrights decide to hold off entering the ideas until they are sure there is merit to the new concept. In this situation a value judgment is being imposed too soon. That critical sense simply must be delayed. Critical editing so early is wrong: The conscious mind is rebuking the subconscious. Only "good" ideas are acceptable. But all too often the conscious mind's definition of "good" is merely "that which already is known." In that case "good" equals "safe." The end result is that the subconscious will send fewer images, and perhaps they all will be "good" in the one value system. Likely enough, they will lack freshness.

The playwright should think of the subconscious as an old friend who now lives far away. The friend tries to telephone long distance. The wires often are down and communication is at best a chancy business. Now and then connection is made and the friends are warm and happy to have the chance to interact—there is no suggestion that one wait until the other has time to communicate—and each connection makes the next one easier. Each time the friends communicate they are better able to understand the other's language and environment. The friendship grows. Benefits accumulate.

The playwright who immediately jots down the communications from the subconscious is, in effect, helping "open the lines." The conscious is telling the subconscious that ideas always are welcome: Send more; keep in touch. The writer who carries the journal ready is reminding the subconscious that new ideas are respected.

The journal has additional psychological values. When the writer jots down ideas in the journal, the process is *writing*. It is easy writing because the journal is personal. It is not to be shown to others; therefore, the writing is conducted in a relaxed and nonstressful atmosphere. No critical sense is applied here, no reluctances to enter this concept or write that idea for fear someone will say it is not right or good. The writer relaxes the self-censor and lets the journal fill with materials, never concerned with whether they are proper or correct.

When you are ready to move from storing materials to actually constructing the script, you will find that much of the play already is in the journal. Writing becomes easier because you have the rich storehouse in the journal; it becomes a smooth transitional device.

Exercises

1. Go to a local office supply company and browse through their stock of logs, journals, and notebooks. Select a notebook that has the right heft to it, the "feel" you appreciate, and the colors and textures you enjoy. Fill the notebook with paper you select from all the possible choices. Buy enough tab dividers—perhaps a dozen or more—to organize the journal.

2.   At home, spend time preparing the journal. Put the tab dividers in the correct order for your personal needs. Begin transferring old notes into the new journal.

3.   Look through magazines until you find at least three stories which interest you and which you feel have some potential dramatic value. Paste them in the proper part of the journal.

4.   Find a photograph that awakens your senses. It could be a picture of a place, a material thing, or a person. Paste it in the proper part of the journal.

5.   Begin carrying the journal wherever you go. It will seem awkward and cumbersome at first, but soon it will fit naturally under your arm. Whenever an idea strikes you, stop and enter it in the journal.

6.   Insist upon a noncritical attitude about this whole process. Until you have given it a good trial—an honest month or perhaps two of genuine acceptance of the journal—you cannot judge the system.

Chapter Six

Guidelines
for the First Play[*]

Introduction

The years of teaching playwriting have probably been more educational for me than for my students. Several hundred young playwrights have taken one or more classes in playwriting since I first started teaching it at William and Mary in 1966, and they have taught me that writing a play can be simplified—maybe not made "easy," but certainly "easier"—if certain boundaries are imposed on the first play.

We began experimenting with guidelines because so many playwrights were expending too much creative energy chasing non-productive fireflies. We have found that these limitations help playwrights over difficult hurdles. Moreover, they are highly important for the overall learning process.

To be sure, for some writers the very idea of imposed limits appears to be a contradiction in significant terms. How, they ask, can I do creative writing if you fence me in?

To a large degree their objections have merit. Limitations often inhibit the creative mind. Indeed, many creative people expend a great deal of effort seeking clever ways of circumventing rules. Certainly I've had students react to the guidelines with the fervor of a bull to a red flag, and we've had to arm wrestle about the rules.

*This material appeared in *Dramatics* magazine in May, 1981. It later was published in *The Writer* magazine in November, 1981. It also is included in *The Writer's Handbook*, edited by Sylvia K. Burack, 1982.

Nor are the objections overcome by telling the new writer that a professional career in writing will bring assigned limitations far exceeding the modest ones I give. Beginning writers are more interested in effective self-expression than they are in jumping into the life of a professional, and I'd not have it any other way.

Nonetheless, imposition of limitations is a way of life in all creative arts. Theatre is no exception. As a play director, for example, I have found that one key portion of my job is establishing parameters of character for actors, holding these walls tightly in place during rehearsals, and encouraging the performer to create depth within those limitations.

We're talking about the contrast between the casual and sloppy meandering of a Mississippi River vs. a tightly confined Colorado. The former changes direction so often that it confuses even experienced river boat captains, but the latter is held so tightly in direction that it cuts the Grand Canyon. Discipline is essential for the creation of beauty.

Guidelines for the First Play

The beginning playwright is encouraged to accept the following guidelines to write the first play. Later plays can be more free. Indeed, deliberately breaking selected guidelines later will help you better understand the nature of dramatic writing. For now, however, let these guidelines help you in your initial steps toward learning the art and craft of playwriting.

1. *Start with a one-act play.* A full-length play isn't merely three times longer and therefore only three times more difficult. But that a one-act is easier doesn't mean it is insignificant. On the contrary, the one-act play can be exciting and vibrantly alive, as has been shown by plays such as *No Exit* (Sartre), *The Zoo Story* (Albee), *The Maids* (Genet), *The Dumb Waiter* (Pinter), *The Madness of Lady Bright* (Wilson) . . . the list can be impressive.

Starting with the one-act, however, lets the writer begin with a canvas that is easily seen at a glance, instead of a mural that covers such a huge space the perception doesn't grasp it all. The one-act typically has only a few characters, is an examination of a single dramatic incident, and runs about half an hour in length. It usually stays within one time frame and one place. Because there are fewer writing complexities, you'll be able to focus more upon actual writing and you'll have less concern about a number of stage problems which come with the full-length.

2. *Write about something that touches your heart.* Writing manuals usually tell the beginner to write "about what you know best." I think that can lead the beginner to think in terms of the daily mundane events. Better, I believe, is for the beginner to *care;* if the playwright is involved with the subject, that interest will pull an audience along.

3. *Conflict is essential to drama.* For your first play there should be conflict. Drama is the art of the showdown. Force must be opposed by force, person (or group) against person (or group), desire against desire.

If there's no conflict, the dramatic qualities are lost. The result may still hold the stage, but the odds against it are increased. More importantly, even if the one-act has no conflict and yet holds the stage, the playwright hasn't learned that all-significant lesson about showing conflict. You'll want to know that when you write more.

4. *Let there be emotions.* People care in your first play, I hope; people feel strongly, whether it is love or hate, happiness or despair. If you are able to get them emotional, your characters more than likely are going to be active, going somewhere. The audience will care more about emotional people than they'll respond to those dull-eyed, unfeeling dramatic deadbeats.

5. *Stay within the "Realistic" mode.* Realism deals with contemporary people, the sort who might live next door, in their contemporary activities. Realism also involves the selective use of ordinary speech. It avoids the aside and the soliloquy. It is quite comfortable inside the traditional box set. Realism is selective, and sometimes critical, in its presentation of objective facts.

Realism is the familiar mode you've seen most often: it dominates television, and only a handful of movies break away from realism. No doubt you've also seen it on stage more than any other mode. Because you know it best, your first play will be easier to write if you stay in realism. Expressionism, absurdism, symbolism, epic . . . avoid these for your first time into playwriting.

(Examples of realism would be full-length plays such as *Ghosts* or *A Doll's House,* both by Ibsen, or one-act plays such as *Ile* and other sea plays by O'Neill. More recent plays tend to be eclectic—primarily but not totally realistic, such as the full-length *Death of a Salesman* by Miller, or the one-act *Gnadiges Fraulein* by Williams.)

6. *Limit the number of characters.* Too many characters and you may lose some: they'll be on stage but saying and doing nothing, so you'll send them off to make dinner or fix the car while you focus on the remaining characters you like better. Consider eliminating those who are dead.

Strenuously avoid "utilitarian" characters, those people who make minor announcements (in older drawing-room plays they say little more than "dinner is served") or deliver packages or messages (Western Union's delivery boy, remember, is as much a relic as the butler). Such characters tend to be flat, no fun for playwright, performer, or audience.

Some utilitarians are confidants, on stage to serve as ears so the protagonist will be able to speak inner thoughts without resorting to the soliloquy. The confidant in this sort of case turns out to be about as vital as a wooden listening post.

Confidants, by the way, are easily recognized: their faces are covered with a huge question mark. They seem to be asking questions eternally, without any apparent interest in question or answer. The playwright uses the confidant to get to the answer. If such a person is necessary, let the human be more than a pair of ears.

Just how many characters should be in the play?

Three is a good number for the first play. The triangle is always helpful; three characters allow development of good action and conflict and variety. More, and there's the risk of excess baggage; less, and the characters may quickly become thin and tired.

7. *Keep them all on stage as long as you can.* All too often I've seen plays developing potentially exciting situations, only to be deflated by the exit of a prime character. The audience will feel let down: promised excitement evaporated through the swinging door.

The flurry of activity with entrances and exits is deceptive. There may be a feeling of action but in truth there's only movement of people at the door. The more such business, often the less drama. In class we comment jokingly about wanting a percentage of the turnstile concession.

The beginning writer needs learn to keep all characters alive and actively contributing to the play's action. So, then, you need try to keep them all on stage as long as you possibly can. If you have a character who keeps running out, perhaps he ought be eliminated.

You needn't invent a supernatural force to keep them in the same room, by the way, although I've seen my student writers come up with fascinating hostage or kidnap situations and locked doors in order to justify keeping everyone present. All of that is clever, but all you need is action that demands all characters' participation.

8. *No breaks: no scene shifts, no time lapses.* Just as some playwrights have people leaving when stage action is growing, so also there are authors who cut from the forthcoming explosion with a pause to shift scenery or to indicate a passage of time. There is a break in the action and that always is disappointing. Such lapses all too often are barriers to the play's communication with the audience.

If you have in mind a play that takes place first in an apartment, then in a grocery store, then in a subway, you have let motion pictures overly influence your theatrical concept. This just won't wash, not in a one-act stage play: that calls for so many sets and breaks that producers will shy away from your script. (Yes, yes, you can cite this or that exception, but we're talking about a beginner's first play, not a script by someone with the established reputation.)

Reduce the locales to the *one* place where the essential action takes place, and forget the travelogue. So also with the jumps in time: find the *single* prime moment for these events to take place.

Later you can jump freely in time and space, as Miller does so magnificently in *After the Fall.* Your first play, however, needs your concentrated attention on action, not on inventive devices to jump around through time and space.

9. *Aim for a forty minute play.* One-act plays are delightfully free of the restrictions placed upon full-lengths, and can be only a few minutes long to something well over an hour. The freedom is heady stuff for a beginning writer.

Aim for around thirty to forty-five minutes. Less than that and you probably only sketched the characters and action; much longer, and you might exhaust your initial energies (and your audience!). Your goal, of course, is to be sure you achieve adequate amplification: too many beginners start with a play only eight to ten minutes long, and it seems full of holes. Your *concept* should be one that demands something over half an hour to be shown.

10. *Start the plot as soon as you can.* Let the exposition, foreshadowing, mood, and character come after the beginning of the plot (the point of attack). Get into the action quickly, and let the other elements follow.

11. *Remember the advantage of the Protagonist-Antagonist structure.* Our era of the anti-hero apparently has removed the Protagonist from the stage. Too bad. The Protagonist is a very handy character indeed, and the Protagonist-Antagonist structure automatically brings conflict which you recall is essential for drama.

The Protagonist is the "good guy," the one with whom we sympathize and/or empathize, the central character of the play. A better definition: *the one whose conscious will is driving to attain a goal.* The Antagonist stands firmly in the way. Both should be equal forces at the beginning of the play: if one is obviously stronger, the conflict is over quickly and so should the play be.

(If you do not fully understand the personality of the true Protagonist, look at Cyrano in Hooker's translation of Rostand's *Cyrano de Bergerac.* He is so strongly a conscious will moving actively that it takes several antagonists to balance Cyrano.)

12. *Keep speeches short.* Long speeches often grow boring. Sometimes they are didactic, the playwright Delivering The Play's Message. Always they drag the tempo. But the worst sin of a long speech is that it means the playwright is thinking just of that one character and all the others are lying about dead.

Short speeches, quick exchanges between characters, on the other hand, keep all of them alive and make the play appear to be more crisp and more vital. The play will increase in pace and you'll automatically feel a need to increase the complications.

How long is "short"? Let the dialog carry but one idea per speech. Or, to give you another answer, let your ear "listen" to the other characters while one is talking, and see who wants to interrupt. A third answer: try to keep the speeches under, say, some twenty words.

One grants the effectiveness of the "Jerry and the Dog" speech in Albee's *The Zoo Story.* It makes a nice exception to this guideline. But there are very few such examples, and there are many more examples of plays where the dialog is rich and effective because the playwright disciplined the talky characters.

13. *Complications are the Plot's Heart Beat.* John wants Mary. Mary says fine. Her family likes the idea. Her dog likes John. His parrot likes Mary and the dog.

So John and Mary get married. They have their 2.8 kids, two cars, a dishwasher, and they remember anniversaries. Happiness.

Interesting? Not very. Dramatic? Hardly.

John wants Mary. Mary is reluctant, wondering if John simply is in love with love. John is angry at the charge. Mary apologizes. John shows full romanticism. Mary worries again. Mary's grandmother advises Mary to take John to see what love really is by visiting Mary's older sis who everyone knows is happy in marriage. Mary and John visit. Sis and her husband Mike are having a violent fight; mental cruelty; damning accusations. Sis gets John to help her and he unwillingly does; Mike pulls John to his side; Mary yells at John for causing the trouble.

That's the first ten minutes.

I think you'll grant it has more potential than the first sketch. *Complications* keep it vital, moving, alive. *A play depends upon conflict for its dramatic effect, and complications are the active subdivisions of the basic conflict.*

So, then: the traditional baker's dozen—thirteen guidelines that will help you with your first play. They will help you avoid pitfalls which have lamed so many playwrights, and they will give you a basic learning experience which will help you with future plays.

Good luck with your first play. May it be the first of many more, each distinctly better than the last.

Chapter Seven

The One-Act Play: Theatre's Iconoclast

The Rebellious Spirit

Bold and brassy like a circus band or gentle like a sea breeze with the sunset; rebellious and stubborn like a kid brother or conservative to the point of being reactionary; irritably didactic with the subtlety of an aroused porcupine intent upon proving the righteousness of its beliefs, or wide-eyed and innocent as in the hearts of children the week before Christmas—the one-act play is all of these, and more. It deliberately defies all literary descriptions: As soon as it appears to be securely walled up inside a neat definition, it bursts free into new territory with a triumphant leap. The one-act is theatre's iconoclast, and damned proud of it.

The one-act is to the full-length as the short story is to the novel. It is to theatre as the poem is to literature. The one-act play's strength is in its brevity, and its soul is in its depth of observations. It must make its points efficiently—no wasted motion is acceptable, and no digressions are permitted. Every moment must contribute to the whole. To make a complex writing task more complex, the one-act must achieve all of these goals without ever appearing to be rushed or directly obvious.

At times the one-act sets forth to be the theatre's nonconformist. Often one winces at a nonconformist's deliberate contrariness, filled with bravado not about Quality but instead about showing its separations from the norm. Likewise, dull and uncomfortable moments of theatre may result from such self-conscious contrariness. On the other hand, there can also be found, in the one-act play's fervor, excitingly alive theatre.

The one-act may attack its venerable full-length "ancestors." It has been known to deny loudly all of the lessons that theatre has painfully learned through the centuries. One smiles indulgently at the folly. In its attacks, it throws out so much of the old that often it seems forced to rediscover the wheel. One shrugs at the wasted energy. But there are also moments when one must blink at new discoveries in the one-act, and new lessons take the place of the old.

One-act plays appeal to those who are boldly experimental. Theatre has found new and exciting modes of dramatic expression as a result of the trial runs of such plays, and often full-lengths have dutifully followed examples set by the brash short ones. For example, absurdism was led by the one-act play, and recent neo-absurdism has its roots in the short form as well. Such playwrights as Ionesco and Albee have contributed significant one-acts to initiate the theatre of the absurd, and Pinter made neo-absurdism a vital form with his one-act plays. Other examples could be cited to illustrate the one-act play's many contributions to new expression via its ability to adapt to experimentation with content and form.

Appropriately for its rebellious spirit, the one-act jealously guards its freedoms. It preserves its right to conform to the conventional or to branch off to an avant-garde movement. It will follow the formula of the "well-made" play, or it will attempt to break all known rules. It can be frankly commercial for Broadway consumption, or it may be new and daring for off-off-Broadway; it may be designed for children or for adults. For playwrights, actors, directors, and audiences, the one-act is like a sports car: Often it is awkward and comfort is restricted, but there will be excitement for the bold travelers who are willing to accept the variations.

The Three Fundamental Premises

The most significant characteristics of the one-act play are quite easy to perceive. We cannot think of the one-act as simply one-third of a full-length play, just as we must not think of the short story as merely a chapter from a novel. The one-act has its special distinctive qualities.

To understand the one-act play, we start with its three basic operational premises. These are inherent in the form. From these we move to other aspects of the one-act play's content and form.

1. The One-Act Play Is a Brief Statement. The one-act play's primary characteristic is its brevity. From that quality will stem other aspects of the form. Its length influences script and performance; due to the shortness of the play, the script will take on certain aspects of plot and character, and in performance there will be limitations of music and spectacle.

2. The One-Act Play's Length Is Approximately Forty Minutes. The one-act play typically will have a running time of less than an hour, usually about thirty-five to forty-five minutes. Of course, the one-act often deviates from that norm; its rebellious nature cannot accept an average, and so there are the successful longer works that run to ninety minutes or more, such as Sartre's *No Exit* and Genet's *The Maids*, as well as those that are fifteen to twenty minutes in playing time, such as Beckett's *Act Without Words I* and *Act Without Words II*.

Such exceptions aside, however, the one-act is seldom less than twenty minutes because it would thereby lose the values inherent in sustained action. If the one-act play is less than twenty or twenty-five minutes, it runs the risk of turning into a lightweight sketch or skit. In the opposite extreme, some one-act plays are barely distinguishable from full-length plays. For example, August Strindberg's *Miss Julie* has some aspects of the one-act play, but in reality it appears to be a full-length play without intermission.

Because the one-act is short, it usually does not provide an evening's entertainment by itself. It is instead considered in groups; producers often seek to present three different one-act plays for an evening in theatre. As we shall discuss, that factor influences aspects of one-act play production.

Most playwrights design the one-act play to be around forty minutes. This results in a script that is about forty pages long, estimating one typed page to be equal to about one minute on stage.

3. The One-Act Play Illuminates One Dramatic Event. A one-act play consists of one major event, in contrast to the full-length play which is built upon a series of dramatic events. To illustrate this concept, in *Macbeth* the dramatic events are: (*a*) the witches' prophesy, (*b*) plans to kill Duncan, (*c*) the assassination, (*d*) shifting blame for the murder to the princes, (*e*) plans to kill Banquo and Fleance, (*f*) the murder of Banquo and Fleance's escape, (*g*) a banquet at which the ghost of Banquo appears but only is seen by Macbeth, and on. That list is three-fifths of the entire action, and undoubtedly additional events could be added from those first three acts.

A successful one-act play might be built upon only one of those events. For example, it is not difficult to imagine a one-act play centering around the assassination of the king. There could be another short play constructed on the appearance of Banquo's ghost at Macbeth's banquet. Another one-act might be drawn from Lady Macbeth's sleepwalking scene. In these cases, the one-act would take a given moment and enlarge it—that is, what is a five-minute scene in the full-length could become a forty-five minute one-act play.

A full-length play will unfold a number of dramatic events like a tapestry, and the whole will be of a major size. The one-act play, however, may look at a single moment of that tapestry, and if the correct moment is shown, the audience is able to imagine the whole. It is not a matter of aiming for a smaller target; the one-act can focus upon the same target as a full-length but express itself more clearly. In this sense the one-act is like the poem: It strikes a larger note than its size would suggest.

From these three premises a number of conclusions can be drawn about the nature of the one-act play. The content and form, in particular, can be seen to be logical extensions of the above premises. A discussion of content and form will follow the format suggested by Aristotle in his list, "The Six Elements of Drama." It is especially appropriate to discuss the six elements here so you can become familiar with their application to plays, one-act plays in this instance; later, in Part Three, you will have opportunity to learn more details of the elements.

The One-Act Play and
the Six Elements of Drama

Aristotle's "Six Elements of Drama" provides a convenient point of departure for discussing content and form of the one-act play. Aristotle's empirical observations led him to conclude that a play can be examined in terms of its elements. He found these six elements:

- Plot
- Character
- Thought
- Diction
- Music
- Spectacle

We shall look at each element briefly in relation to the one-act play.

Plot. Because the one-act play is a brief statement, plot will be distinctly less complex than that of a full-length play. The full-length will have a number of events, but the one-act will be an illumination of one dramatic event. The full-length play's plot will demand dozens of complications, but the one-act play's plot will have perhaps only three to six.

The point of attack in the one-act play must be early. Exposition usually is limited to a few bare facts. The play's climax will be in the last few moments.

Character. The one-act play has room for but a few characters. The full-length play often brings in new characters to help move the play forward, and it is not unusual for the long play to have dozens of characters. The one-act aims for two to five characters. All must be essential to the basic action; no utilitarian characters appear in the well-unified one-act play. Usually one character will be well drawn, although in some plays there will be two or three characters who are given equal dimension.

Thought. That the one-act play is less complex than the full-length play is true, but the fact must not be misunderstood. *We must emphasize that "brief" does not at all imply "simplistic."* The one-act is pared down to dramatic essences, but that does not reduce it to simple-mindedness any more than brevity makes the poem a simple-minded expression.

We need to emphasize that the one-act play is quite capable of mind-stretching thought. Proof is found in so many plays that one hesitates to list them. Jean-Paul Sartre's *No Exit,* for one example, is a complete and powerful statement about the philosophy called existentialism. Other one-act plays known for their intellectual content are Genet's *The Maids;* Albee's satire, *The American Dream;* I. Shaw's angry antiwar play, *Bury the Dead;* and Beckett's *Act Without Words I* and *Act Without Words II,* which suggest that mankind is a mere laboratory experiment.

Student playwrights often come with misconceptions about the one-act play. Too frequently they believe that it is for minor statements at best. They view it as a kindergarten exercise, no more. With their minds locked firmly onto the belief that the one-act is for lightweight or inconsequential subjects and themes, these playwrights all too dutifully aim their efforts at that level. The resulting plays are, unfortunately, kindergarten exercises.

How have these beginning writers come to such incorrect attitudes about the one-act play? The problems stem from the educational system, or more specifically from those who teach drama on the high school and college levels. In classes, the full-length plays are assigned and given long discussions, but important one-acts by famous playwrights are skipped. Play directors focus upon the full-length play, not the one-act play; when one-act plays are done, the teachers manage to shift them to student directors in a clear statement that one-act productions belong to beginners. And the student playwrights are given short shrift; one of my better playwrights reported she was asked by a professor, after her one-act play had had a successful production, when she would be ready to move up to a *real* (i.e., full-length) play. It is a method of rewarding length, not Quality.

This is sad artistic snobbery. It is related to the often-expressed concept that anything from the Continent will be "good" drama in contrast to the "weak" homegrown variety. The same snobbery leads to *ex cathedra* evaluations that somehow musical comedy is not art and therefore not worthy of serious effort; it is the same mental attitude that preaches that only the classics are "good" and modern plays are "poor." As is the case with any snobbery, the real evaluation is of the snob. Only muddled thinking could produce such attitudes.

Those lessons may have become ingrained in the writer's subconscious. They must be rooted out and discarded. The playwright must be guided by this basic premise about the shorter play: *The one-act play is brief but not necessarily simplistic.* The one-act play can, and does, carry significant subjects and themes.

Diction. Diction in the one-act play tends to be of the standard "people who might live next door and would probably speak this way" realism which is typical of modernism. Seldom is there an effort to use elevated diction, but poetic diction indeed has a place in the one-act play format. The one-act play can take on so many different forms that it also can shift from the standard conversational realism to the higher diction. Some playwrights, such as Eugene O'Neill, used the one-act play to experiment with dialects, but more often langauge is used efficiently even if it is nondistinguished.

Music. Music plays very little part in the one-act play. It is, one suspects, less important in the one-act than any other element. I often have urged my musically-inclined playwrights to attempt one-act musical comedies or musical plays, but there have been few such works completed. That there have been no particular successes in one-act musicals does not mean that there will be none in the future.

Spectacle. A direct result of the one-act play's short running time is little spectacle. Most producers think of the one-act in terms of presenting three or possibly four one-acts together in one production. These usually are done with minimal production values; the business-minded producer seldom wishes to finance scenery, furniture, costumes, and the like. To do so for three or four plays would be expensive. The beginning playwright would be wise to write one-act plays that can be done on a bare stage with a few pieces of furniture. Calling for elaborate spectacle may result in the play not being presented.

Artistic Balance:
Beginning, Middle, and End

A proper balance of the one-act play's beginning, middle, and end will be essential. One can argue that the one-act play must be more concerned with the totality of these three portions than would the full-length play, because the one-act play, like a poem, achieves some of its appeal with effective use of form. Certainly, too, the one-act play's form is more easily perceived; the full-length play, on the other hand, is expanded over a longer period of time and therefore more difficult to grasp. A correct proportion of beginning, middle, and end will give an artistic integrity to the whole.

The Beginning. For the one-act play, the beginning should be quite short. The playwright will remember that the one-act is a brief statement and therefore it has no room for nonessential materials. The beginning, in particular, needs to be as neat and effective as the author can make it. All too often the playwright attempts to pack too much into the play's beginning, loading it with mood, characterization, tempo, exposition, introductions, and general atmosphere. The result of so many effects is a slow beginning; the play sits idle because nothing of significance is happening.

The one-act play's beginning will be relatively shorter than the full-length play's where a proportionately larger percentage of energy can be given to introductions. Today's one-act plays initiate the plot earlier than did older one-act plays, and the result is a beginning that is markedly more intense and sharp. The play's action must start quite soon. I urge beginning writers to *start one-act plays in the middle of ongoing action*. Exposition and other introductions can follow later.

The Middle. The middle of any play contains the "meat"—the movements of the plot, and the character developments. In the middle of the play the plot is operating at its peak efficiency, and the result is bringing the play's thought to the audience's attention.

The middle of the play is the longest of the three parts. It is the active see-saw, up and down, reversing directions, as the characters respond to new conflicts and other stimuli. The middle is the meal for which the audience came.

For the playwright, the middle is the most significant of these three parts. It must be active. As a guideline, the playwright should be sure the middle is not a whisper but is instead a declaration; there must be changes and complications. Beginning playwrights tend to make the middle too quiet and too inactive.

The End. The end is not the playwright's final opportunity to deliver the message. If the play contains a "message," it has to be integral to the overall play and inherent in the action.

Some playwrights tend to try the "O. Henry" ending, a trick or twist that surprises everyone. The gimmick is out of fashion and unpopular because it depends upon awkward contrivances. Only O. Henry was able to make effective use of that trick ending, and then only in short stories. The device is not recommended to today's playwrights.

The cleanliness of the one-act form suggests that the ending is best when neatly efficient. The full-length play, with its many complexities, often will require a lengthy denouement to tie up loose strings; the one-act play, however, has no need for that denouement because it has few complexities and therefore no loose strings are expected after the climax.

The "Unities"

Many are familiar with the so-called classic unities of time, place, and action. These unities are, according to legend, sacred to the memory of Aristotle and the Greek theatre. Actually, the unities came into power during the neo-classical movement in seventeenth-century France. The one-act play tends to be conscious of time, place, and action, but with different emphasis upon each.

Action. The one-act play's focus upon a single basic line of action is part of the short play's third basic premise, mentioned earlier, having to do with illuminating a single basic event. The one-act is too brief to permit anything other than a unity in action; short plays which shotgun a number of different actions are likely to be confusing, apparently formless, and suggestive of several plays pushed into one.

Place. One-act plays are not limited to a single place. However, if the action moves from place to place it must do so *without* elaborate stage devices to indicate the changes. The play must awaken the audience's imagination for these sorts of shifts in place, not depend upon technical effects.

Movement through place is not necessarily a virtue. Indeed, plays that try to jump from place to place may well expend their energies on these shiftings and leave too little actual plot and character. Nonetheless it can be done successfully, but the playwright should not call for scenic assistance. As was noted earlier, one-act plays receive very little spectacle.

Time. The one-act play tends to be less flexible with movement through time than it is with movement through space. The brevity of the play prevents much success with changes in time. Certainly the one-act plays that feature the "flashback" seldom succeed; these plays would be better if revised so the action can take place in one or the other of the times, thereby eliminating any need for a flashback.

Jumps in time, like jumps in place, cannot depend upon scenic devices or lighting techniques to communicate the change. If the play does move through time, it will have to do without assistance from technical theatre devices. Better is a play which holds to its time.

Breviloquence

The one-act play is eloquent because it is fluent, forceful, and movingly expressive. It is all of those because it is brief. The one-act must be stated concisely, and the playwright must edit the script most carefully.

In the full-length play a few words too many can ruin a moment, a moment too many can ruin a scene, and a scene too many will turn the entire play into a failure. To the degree that this is true for the full-length play, it is even more appropriate to the one-act. There can be no padding, no excess baggage; the one-act has no room for anything but the relevant—not necessarily the *obviously* relevant. Please note: The one-act play's need for accurate statement does not mean that it should be obvious about hitting everything on the nose. On the contrary, a precept of art is that it achieves best by indirection. So, then, the one-act carries only the relevant but not the obvious.

The one-act is the poem of the theatre, eloquent and meaningful in its brevity, emotionally moving and intellectually stirring, comic or tragic or a mixture of the two. If the word "breviloquence" did not exist, the one-act would invent it; much of its impact is a product of its distillation of human emotions and fears and dreams.

One-Act Champions

The one-act play draws active champions. One of the short play's best friends was the late Stanley Richards, who edited an annual anthology of new one-act plays, each year's collection under the title of *Best Short Plays of* "*[year]*", following an example established earlier by Margaret Mayorga. The support of such people as Richards has increased the one-act play's popularity.

Certainly the one-act play has been popular with leading playwrights who find the short play appropriate for their dramatic ideas: William Butler Yeats, Lady Gregory, John Millington Synge, George Bernard Shaw, Eugene O'Neill, Thornton Wilder, Jean Genet, Jean-Paul Sartre, William Saroyan, Bertolt Brecht, Eugene Ionesco, Samuel Beckett, Harold Pinter, Edward Albee, Arthur Miller, Lanford Wilson, Robert Anderson, Luigi Pirandello, Noel Coward, Neil Simon, Clifford Odets, Sam Shepard, Tom Stoppard, Joe Orton, John Guare, Terrance McNally, Murray Schisgal, Tennessee Williams, and Joanna Glass, to name a few. The list goes on. That the one-act has been so popular with so many leading playwrights is itself a testimony to its values.

The one-act play is a favorite of off- and off-off-Broadway audiences. Evenings of one-act plays are typical fare, and one finds many of tomorrow's theatrical concepts in today's one-act play productions. One also can find excellent theatre.

A Brief Reading List

One can read fine one-act plays to understand the nature of the form, although it always is better to see them in production as well. A careful study of selected one-act plays will illustrate the variety possible. The anthologies edited by Stanley Richards provide a number of one-act plays. The list of playwrights mentioned above includes a number of authors whose short plays could be searched out.

For those interested in some recommendations, I include here a number of one-act plays which are particularly strong. The list is brief; it could easily be tripled but space limitations narrow the choices.

"Classic" one-act plays that set the standards:
No Exit, by Jean-Paul Sartre—illustrates how much depth is possible in the one-act play. *The Zoo Story,* by Edward Albee—a gripping examination of character caught in society. *Hello, Out There,* by William Saroyan—a brave mixture of comedy and pathos. *Riders to the Sea* by J. M. Synge— perhaps the outstanding classic one-act of all time. *The Maids,* by Jean Genet—stunning, deliberately offensive, and highly powerful.

Suspense is achieved, primarily by withholding vital information:
The Dumb Waiter, by Harold Pinter—a very tough gangster play that should be seen, not read. *Hopscotch,* by Israel Horovitz—two people appear to be strangers but they share an angry past which is slowly revealed to the audience.

Marvelously comic:
Where Are You Going, Hollis Jay?, by Benjamin Bradford—a richly insightful look at an aspect of the rites of passage, extremely funny, yet honest. *Crawling Arnold,* by Jules Feiffer—modern society is ripped by a straight-faced satire.

The play's thought is the prime quality:
Bury the Dead, by Irwin Shaw—an angry antiwar play that imagines there has been so much death that the earth is now saturated and can accept no more. *The Happy Journey to Camden and Trenton,* by Thornton Wilder— the family is all, and when it works together there can be warmth and happiness. *Picnic on the Battlefield,* by Fernando Arrabel—there is a solution to war here, but suddenly a machine gun kills those with the answer. *Canadian Gothic,* by Joanna Glass—an extremely potent drama of family tensions full of rich characterizations.

Chapter Eight

The Scenario

Problems and Solutions

Described below are some problems afflicting playwrights. They are not uncommon, and in cases of this sort we all can easily empathize with the unfortunate author. Perhaps you have had experiences such as these?

- You have no difficulty starting a play. As a matter of fact, you've begun a dozen different scripts. Your writer's journal overflows with these exciting starts. The problem is, however, that you simply cannot keep the characters alive and moving. By page six they seem to dry up, and by page eight they have become dully repetitive. And so you ask what went wrong with characterization?
- You've started a full-length play. Act One burns with excitement and promise of rich action to come. You are anxious to discover what will happen in Act Two. But in Act Two there is nothing happening. The play simply dribbles off. You've returned to Act One to revise, adding new characters and situations, but again you discover voids in Act Two. What went wrong with the writer's creative juices?
- You have finished a full-length play. You admire its sparkle, its sense of life, the clever diction with telling phrases, and the patterns of the characters. But your most trusted critic tells you that the play is wordy and aimless. Now you are ready to revise but you don't know where to start. You wonder how you are to correct the diction. What do you need to learn about dialogue?
- Your one-act play seems to want to be three or four nonassociated plays. It lacks focus. It rambles from play to play. How do you bring a play into focus?
- Your play is performed, and as you sit with the audience you have the horrible feeling that they are uninterested. With them you feel that there are long dull

spaces with no action, followed by a flurry of complications too close together, and then several climaxes. Your groans almost can be heard. What went wrong with the director?

Described above are plays started with great excitement but with unfortunately too little craft. Nothing "went wrong" with characterization, creativity, dialogue, focus, or the production. Instead, the problem is that the plays were not given sufficient planning before the writing started. The playwrights plunged directly into writing the scripts without first constructing viable plans and goals. No doubt the authors started with a fine zeal, but enthusiasm alone will not substitute for a carefully thought-out design. Without adequate planning in advance, all too often a play will falter, slip sideways, and finally collapse. The root problem is that there was no scenario.

The Scenario Defined

The scenario is an outline of the play. It begins as a simple sketch and it grows until it is complete with all of the major actions and character movements. The scenario is a narrative description of the play, action by action—"this happens and then this and then this"—and the actions always involve character motivations and responses.

A scenario is to a play as a blueprint is to an office building. The playwright is no less of a master designer than the architect. There is the same concern for a proper foundation, interlocking structural devices, pleasing lines, adequate strength to survive windstorms and human abuse, marriage of form and content, and an aesthetic sense of balance. The playwright is the architect and more—the author also is carpenter, bricklayer, painter, roofer, interior designer, electrician, plumber, landscape planner and grader, and overall contractor.

The scenario is to the playwright today as it was to performing troupes in mid-sixteenth century *commedia dell'arte* presentations. Those troupes worked from outlines of action to improvise a performance; the playwright works from an outline to construct the play. In either case, the final public presentation is derived from an operational scenario. More recently, playwrights will start with a concept and write a scenario that illuminates the basic subject and theme, then work with performers who improvise characters and additional situations to flesh out the original idea. Such "made pieces" were popular years ago, and one hears of the better-known results such as Jean-Claude Van Itallie's *The Serpent* or Megan Terry's inventive antiwar piece, *Viet Rock*. The scenario is a skeleton upon which action and characters can be constructed. Although *commedia dell'arte* and "made pieces" are uncommon today, the scenario continues to be a significant guide for the playwright.

For some playwrights the scenario can be a brief sketch, perhaps less than a page long, that merely lists in order the major actions of the play. Other play-wrights will construct a far more detailed outline, often ten to twenty pages long, that lacks only dialogue to become the final playscript. There are playwrights who demand a scenario that is almost dictatorial, including final scenes and all approaches; other writers use the scenario as a springboard, intending to deviate from the path as they do their actual writing.

Scenario Advantages

The scenario is a safety net for the playwright attempting a high-wire walk. The more complicated the intended play, the more the writer needs the protection and assistance of a well-designed scenario. Some of the advantages of the scenario can be listed briefly here.

1. A successful play rarely, if ever, can be written from beginning to end with no changes necessary. Those inevitable changes are easier to make on an outline than in a script.

2. Making changes on the outline is not only easier but also markedly more efficient than making changes in the completed script. The outline permits shifting about of various units into a new order, often accomplished simply by drawing arrows to indicate the new arrangement. Comparable shifts in the script, however, demand major revisions of at least portions and more likely the whole play. Such revisions are a wasteful expenditure of time and creative energy.

3. The process of building the scenario, although difficult, is nonetheless easier than writing the script. The scenario therefore eases the playwright into writing, and it avoids the shock of starting the entire project with a blank piece of paper on which is typed only "Act One, Scene One. The curtain rises."

4. The playwright can study the bare bones of the scenario before the other dimensions of the play are added. The skeleton allows the author to check the structure, because it is all that can be seen at this time. Later, when dialogue and other materials flesh out the outline, it is more difficult to judge the basic structure.

5. After the playwright has revised the scenario into its final draft, attention can shift to characterization and dialogue and other aspects of the play. The scenario frees the creative flow of writing.

6. A well-organized scenario allows the playwright to attack individual scenes to be sure the play actually will work. Instead of starting with the first scene and writing the entire play to get to the most significant moment, the writer can write that moment first. Once that scene is completed, the playwright is free to work on the preliminary materials leading to that crucial place in the play.

7. The scenario organizes the writer's daily work. The outline will always be there to give the playwright the proper sense of direction for each new writing period.

Do not think the scenario is engraved in granite. Changes often are made as the writer works through the project. Those changes will enhance the play and will not change its focus as long as you have the scenario to guide you.

The First Scenario

Your first scenario will be perhaps a paragraph or two in length. Here you set forth the basic concept you will explore. Some writers call this the play's *premise*. The scenario will contain all of the basic information but not details of the action. You will want to include such materials as:

1. The basic conflict of the play. Describe the explosive qualities and the clashes of wills. Who wants what, why, and what stops the person from achieving the goal?

2. The play's thought. Divide thought into subject and theme, and state each as briefly as possible. ("My play's subject is *justice*. The theme is that the distinction between justice and revenge is too often blurred.")

3. The characters. List all names, ages, relationships, what each wants, emotional tonalities, how each differs from the others, and other distinguishing characteristics; perhaps details such as occupation and personal habits could be included.

4. The play's genre. Is it drama? Comedy? Realism?

5. Length. Is it a one-act play? A full-length play?

6. The time and place. Describe the "feel" of the environment, that is, the significance of the setting and time, and how these touch the action and characters.

7. The basic story. You will need perhaps two paragraphs to tell the basic story. At this point you need only the essences.

The first scenario is a beginning. Here you organize the approach to writing your play. If you cannot supply these bare specifics, you certainly are not ready to begin writing. If you plunge directly into writing the script knowing less than these essentials, your play will soon collapse into a muddled mess.

Revisions and Growth

Do not rush these scenario steps. Contemplative time here is well spent and will benefit the play later. Changes in the scenario should give your play more depth and interest; however, if you hurry through the construction of the scenario, your play will suffer. Your goal is to create a carefully organized outline which will make writing easier.

The scenario will grow more detailed; scenes will come to mind and conflicts will spark. You will find that you are beginning to know the characters, and you will soon "hear" them speak and "see" them as they move through the environment. Their emotions will become yours, and you will laugh and cry with them. You will begin writing their dialogue.

The Final Scenario

One last organizational effort to put the scenes into their proper order will produce the final scenario. It will be rich in detail. You will have at least the following materials:

1. The play's title.
2. The length of the play.
3. The play's genre.
4. The time and place of the action. You may need a great deal of information here to describe the time (if other than the present). The place should be described in detail, although you should not think in terms of the stage (for instance, avoid such descriptions as "a window is down left" and simply say "there is a window").
5. The characters.
   a. Ages, relationships, emotional qualities and tonalities, attitudes, biographical details, and the like.
   b. The protagonist. Her goal, motivations to achieve the goal, strength of purpose and need, and steps she is prepared to take to achieve that goal.
   c. The antagonist. His reasons to stand against the protagonist, strength of purpose, and steps he is prepared to take to thwart the protagonist.

6. A statement describing the play's thought, divided into subject and theme.
7. A sentence or two stating the basic conflict of the play.
8. An explanation of "why *now*"—that is, why does the action take place now instead of yesterday or tomorrow? What is the play's sense of urgency?
9. The beats of the play, in proper order. A "beat" is a major action-unit, a single emphatic stroke of the story. When one says "this happens, and then this, followed by this," one is describing three beats of the play. Beats center around complications.

10. The "French scenes" of the play, in order. These are named for the construction system of the seventeenth-century French plays. Each French scene is marked by the entrance or exit of a major character, on the logical premise that the play's action changes significantly with those entrances and exits. If one thinks of the stimuli from major characters, then the French scene makes more sense. Although it is old-fashioned, the French scene device nonetheless can organize the scenario.

The scenario will be long, perhaps five pages or so for a one-act play, and approaching twenty for a full-length one. The writer should not begrudge the effort and time expended, because once the scenario is done a large portion of the play already has been written. True, the scenario often has so many mechanical aspects that it bores playwrights, but when it has been completed the actual writing is made easy.

Do most playwrights construct a scenario for a one-act play? No. Experienced playwrights often are able to draft the action mentally for the relatively simple one-act play. Note, please, the operative word in that sentence: "experienced" playwrights. Those with less experience should not bypass the scenario.

But I have the play well in mind: Why should I bother with a scenario? If you actually have the play securely in mind, the scenario will be easy to write. Go ahead and practice.

Should I use a scenario even if I'm writing a short play? Yes. The training will make the construction of a scenario for a full-length play easier.

Do most playwrights make a scenario for a full-length play? Most assuredly, yes

Must I always use that particular ten-point format spelled out above? No. But use that system for your first several plays until you have experienced enough to know how to adapt it for your own particular needs.

Isn't the ten-point format too detailed? Not at all; every piece of information from that outline will be useful in writing the play.

Why can't I just make the scenario in my mind? Why write it? First, you want to be a writer; write the scenario. Second, the act of writing will help you think of new aspects to add to the scenario. Third, once it is on paper you can make changes and revisions to improve the outline. Fourth, you will want to mull it over repeatedly, and you may spend days or weeks working on it; if it is written, you will be better able to study it, but if it is "in your mind," you quite likely will forget parts of it.

If you intend to make writing your life's work, you will want to establish proper working habits and a professional's attitude. Scenario construction is part of the craft of writing. Learn the process now and it will soon become second nature to you. Ignore it now and you will be establishing sloppy working habits that will haunt you as long as you stay in writing.

I stress the scenario because I have seen so many talented writers fall away from playwriting because they simply would not write the scenario and instead wrote the play that did not hold together. I urge you to make writing easier: Develop the proper scenario construction habits now!

Exercises

1. Read carefully the first act of *Macbeth*. You might wish to read it several times until you feel comfortable with the play.

From memory, recreate the beat-by-beat outline of action of Act One. Then refer to the script and revise your scenario to take care of the errors. How many beats did Shakespeare use in the first act?

From memory, recreate the French scene outline of the action in Act One. Then refer to the script again and revise the scenario as necessary. How many French scenes are there in the first act?

Do you see how beats and French scenes work and how they create a flow of action?

2. Read the rest of *Macbeth* carefully.

Some critics claim that Shakespeare's play is flawed because he removed Lady Macbeth from the action. So revise Shakespeare's play; create your own scenario that will keep Lady Macbeth alive until the final scene of the play. This will, of course, call for major revisions, rather rude changes in Shakespeare's classic. Go ahead and revise; he has had more violent treatment and he continues to survive nonetheless. When you finish, do you now have a better idea of how a scenario can be constructed? And do you see why Shakespeare had to get rid of Lady Macbeth (or else change the title of his play)?

3. Now begin constructing a scenario of a play that you wish to write. Follow the ten-point outline described earlier in this chapter.

Chapter Nine

The Sound of
a Breaking Harp-String

The sights and sounds of the stage are as much the playwright's province as are the characters and their words. The modern playwright stimulates the imaginations of the technical personnel, demanding carefully specified effects, in order to maintain control over the whole. The result can be vital and exciting.

Effects of Sound

Anyone who has had the good fortune of attending a conscientious production of Anton Chekhov's *The Cherry Orchard* will remember the impact of the ending. The playwright has everyone on stage dashing about, with emotions ranging from despair to happiness, in a rather hectic exit. The last one leaves. Now Chekhov forces the pace to slow and he demands much of his stage crews:

> *The stage is empty. There is the sound of the doors being locked up, then of the carriages driving away. There is silence. In the stillness there is the dull stroke of an ax in a tree, clanging with a mournful lonely sound. Footsteps are heard. FIRS appears in the doorway on the right. He is dressed as always—in a pea jacket and white waistcoat, with slippers on his feet. He is ill.*

FIRS

(Goes up to the doors, and tries the handles.)

Locked! They have gone . . .

(Sits down on sofa.)

They have forgotten me . . . Never mind . . . I'll sit here a bit. . . . I'll be bound Leonid Andreyevitch hasn't put his fur coat on and has gone off in his thin overcoat.

(Sighs anxiously.)

I didn't see after him. . . . These young people. .

(Mutters something that can't be distinguished.)

Life has slipped by as though I hadn't lived.

(Lies down.)

I'll lie down a bit. . . There's no strength in you, nothing left—all gone! Ech! I'm good for nothing.

(Lies motionless.)

> *A sound is heard that seems to come from the sky, like a breaking harp-string, dying away mournfully. All is still again, and there is heard nothing but the strokes of the ax far away in the orchard.*
>
> CURTAIN.

Chekhov here creates one of the great moments of theatre; the sounds give the play a richness which could not be achieved had he thought only of characters and words. The sound of the ax in the cherry orchard and the mournful harp-string add poignancy to the play.

Visual Effects

Colors, too, can be significant. Federico Garcia-Lorca demands a visual symbol to give strength to the final scene of *Blood Wedding*. Earlier in the play the playwright had used a forest scene at night. For that scene he had called for "great moist tree trunks," darkness, intense blue lighting, and the visual qualities presented by a personified Moon and The Beggar Woman who represents Death. He then switches to a sharply contrasting scene. He turns his painter's eye upon the interpretation of his theme as he describes the visual aspect of the play's final scene: In an all-white room are girls dressed in blue who are winding balls of red yarn. The symbol is appropriate for *Blood Wedding*: white is the temple of the body, blue are the veins, and red is blood. The playwright thinks not only of words but of the totality of the stage.

Stage Directions: Hearing and Seeing Characters

The playwright uses sound, color, and performers. For the latter, stage directions give the dramatist opportunity to communicate to performer and director. For example, the playwright can avoid mundane words by giving instructions to the actor. Here is a simplified example:

MARY

John, won't you please give me the bottle?

JOHN

I will not! It belongs to me! You can't have it. You go get your own bottle!

The author eliminates words by "seeing" the people, as indicated below:

MARY

John.. . .

(Points at the bottle.)

Give it to me? Please?

JOHN

(Shakes his head; holds the bottle close as if a baby; he speaks petulantly.)

Go get your own.

Neither example would win an award, but at least the second is more economical, stronger, with more coloration. John, in particular, becomes more alive.

The process requires that the playwright not only hear the characters but also see them. The author's concept of character can be shown visually, as Lorraine Hansberry shows Walter Lee Younger so vividly in this moment from *A Raisin in the Sun:*

RUTH

Oh, Walter—

WALTER

(An irritable mimic.)

Oh, Walter! Oh, Walter!

(To Murchison.)

How's your old man making out? I understand you all going to buy that big hotel on the Drive?

(He finds a beer in the refrigerator, wanders over to Murchison, sipping and wiping his lips with the back of his hand, and straddling a chair backwards to talk to the other man.)

Shrewd move. Your old man is all right, man.

(Tapping his head and half winking for emphasis.)

I mean he knows how to operate. I mean he thinks *big,* you
know what I mean, I mean for a *home,* you know? But I think he's
kind of running out of ideas now. I'd like to talk to him. Listen,
man, I got some plans that could turn this city upside down. I
mean I think like he does. *Big.* Invest big, gamble big, hell, lose
big if you have to, you know what I mean. It's hard to find a man
on this whole Southside who understands my kind of
thinking—you dig?

(He scrutinizes Murchison again, drinks his beer, squints his eyes
and leans in close, confidential, man to man.)

Me and you ought to sit down and talk sometimes, man. Man, I
got me some ideas . . .

GEORGE

(With boredom.)

Yeah—sometimes we'll have to do that, Walter.

Here is a fine dramatist who hears her characters and sees them. There is no
question about it, we know Walter: pie-in-the-sky dreams, talking big dreams as
he drinks beer, posing in the chair to be a big man speaking to a man, a person
speaking of *big* but doomed to small. The playwright makes Walter vivid and
alive by the addition of actor instructions.

The advantage to the playwright cannot be ignored. Not only does the
character become more alive for audiences as a result of the actor instructions,
undoubtedly the character became more alive to the playwright as she en-
visioned Walter's visual actions. She was able to see him in both a literal and
figurative sense. Writing becomes easier as one thinks of the character moving,
doing things, smiling or frowning, sitting leaning back or straddling a chair.

A *Streetcar Named Desire* is filled with stage directions that are essential
communications. Without the sounds and sights, the play would be markedly
smaller; the sounds of the blue piano and the sight of the small overhead lights
carefully shaded by Blanche are part of the effects created by the playwright so
often praised for his theatrical abilities.

The opening moments immediately characterize Stanley and Stella. He
enters, carrying a red-stained package from the butcher shop, and yells for
Stella. She comes out and Stanley throws the meat to her despite her protests.
Almost without looking to see if she caught it, Stanley starts off. She calls after
him to ask if she can come with him. "Come on," he replies, and continues
without stopping.

Here Williams encapsulates the relationship of husband and wife by showing an atavistic moment. No one seeing those initial moments can mistake the
two. The hunter brings home meat for his mate, and she depends upon him. The
pantomimic dramatization is quite strong.

The conclusion of the play neatly balances the beginning. Again, *pantomimic dramatization* is used. The interloper is taken off and the nest is once more secure. The men continue their poker game while Stanley and Stella, outside the apartment, curl closely together. She holds their baby; he comforts his wife; his fingers slip into her blouse; the family unit is again secure. We hear the blues music of the piano and trumpet.

It is superior pantomimic dramatization and demonstrates quite effectively how the imaginative playwright uses lights, sound, and performers to create a totality far stronger than would be possible for a novelist or poet. The theatre's strengths are exploited well, indeed.

The stage direction provides the playwright with a fine working relationship between author and stage workers. The playwright gains more flexibility and more "arrows for the quiver." The author is encouraged to think of the sounds and sights of the stage.

Overusing Stage Directions?

Not all scholars believe the playwright should depend so heavily upon stage directions. The Greeks did not use stage directions, such scholars emphasize, nor did Shakespeare. "Let the playwright learn to communicate via dialogue and with action. There's too much focus upon insignificant trivia in the modern theatre," they say.

However, these nay-sayers ignore salient facts. In the first place, Shakespeare was present during productions of his plays. He could speak directly to the performers. Obviously, the modern playwright is separated from productions to a degree never felt by those who wrote in years past. It is small wonder that the playwright attempts to bring control back to the script via stage directions.

A more significant factor, however, has to do with the modern age. Today's playwright operates within concepts that brought "modernism" into being. We today are highly aware of the importance of heredity and environment as determinants of human behavior patterns. Certain dramatic actions can take place in, say, a bus station in a metropolitan city but not in a small town residence. *The Iceman Cometh* demands the specific locale O'Neill describes, a bar, because the author saw the effects of place upon person: that bar *forces* the action forward.

Walter Kerr, with customary keen insight, describes incorrect use of the stage direction. In his fine book, *How Not to Write a Play*, Kerr talks about the playwright's discovery of the instruction to the actor. The author writes an ordinary line, something such as, "I think I'll be going now." Then, by use of the stage direction, the author can call for the line to be read "unhappily" or "angrily" or "indifferently" and so on for a host of possibilities. Armed with the stage direction, Kerr points out, the playwright needs never write a line which is itself unhappy or angry or indifferent. The result is thin dialogue, watered down to insipid tastelessness.

No doubt Kerr is right, but the problem he describes is one which concerns dialogue rather than stage directions—let the playwright be encouraged to write dialogue with correct flavor, but let the playwright also be encouraged to use the stage and theatrical effects. The playwright needs to remember that too many demands might increase the difficulties and expenses of a play's production to a point where the producers will either ignore the play or ignore the playwright's wishes.

For an illustration of difficult stage directions, consider Federico Garcia-Lorca's magnificent poetic tragedy, *The House of Bernarda Alba.* In the opening moments of the play the stage directions call for women of the village to begin entering slowly into Bernarda Alba's home. As they enter, the maid speaks a total of four sentences, or forty words. After that short speech, Garcia-Lorca's stage direction says, "The two hundred women finish coming in . . ."

The two hundred women? And they were to enter, two by two, during the maid's one short speech? A production I directed used approximately thirty village women at that moment, and we brought them in as quickly as we could. Even so, the play's forward motion was endangered, and I suspect the effect would be even comic if the production paused for two hundred women to enter. The expense of hiring that many extras could bankrupt a professional production, and how many amateur productions can find so many women to perform but one moment on stage? Here is an example of a stage direction that can overwhelm producers.

Summary

The stage direction provides the playwright with a communication to stage technicians, performers, and directors. To the degree that the playwright's imagination sees and hears the universe of the play, so to that degree should he describe those sounds and visuals.

The playwright should use stage tricks for flavoring not just because they are available, but because the sounds and sights help the playwright's development of thought, character, and plot. Excesses of stage directions, like excesses of any writing technique, will cloud the play; use of the best single effect will, as always, be a wise choice toward making the whole stronger.

Exercises

1. Read Samuel Beckett's two pantomimes, *Act Without Words I* and *Act Without Words II.* It might help you better understand the riches of those plays if you know that each will take approximately thirty minutes to perform (to judge by the playing time of productions I have directed). Visualize the half hour.

2. Take any page from a script you have written. Arbitrarily eliminate twenty words or more by use of actor instructions to replace dialogue. (For example, write the instruction "nodding" to replace the words "Yes, I agree," or the instruction "holding up the book" to replace the words "do you mean this book?") After you have completed the revision, ask yourself if that page's writing style is now sharper. Also ask if you feel you are a bit more sensitive toward the character(s) whose lines were revised.

3. Write a brief (perhaps three-page) pantomime.

Chapter Ten

The Scene
Not Written,
the Speech Unspoken

The Silent Macbeth

Macbeth, Act One, Scene Three: Macbeth and Banquo are on the "blasted heath," a strange place not quite of the real world. A moment ago they had encountered the three witches and Banquo had marveled at their peculiar appearance. Macbeth then speaks to the Weird Sisters.

MACBETH

Speak, if you can. What are you?

FIRST WITCH

All hail, Macbeth! Hail to thee, Thane of Glamis!

MACBETH

How know ye of events not yet pronounced? But yesterday the title pass'd to make me Glamis.

SECOND WITCH

All hail, Macbeth! Hail to thee, Thane of Cawdor.

MACBETH

Nay, not Cawdor. I bid thee to instruct me why you greet me thus imperfectly.

THIRD WITCH

All hail, Macbeth, that shalt be King hereafter!

MACBETH

But Duncan lives! How canst those wrinkled eyes,
Blue-fogg'd with age and weary of the world's dull
Daily repetitions, now perceive what beats within
My secret heart? Indeed, King. Yet Duncan lives!

Of course that is not the way Shakespeare wrote this significant opening moment. In truth, had he been this clumsy, it is likely that author and plays would have sunk in deserved obscurity long ago.

Here is what Shakespeare wrote.

MACBETH

Speak, if you can. What are you?

FIRST WITCH

All hail, Macbeth! Hail to thee, Thane of Glamis!

SECOND WITCH

All hail, Macbeth! Hail to thee, Thane of Cawdor!

THIRD WITCH

All hail, Macbeth, that shalt be King hereafter!

BANQUO

Good sir, why do you start and seem to fear
Things that do sound so fair?

. . . . .

My noble partner
You greet with present grace and great prediction
Of noble having and of royal hope,
That he seems rapt withal.

Macbeth does *not* speak!

Banquo listens to the predictions and awaits Macbeth's answer. Macbeth does not reply! Banquo observes Macbeth's reactions—he is afraid and then entranced—and then speaks to the witches himself.

Why does Shakespeare elect to keep his protagonist silent at this crucial moment? We have just met Macbeth for the first time and hardly know him, so why would the playwright let slip this opportunity to give his central character a sensitive and insightful speech about the temptation he suddenly faces? Why does Shakespeare leave out that sweeping speech which would echo the strong emotions now beginning to blaze within Macbeth?

The playwright's decision to omit Macbeth's verbal responses is the more surprising when one examines the play's structure. Note that the plot begins at this very moment; here is the play's point of attack. Here, too, begins the play's thematic struggle. Why would Shakespeare, the consummate theatrical artist, let slip this golden chance to hammer clearly the point of attack and the play's theme?

"Streetcar's" Final Confrontation

Lest it be concluded that Macbeth is silent because that is the way of old-timey poetic tragedy, consider now a modern classic. We move from the elevated world of royalty to a much more elemental level of animalistic survival.

A *Streetcar Named Desire* has an even larger "hole," an even more remarkable omission. The play is missing not merely one speech—there is an *entire scene* conspicuously absent. I marvel at the omission because this missing scene is one that playwright Tennessee Williams could have filled with exciting emotional pyrotechnics. For Williams, the scene would have been marvelously easy to write; for the performers the scene would have been an exciting challenge.

Williams structured *Streetcar* by scenes instead of acts. There are eleven scenes, each roughly equal in length. Early scenes establish the characters' emotional needs and psychic territorial boundaries. Blanche's need for a safe haven leads her to try to exclude Stanley from his own home; Stanley's masculine concept of self makes him shove against any force that pushes him. As he becomes aware that she represents a threat to the sanctity of his nest, the conflict turns into a war of survival. Blanche suggests to Stella that she ought leave the brutish Stanley; Stanley, incensed at Blanche's airs, discovers she has led a common life and has been lying to him. He buys Blanche a bus ticket for her birthday and tells her to leave.

These are intricately sensual people. The act of sex is essential, but for different individual reasons. For Stanley, sexual intercourse is part of his masculine definition, and with Stella it is his expression of love. For Stella, the act is a prime source of her contentment with Stanley, the reason she is "narcoticized." For Blanche, sexual activity is a device to push back, even if momentarily, the terrors of loneliness, and it is her way to attract someone who will give her the protection she so desperately craves.

Scene Eight ends with Stella going to the hospital, where she will have Stanley's child. Scene Nine is a duet between Blanche and Mitch, the latter primed by Stanley to think of Blanche as a cheap whore. And Scene Ten begins with byplay between Blanche and Stanley. The "playfulness" is not light, however. They are alone in the house. As the scene draws to an end, Stanley is stalking Blanche, who becomes frightened of his rough sexual advances. She smashes the top off a bottle and faces him. He forces her to drop the bottle. She moans and falls to the floor; he says "we've had this date from the beginning" and carries her to the bed. The scene ends.

The following scene could be subtitled "The Final Confrontation." In it, Blanche confronts Stella with the brutal fact of the rape. "Your husband, that pig! He! Raped! Me!" Stella says she will not listen. Blanche persists. "Even while you were in the hospital having that Polack's baby! He was wearing his bridegroom's night-clothing with an evil lustful look on his face!" The baby, awakened by the shouts, begins to cry and Stella picks it up to coo over it almost musically as Blanche sobs. "What will we do, Stella, sister Stella, Stella-for-star? What will we do?" Stella rocks the baby, singing softly to it. "I! Fought! But in the end, his greasy hands were more powerful and he was the victor!" Stanley now enters, demanding less noise. Blanche cowers in the corner but he doesn't even glance at her. She demands that Stella get the truth from Stanley: "Ask him!" Stella, unwilling to ask, turns slowly to Stanley. She looks at him. Will he lie? Will he tell the truth? Whichever, what will she say in return to him? More significantly, what will she do? Will the truth force Stella to leave Stanley, to go off with Blanche? Will Stanley casually dismiss the charges, saying they come from a crazy woman who knows only the beds of the Flamingo Hotel? Will he simply stare at both women coldly, refusing to speak at all?

But of course the above scene is *not* in the script.

That scene is missing, conspicuously: there is not a "final confrontation" at all. Why?

The scene that *does* follow is "some weeks later." Stella is packing Blanche's things. Eunice, the neighbor, helps. The men are playing poker. Soon the doctor and the nurse appear to take Blanche away. She's rather distant, not quite in contact with reality. Gently they guide her off. Stella sobs, "Oh, God, what have I done to my sister?" Stanley comforts Stella, crooning to her, holding her, his fingers at the opening of her blouse. Tableau.

Final curtain.

Why did Williams leave out that "confrontation scene," when Blanche confronts Stella with the rape? Why did he leave out the explosions which would be fired by the exposure of truth? Why did the playwright elect to omit the fires and pyrotechnics? Considering that this would be a scene that could show Williams at his best when emotions are rubbing against raw nerves, why isn't the scene in the play?

We know that there was a confrontation, that Blanche told Stella about Stanley. As Stella says in that final scene, "I couldn't believe her story and go on living with Stanley." So there was indeed a moment of truth. But only once does Williams mention it, and never does he show it to us.

Why is the scene not in the play?

Why did Shakespeare keep Macbeth from speaking, and why did Williams omit an entire scene? *Because the playwrights knew that more could be said with less.*

Macbeth is not precisely "silent." He doesn't speak but there is a great deal of active communication, character to character and character to audience. The audience senses that the witches have awakened some dark and terrible secret deep within Macbeth. True, the audience may not be totally confident it knows all details of those emotions, but it is led to look at Macbeth now far more than had he spoken of his feelings. More is said with less; that unspoken speech lets the audience sense there is a mystery inside Macbeth. The audience is curious. It decides to watch that man with the strange silence; it will find out just what burns inside of him; the audience is intrigued by the way he keeps his thoughts secret in contrast to the more outspoken Banquo.

To digress for a moment, here lies the answer to those interpreters who like to suggest that the witches are agents of the devil and that all of this play's evil derives from supernatural force. Nonsense! This very scene shows that Shakespeare portrays Macbeth as a man with a powder keg of ambition inside;

the witches help him light the fuse, but they do not create the keg. His silence at this crucial moment shows he is now facing dark demons he previously had managed to subdue. They rage alive, now that half-imaginings have been put into words. Shakespeare's play too strongly establishes *character* as the driving force to permit any rational person to conclude that the play implies that the devil sent witches to work supernatural powers over helpless mortals. Macbeth is immensely powerful. If he were so weak as to be made putty in the hands of witches who say only a few words, the play itself would be quite small. Shakespeare wrote a gigantic tragedy about a man's downfall, not a small thing about Weird Sisters. Macbeth also is speechless because, simply, whatever words he might be given would be tiny. "O, be still, my heart." "Who, me?" What would we have him say?

Williams omits his scene for several reasons. First, it would have been structurally unsound. The playwright is at the end of the play and must move rapidly to its conclusion. He does not have room for the confrontation scene; if it were included, then the departure would be anticlimatic. The departure has priority and therefore the confrontation is best skipped. Secondly, Williams simply does not need that confrontation scene; he has established characters and the situation so completely that he can confidently expect the audience's imagination to fill in the scene. And it does. As soon as the audience sees that Williams is skipping the moment of confrontation, in a flash the audience "writes" the scene itself, filling in all the blanks, staying within the parameters of the characters Williams has so richly drawn in earlier scenes. It takes the audience only a moment to write the entire scene; had Williams written it, it probably would have been a ten-minute scene on stage.

A Great Play Stimulates Imagination

All of this leads to a partial definition of a great play: *A great play is one that stimulates the audience's imagination to add more material and depth than is actually in the play.* By having Macbeth speechless, Shakespeare makes the audience imagine what the man is thinking and feeling. By boldly leaping over an entire scene, Williams asks the audience to imagine all of the details of that explosive confrontation between Blanche, Stella, and Stanley. Audience participation is demanded. How remarkable that playwrights can be so sensitive to the audience's imaginative powers that the authors knew to *not* write the materials!

A Great Play Does Not Answer Everything

A second partial definition follows the above: *A great play forces the audience to enter the play and to participate with the characters; a lesser play keeps the audience at* arm's length by solving every problem. A play will be strong if it demands that the audience use its intellectual powers because of emotional involvement and a desire to know more. Too much detail prevents the audience from participating.

A "Talky" Play Defined

Sometimes beginning playwrights are hard pressed to explain why a play seems "wordy" or "talky." After all, don't plays depend upon words? Aren't we taught that it is through dialogue that a play communicates? But the difference is one of need: A talky play is one that says more than the audience needs to hear in order to understand; it uses more words than the situation demands; it leaves nothing for the audience's imagination.

A play is not at its best when it plods along on leaden feet. Plays must be free to fly, to jump, to take bold new directions.

If it is true that a speech can be unspoken and that the entire scene can be unplayed, it follows that smaller units can be omitted: words, phrases, or sequences. The result will be exciting and vibrantly alive. (See Pinter's The Dumb Waiter and study carefully the many times a character does not speak.)

You may need to shake loose the chains of modern realistic drama's influence upon you. One good way is to use the poet's brevity. The goal is to say less and mean more. Undoubtedly there will be times that the goal is frustratingly difficult to achieve, but time and practice will bring rewards.

Chapter Eleven

Script Format: Preparing the Final Version

The final version of the playwright's manuscript is designed primarily for production personnel and not for a publisher. For that reason, certain traditions have accumulated that influence the appearance of the final script.

The play must be typewritten. A handwritten script simply is not acceptable. The playwright who has yet to learn to type is at a distinct disadvantage, but there are typing services in almost every community and, if necessary, the author can hire someone to type the playscript.

The typewriter should be equipped with pica (large-size) typeface. Elite (small-size) typeface is permissible, but because it is more difficult to read it is not preferred. Avoid "cutsie" typefaces *such as script* or those that shout out their uniqueness SUCH AS THE SORT OFTEN FOUND AROUND RADIO OR TV STATIONS. The typewriter keys ought to be clean and reasonably well aligned. The ribbon should be in good health and totally black.

Neatness is important. A messily typed playscript implies overall messy workmanship; a neatly prepared script suggests the work of a careful professional who takes pride in the art and craft of writing. The romantic in me likes to think that a new *Macbeth* or *After the Fall* would receive an attentive reading from a producer even if the manuscript was in horrible condition, but the pragmatic part of me tends to be more cynical.

Avoid "easy erase" brands of typing paper. Such paper is easy to erase because the surface is coated to prevent the ink from setting into the paper. As a result, the ink reproduces itself on shirt cuffs and hand palms, and the page smears easily. Producers hate it. Expensive heavyweight bond paper, which is standard for novels or poems being submitted to a publisher, seldom is used for playscripts. Most producers accept photocopies, although the playwright ought to be sure there are no long black lines or smears. Usually the playwright keeps the original and sends the copies to the producers or publishers.

The goal is to achieve a neat and legible playscript which clearly communicates the playwright's vision. Certain conventions for spacing, indentation, and capitalization help achieve that goal. Anything counterproductive that distracts from the play should be avoided.

There are several typographical forms that are acceptable. The following material gives specific instructions, but it is understood that variations are permissible.

Typing the Script

Margins. The playscript is bound. Ample room is given for the binding device on the left side of the page, and the right, top, and bottom margins are about one inch.

The Title Page. The title page is the cover sheet. The title of the play in all capital letters is centered, perhaps five inches down from the top of the sheet. It is underlined.

Double-spaced under the title, and also centered, is a brief objective phrase about the play (such as, "A one-act play," or "A verse drama in eight scenes"). Qualitative descriptions are avoided ("A new and unique magnificent rollicking comi-tragedy about sexual failures caused by social pressures"). The descriptive phrase is not underlined. It has one capital letter, at the beginning.

Under the title, after a double-space, the word "by" is centered. Then after a single space appears the playwright's name, which is centered, neither in all capital letters nor underlined.

In the bottom right corner of the page appears the playwright's name and mailing address. Usually the telephone number also appears. Under that is typed the copyright information (such as "Copyright 1984").

On the cover sheet also appears an identification of the draft ("Draft #6, January, 1984"). This is less for the reader's information and more for the playwright's convenience in keeping the various versions of the play properly identified. It is apt to be beneath the author's name or perhaps with the other information at the bottom right corner of the page.

Dedication Page. If the play is dedicated, that appears on the second page. The dedication tends to be a simple statement (such as "For T. T. Cooke. Thanks."), typed on the approximate center of the page. Most authors avoid the dedication until the play has proved its success. A double or triple dedication is not unusual for playwrights who feel indebted to several people.

Characters, Time, Place, Acts. Usually this information appears on one page. However, if the play has so many in the cast that listing them fills an entire page, "Time" and "Place" will move to the next page.

Cast of Characters is centered, typed in all capital letters, and underlined. Under the heading will be a simple listing of the characters. There is little description of them at this time, at most basic facts about ages and/or family relationships.

The *Time* heading is also centered, in all capital letters, and underlined. A sentence or two states the time. For instance, "The play takes place one dark January afternoon in 1864" is adequate.

The *Place* heading is typed as the previous two entries are. Again, a simple sentence suffices: "The play takes place in the parlor of Abraham Lincoln's home in Springfield, Illinois."

The above elements will take care of a one-act play's needs. For a full-length play, the playwright adds "The Acts" and indicates, as necessary, times and places of each act.

Previous Production. A play that has been produced usually has a page or two listing details of its premiere performance. The cast, director, designers, producers, and crews are included. The reader can tell where the play was presented, and when, as well as other details.

Pagination. Each page is numbered. The page number is in the upper right-hand corner because the left-hand corner may be obscured by the binding. Along with the page number there are always one or two key words from the play's title. For instance, *Death of a Salesman* could use "SALESMAN, p. 10." Pagination is not indicated on the title page but appears on every other page.

For a one-act play, the pages are numbered sequentially. For a full-length script, pagination is a bit more complex. There is the name of the play, followed by the (*a*) act number, (*b*) page of that act, and (*c*) sequential number. For example, II-5-45 refers to the forty-fifth page of the entire script and to the fifth page of Act II.

The Script. And now begins the script. There are three basic parts to the typography of the script: (*a*) dialogue (and character names), (*b*) actor directions, and (*c*) stage directions.

Character names for dialogue are placed in the approximate center of the page and not along the left-hand margin as one often sees in published scripts. There is one tab-key setting for all names in that approximate center; individual names are not centered individually. The names are typed in all capital letters, and nothing else is typed on that line.

Dialogue begins a single space beneath the all-capitals character name. It uses the full width of the page, left to right, and is almost always single-spaced, with some exceptions for (*a*) actor directions, or (*b*) paragraphing. Dialogue can be paragraphed, if that helps clarify meanings, but usually it is not. The playwright freely uses typographic techniques such as underlining, dashes and dots, all capital letters, and exclamation marks to help express what he hears the characters saying and how he hears them saying it.

Actor directions are aimed at the specific actor (versus stage directions which are more broadly addressed). Usually these have to do with the way the playwright hears the line. She may indicate the line to be spoken "angrily," "crying," "whispering," or "with sharp intakes of breath." Sometimes the actor direction indicates the playwright's concept of the visual aspect of the character, such as "smiling," or "looking away," or "hiding his face within his hands." Actor directions are single-spaced beneath the character name, indented approximately seven spaces from the left, and placed within parentheses.

Indicated below are the spacing and arrangement for dialogue, character names, and actor directions.

WILLIE

(Blinking quickly.)
I can't . . . I mean . . . Not *this* way. No!

WOODY

(With pencils he taps a marching beat.)
Listen to me, m'boy. We're goin' *on*. Hear that? WE'RE GOIN' ON!

(The drum beat increases in tempo.)
You 'n me. Movin' *on*, hup-two-three-four, raight-shoulder HARMS, a-boot FACE, ONE-two-three-four.

WILLIE

No!
(He looks up; imploringly.)
Why do You do this to *me*?

WOODY

(The drumming stops; a whisper.)
I tol' Him to.

(He becomes a conductor; the symphony orchestra plays largo and with feeling.)
There's the way of it, Willie m'boy; we're singin' forth a song and movin' on.

Stage directions contain basic information for producing the play. From this information will come artistic and practical decisions of designers, directors, operating crews, and performers. Stage directions may be long or short, depending upon the individual writer's desire to show the production personnel the images which surround the dialogue.

Typists keep stage directions to the right-hand half of the page. If character names appear on a centered vertical line, stage directions are usually indented another five spaces to keep them away from the names. Paragraphing in the directions separates thoughts.

Within the stage directions, all capital letters draw the attention of appropriate theatre personnel. All character names are written in all capital letters, as is such information as "lighting," "sound," "curtain," and the like. The goal is to insure quick and easy communication to appropriate personnel.

Stage directions are purely informational. Never will the playwright use this area for discussions of the philosophy or theme of the play or the meaning of life's truth. Even George Bernard Shaw had difficulty getting away with that sort of writing, and today's playwright should not seek to compete with Shaw. Occasional humor is not totally inappropriate in stage directions for a comedy, but the playwright is not obliged to amuse production personnel.

The first part of stage directions describes the environment, the mood, the setting; several paragraphs here may be necessary. Subsequent paragraphs typically focus upon descriptions of characters. A full description of a character is given at the time of that character's initial appearance.

Example of a Typed Script

ACT I.

THE CURTAIN RISES. *We see a small room, with a desk and chair dominating.* LIGHTING *emphasizes the gloom. It is early morning in January.*

AT RISE: *onstage is* ROBERT BARROWS *and* MR. HUBERT ANDERSON.

ROBERT *is sitting on the edge of the desk. He is small, thin, compact, a bundle of wires like a jockey. He wears a white suit with a dark shirt and tie. There is a blood-red rose in his coat lapel. He is amazingly blond for his dark skin. He is 29.*

MR. ANDERSON *sits in a chair avoiding looking at* ROBERT. *His posture suggests he is extremely fatigued; his shoulders slump, his arms may fall down off his lap; he sometimes rubs at his eyes as if they hurt. He is around 49. When he walks it is heavily, perhaps limping. He is dressed in a three-piece suit which likely was expensive but now is torn and smudged, most especially at the knees.*

> SOUND: offstage *there is the noise of hammering, one man constructing something from short pieces of wood.*

ANDERSON

(After a pause.)

Back home . . . about now . . . they'll be waking.

ROBERT

(With the suggestion of a smile.)

Will they be thinking about you?

ANDERSON

(Heavily.)

I imagine.

(A glance at Robert.)

Will they?

ROBERT

(An unexpected explosion.)

My God, man!, listen to that damn carpenter!

> ROBERT *quickly moves from the desk to the door.*

ANDERSON

(A small nod.)

I hear him.

> ROBERT *turns to look at ANDERSON.*

ROBERT

Mr. Anderson?

> ANDERSON *walks slowly from the chair to the window. Once there he replies.*

ANDERSON

No.

> SOUND: *the offstage hammering stops.*
> *Silence.*
> SOUND: offstage *a heavy door is unlocked, swung open, slammed, and locked.*

ROBERT

A time-minded people.

(He slowly slumps next to the door, onto the floor.)

They said, 7:00 A.M. sharp.

ANDERSON
(Turns to stare at the door, his chin deliberately up.)
Well, then . . .

After the final curtain. Often play publishers print an appendix of information about the production of the play. One finds diagrams indicating lighting cues, scenic floor plans, costume notes, property lists, and other production data.

Few people realize that the playwright has nothing to do with that appendix. Such information is derived from a stage manager's prompt book. Indeed, sometimes material inside the script itself—stage directions about actor movements—comes from a stage manager instead of from the playwright.

But play publishers may ask playwrights to add a prop list (if that has not been done by the stage manager). It is easily done, and it does not harm a playwright to develop the habit of including a list of all properties at the end of the playscript.

Other notes about production concepts can be added. They will not intrude upon the play if they are written as an appendix following the final curtain.

Miscellaneous Notes

If a character's speech is carried over to the next page, the character's name is typed in all capital letters to start the dialogue. ROBERT (con't.)

Parentheses are not used to set off stage directions. The manner of indentation suffices to keep this material away from dialogue.

The playwright uses stage directions to show what he sees, but not to direct the play. The playwright can say "ANDERSON moves to the window" but *not* "ANDERSON walks downstage left and looks out the downstage-left window while ROBERT crosses upstage center."

Stage directions are written according to accepted rules of grammar and spelling.

Remember the script will be bound. Leave ample left-hand margins.

Chapter Twelve

Don't Talk about It, Write It!

Scenario: Call it, "Tragedy in a Minor Key."

Scene One: A coffee house. We discover our Author. Happy smile, animated gestures. Babbling. Flushed with warmth of having had a successful play. (A Confidant listens, asks questions, to help get this exposition across.) Bubbling about the next play, excitedly rich with ideas and situations. Talking and talking.

Quick shift into Scene Two: A street. On stage stands Author. Babbling. Talking about the next play, its plot and ideas. Confidant makes suggestions; they argue. Our Author talks.

Quick shift to Scene Three: Abstract of a bar. Sounds of a noisy pub. There leans Author. Talking about next play. Confidant (bartender) asks questions, makes suggestions. Author is expansive.

Quick shift to Scene Four: A living room. Party in progress. Smoke, disco sounds, blinking lights. Author is talking with this person, that person, describing the play. Gets many suggestions.

Scene Five: Desk, forlorn. Solo spot on desk; it is surrounded by vast empty darkness. Extreme quiet. Author sits at typewriter. Pause while nothing happens. Author sighs (echo chamber effect). Pause. Author shakes head, turns from typewriter to desk. Pause. Picks up pencil, slowly writes half a dozen words. Pause. Sigh. Throws paper on floor. Back to typewriter; inserts paper; types four words; tears out paper and throws it on floor. An expressionistically distorted clock descends from overhead; minute hand spins; hour hand spins; voice as of God says, "Hurry up, please. It's time." Lots of clock sound effects, tickings, gongs. Silence. Lights flicker. Snowstorm of typing paper (drops from flies).

Lights turn red; projections on rear cyc of fire and flames. Kettle drums. Author staggers off stage, yelping in pain. Silence.

    Blackout.

I've seen this scenario played out all too often. My students disappear offstage and can't find a way back, or I am consulted by a writer whose well of ideas has run dry. For the victim there is a heavy load of despair, frustration, and misdirected guilt. Sometimes the silence is permanent. Often one can feel sorrow over the loss of a good writer.

The problem, to simplify it, is that writing is—writing *must* be—an intense act of communication. Writing is hypercommunication, full and rich and total communication, ardent communication. It is love, desire, and sex; it is the nova of communication; writing is the Big Bang that creates suns, moons, and rippling galaxies.

In the beginning there was the Word, and the Word got written. Or else it wouldn't exist thereafter.

If you do not believe this about writing, you had better start convincing yourself that it is all of these things, and more. Don't minimize writing or else you will shrink your own works to practically nothing. Anything that weakens that intense communication will, perforce, weaken the writing. Weaken the writing enough and it becomes a mere pale wisp that flits without substance.

What weakens that intensity? A lack of concern for the craft, a lack of love for the written effort, a defeat by the frustrations set forth by the savage mistress, or a lack of psychic energy could weaken it.

Most often, however, the intensity is weakened because another form of communication is substituted: "talk." A tremendous amount of writing is squandered in babble.

Writing is a process of communicating from writer through a medium (paper, a novel, the stage and its performers) to an auditor. If you interrupt that magical process at any point, communication will stop. If you substitute oral chitter for the actual process of writing, you simply will no longer *need* to write.

"Tragedy in a Minor Key," then, is a little playlet about a writer who has shifted gears from writing to social butterflying. The latter is easier and certainly more fun than the often bloody work of writing. And it has immediate gratifications; namely, having wide-eyed listeners all golly-gee agog at being Around A Writer.

In such an environment, Quality is not essential.

Why does this sort of tragedy happen? First, our Author in those scenes was expending creative energy and time without profit. There was chitting and chatting *about* writing, but no writing. That led to some bleak silence.

Second, our Author was becoming something of a dilettante. There was a transformation, taking writing from an art and craft down into a social password. It was a shameful waste. There is an uncomfortable creature found at those places we saw our Author. Call the poor soul a Dilly, all set to talk about his Novel In Progress and the Muse and those horrible, mean old publishers who are so nasty they won't read really good stuff because, after all, It's Who You Know and . . . Our Author was becoming one of *those*.

The arts are cursed by these frilly dilettantes who dabble and mess about, motivated by a temporary fascination. One finds such types around theatre in particular, I suppose, because to them it all looks so "easy," and of course it has glitter and sparkle; they worm into a momentary influence without ever once worrying about the long-range effects of their dilly work. They last three years before they are weary. In five years a shambles exists where they touched and moved on. You now find them presidents of the community players. Four years ago they admitted they knew nothing of theatre, and now they are Resident Experts; four years hence they'll be far away from theatre, but they'll have letters framed and displayed about how good they were.

Our playwright had fallen into that sort of bad company. I urge writers to avoid such people, to rush to a different world than that which these dilettantes occupy. They carry a plague which erodes love of the art into an attempt for self-glorification. With them around, Quality becomes mere quantity.

The third problem for our Author was no less worrisome. The playwright was talking about a writing project to people whose opinions were of absolutely no value. It does the writer no good to talk to the incorrect sort of people as a social act, people who have not demonstrated an acute knowledge and love of writing, who think only casually about theatre and playwriting. It is a waste to use writing talent as a party trick.

Fourth, the writer was developing ideas. What is wrong with a process that sounds so rich? A lot. Look at our Author tossing out an idea to the party person. Of course our Author hasn't formed that idea fully, nor can he describe it with the surgical precision with which it will be written. And what happens? The friendly party person, with great eager earnestness, tells the writer the flaws of the idea. Does that help the writer? It is about as productive to his forward progress as a pound of sugar in his car's gas would be to his mileage.

The playwright made the mistake of giving a rather superficial description and letting someone evaluate it. If the evaluation is blunt—"No, that's a dumb idea"—that can deflate the writer and pull the idea out of the project. Or if the evaluation is good—"Man, that's swift"—it can make the playwright over-amplify the concept when writing the script. Either way, nothing is gained and a lot can be lost.

Fifth, suppose the party person gives a lot of new ideas to our Author: "Try this"; "Let that happen"; "Why don't you have the character do this?"; "How about throwing away the first fifty minutes and starting at the end?" Those suggestions merely let the party person play Writer in Progress and load our Author's brain with nonessential junk that may get stored in the subconscious and float out to appear as part of that project. Imagine how helpful that will be.

Sixth, suppose our Author is telling this idea to a good friend. Now the friend is in a messy situation: Should she risk the friendship and give an honest response? Suppose the friend has a rash of ideas and the writer faces that messy situation: Now what to do? In that scenario, the playwright is in a no-win situation. There is a wasteful expenditure of material, thrown away by casual chatter. Regardless of party-goers' responses, the writer is losing the original drive to communicate. Think of computerese next time you want to talk about ideas casually and listen to suggestions; computer operators speak of GIGO: "Garbage In = Garbage Out."

Take yourself, and your precious talents, more seriously. Don't expend yourself casually. Rather than talk about writing, why not sit yourself down and write?

"The Six
Elements
of Drama"

Parts One and Two give a general overview to playwriting. Now, in Part Three, you will find detailed discussions of each aspect of a play. The following chapters will focus upon the contents of plays—plot, character, thought, diction (often called dialogue), music, and spectacle.

It is not necessary to read the chapters in order. After reading the next chapter ("An Introduction to 'The Six Elements of Drama' ") you may elect to read material on any element you think most significant for your particular writing.

Parts One and Two should have gotten you writing. Part Three now covers in depth methods that will help you improve your plays.

Chapter Thirteen

An Introduction to "The Six Elements of Drama"

How does one learn what makes a play? Are there individual essences of theatre? What are the construction units that build a drama? Is there an organized approach, a step-by-step methodical system, to understanding the nature of play-making? One sees such variations in style and types of theatre that one wonders if theatre is a hodgepodge of individual tastes or if there is a cohesive aesthetic core.

The following discussions provide answers to those questions. These chapters are based upon the premise that the key to understanding the nature of drama can be found in "The Six Elements of Drama," as set forth in Aristotle's *Poetics*. His analysis of the six elements provides a systematic approach to an enriching study of the art of drama.

Aristotle observed drama and used empirical observation to come to conclusions: "I have seen this play which my best and most trusted instincts tell me is 'bad.' Now, how do I go about isolating the variables in order to understand what makes a play better than others?" He did not formulate rules; he instead observed and came to conclusions. You can do that equally well and certainly there are more opportunities for you to see dramatic productions than Aristotle ever had.

As we discussed briefly in describing the one-act play, there are six elements of drama listed in the *Poetics*. Each will be discussed in detail in the following chapters. Those elements are:

- Plot
- Character
- Thought
- Diction
- Music
- Spectacle

Of them, Aristotle said that plot was most important. Today we tend to emphasize character, but plot's popularity can be seen often. The first three of the elements are the most significant; a play that is quite strong in the latter three and weak in the former three will be a skimpy work. Strong plays are written with emphasis upon at least two of the key three elements of plot, character, and thought.

Chapter Fourteen

Plot: Part One

Introduction

A clockmaker would enjoy the workings of the plot in a well-crafted play. Imagine an old-world craftsman—give him a beard, a pipe, and a Black Forest environment—who fashions brass cogs and wooden wheels inside hand-rubbed walnut cabinetry. There are cogs within wheels, each efficiently acting and reacting, all working quietly without drawing attention to the operations. Such craftsmanship is similar to the playwright's.

Likewise, an architect could turn from his blueprints to the plot of a play and barely notice the difference. Both plans construct a foundation that supports the facade of the whole; both include subtle inner workings that cannot be seen; and both build sturdy structures, and no one notices how they operate.

Others who would relate to the strategy, tactics, and plans that make up a plot might be a chess master, who would equate plot's workings to a strategy on the board; a skipper in the America's Cup Race; a psychologist working out sessions in group dynamics; a shipwright; generals at a war college; or the people who design the exercises for the generals at the war college.

Your Knowledge of Plot

Often "plot" is discussed as if it were unrelated to experience available to the playwright. But you know what plot is. You are fully aware of the ways that plot develops forward motion for a play or story. You've told stories, perhaps at a campfire or under a summer's flickering street light, maybe ghost stories to frighten and chill, or boasting war stories to impress and awe. For those stories you have had to use foreshadowing, complications, reversals, and delayed disclosure of fact.

For a moment consider a child's fanciful explanation of how the lurking blob monster came out of the closet and broke the lamp, how really big bears must have broken into the kitchen to eat all the cookies, or how a really big cat ate her homework. Compare the child's stories with the no-less-fanciful *Peter Pan*, *Harvey*, or *Sweeney Todd*.

You know the basics of plot. You know, too, what is "good" and "bad" plot—effective and ineffective, subtle or obvious, plausible or unbelievable— because you have encountered both. You have a full and operational working knowledge of plot.

Initial Definition of Plot

Plot is the accumulative organization of the play's actions. It is the series of actions and resultant reactions that combine to express the play's thought, or intellectual cohesive content, and characters. It is the selective patterning of the actions into a carefully designed order that best fits the playwright's purpose for writing the play. Plot is an expression of the playwright's philosophical tenets, just as is character and thought.

A play is a series of happenings, small and large. Plot provides those happenings.

A play is a series of choices, decisions whether to take this course or that, the road to the left or the one to the right. Plot provides those "forks in the road," makes them major or minor, and forces characters to choose.

A play is a series of meetings between people. Plot plans those meetings; it arranges those to be happy or disastrous encounters; it makes those meetings highly significant or casual.

The playwright crafts these series of events into a given specific order—no other will do—according to the needs of the particular play. Arranging that order is plotting.

The Relative Importance of Plot: Aristotle

So important is plot to drama that the world's greatest theorist ranks plot first of all possible ingredients in a play. As we mentioned, Aristotle says plot is primary of the six elements. Plot, he points out, illustrates thought and brings character to life. The events of the play dictate the scope of the drama.

Plot is Character in Action

Character is fascinating. Plays capture audience attention and hold it tightly by introducing the audience to people who they would not have had the opportunity to meet but who are nonetheless colorful additions to the world. Does that suggest that playwrights should conclude that character is more important than plot? No. I think playwrights should instead conclude that character and plot are a permanently married twosome. The best approach, I suggest, is for playwrights to believe this: *Plot is character in action*. This concept will ensure a unified approach toward writing.

Plot Marries Character and Thought

Plot provides actions that stimulate reactions; the actions and reactions illustrate the intellectual concepts of the play and simultaneously exhibit the characters under a variety of stimuli. As the characters move and act, the sum total of their behaviors will illustrate the play's theme. The sum total of the characters' movements in *Waiting for Godot* speak the play's theme: Is mankind lost and unable to go meaningfully in any direction because structure has disappeared? The actions of the characters in *Death of a Salesman* state the theme: Does a man without viable life-goals pass along moral failure to his family?

Plot creates the actions that allow the playwright to show the play's subject and theme, rather than tell it. If the actions are insubstantial, the playwright is left with only the option of using curtain speeches to tell the play's meaning.

A human who never faces an emergency will fall into one static behavior pattern. But the human who must cope with the unexpected crisis will have to face his or her own psyche while dealing with real or imagined dangers. The reactions will make the person more colorful, more dimensional, and each new challenge will illuminate new aspects of that personality. The result is a more complex character. Plot provides those constant changes.

Plot is not a series of awkward contrivances that blatantly force the characters to act as mere puppets, existing only to serve the action. That is not a definition of "plot," but instead it defines "bad plot." A well-crafted plot puts together character and thought so that the three elements appear to be welded into one.

MACBETH: Plot Creates Character
and Illustrates Thought

The casual observer might think that *Macbeth* is primarily a *character* play—that is, of the six elements, character is given most emphasis—and that thought is second in importance. Plot, to such an observer, is so thin as to be unimportant.

But that observer would not have sensed how the plot's movements created the strength in characterization and how the overall process conveyed the play's thought. It is all worth noting.

When the play begins, there is a certain equilibrium. Macbeth is loyal to the King. Clearly he is a popular and strong military leader. And even though the kingdom has been involved in a bloody war, the country and its people have managed to survive morally: Everyone we see is free of the taint of war's cruelties.

The focus of the play is Macbeth. He is shown to be a strong man, powerful and noble. Look then at the action beginning in Act Three, Scene Four. Fleance escapes. The Ghost of Banquo appears to Macbeth alone. In Act Four, Scene One, the witches appear and make predictions that deeply trouble Macbeth. Macduff leaves the country and there are suspicions he will rally forces against Macbeth. Macbeth—the strong and noble man we met in the early part of the play—sends his murderers to kill Macduff's family (Act Four, Scene Two), and Lady Macbeth is seen in her highly distraught stage (Act Five, Scene Two) which troubles Macbeth already wearied from other problems. In Act Five, Scene One, those in rebellion against Macbeth are seen assembling for a final attack, and now we begin to see the internal rot which affects the once mighty Macbeth.

The badly disturbed mind and irrational behaviors *show* the way the strong man has become weak. A Servant tells Macbeth that "there is ten thousand. . . ." and Macbeth cannot cope with the news but instead shouts down the servant. The warrior begins to buckle on his armor, surely something he has done hundreds of time in the past, but his frenzied mind cannot concentrate upon the task. The Queen dies (Act Five, Scene Five), which brings home to Macbeth the horrible totality of his acts. He is then told that Birnam Wood is moving to Dunsinane.

These actions are the movements of *plot*. Each provides a stimulus to Macbeth; Macbeth's responses to each stimulus further shows his character. We *see* that he is increasingly weakened. He becomes more and more unable to cope with the rush of disasters that stem from his own earlier actions. We are *shown* the steps of his destruction.

It is the play's *plot* that provides the action that demonstrates the weaknesses that grow and gnaw in Macbeth. And it is the play's plot that allows us to conclude that the theme of *Macbeth* concerns the total destructiveness of a blind hunger for raw power: We see Macbeth so eager for power that he goes against his own code (he kills his guest and King, he sends murderers out to kill his best friend) and the process destroys him. No curtain speech is necessary to determine the message. To repeat a concept expressed earlier, plot is as expressive of the playwright's philosophy as is thought or character. Shakespeare's plot in *Macbeth* tells his concept about power—power begets power until it must eat itself just as it had devoured earlier victims, a deadly snake swallowing its own tail.

1. Plot Is Conflict. The first rule of drama is that it stems from conflict. Without conflict there is no dramatic action, no clash of wills between characters, no dismaying fall from grace or exciting rise to success. A play without conflict is like yesterday's meringue—perhaps initially promising but ultimately bland, tasteless, and incapable of supporting enough weight to make it interesting. Without conflict there can be no drama. Without plot there will be no action that will create conflict.

2. Plot Must Be an Integral Part of the Whole. Discussions of plot focus upon it as a unit distinct from the whole play. But we must always be aware that plot has to be cleanly interwoven into the fabric of the entire work. It is an integral part of the whole, indistinct from the rest of the script.

If one can hear the creaking gears of the plot, one concludes that the play has problems. A machine-like grinding sound will drown out all the rest of the play, no matter how nicely it is written. Art consists of hiding craft.

3. Plot Creates, Interacts with, and Results from Character. As incidents occur—"complications," in plot terminology—they affect characters. Whether the incidents are good or bad, the characters have to respond. As the characters respond, changes necessarily occur. The result is broader and more effective characterization.

If the curtain goes up to show us John and Mary just sitting, he reading a book and she looking out the window, we get a single impression of the characters. Time passes and he continues to read while the window fascinates her; we have still the same impression of them. They chat idly about nothing of significance; we still have the same feeling about them. We'll call them shallow, one-dimensional characters.

If he throws the book at her, if she responds by laughing at his poor marksmanship, if he then runs to choke her, and if she begins to cry in fear, which makes him apologize softly—now we see different aspects of the characters and we begin to think that they have dimensionality. They are more interesting. As audience members, we feel that there is action, and we wait to see where all of this will go. It is a beginning at least.

The first John-Mary situation had no plot. The second had plot devices based upon confict. Without plot, the characters would never change.

4. Bickering Is Not Conflict. A play with characters who only nag and bicker is a play with no plot, because there is no change in the direction of the action and the intensities of the characters' emotions. It is a play with shallow and uninteresting one-dimensional people. There is no change in the characters, no revelation of inner secrets, no discovery about the self and others. There is a dull sameness to the whole.

If, however, there is a major basic *conflict* shown in a vitally alive plot, one has a *Who's Afraid of Virginia Woolf?* with richly drawn multidimensional characters who do not merely snipe at each other disinterestedly, but who are in full-scale war with ritualistic positioning of "armies" that clash by day and night. Personal survival is at stake.

For the playwright, characters who merely snipe at each other are boring to write. What is worse, the writer will fall into a pattern: Once that sort of dull writing begins, the playwright seems to have problems changing to more vital conflicts. For the actor, such people are so dull that the performer will try to add *something* to give the character some zing, perhaps a quality totally different from one the playwright had in mind. For the audience, a play of mere bickering is about as exciting as watching drones in a beehive; there just is not enough individuality.

5. Plot Orders the Actions.   Plot puts the actions of the play into an order best suited for the needs of the story. For instance, in one play, X could happen and *then* Y. In another play, with a different story approach but about the same people, the order might be Z and *then* Y. To use a specific example, in *Medea* Kreon enters and threatens Medea with exile from his kingdom and *then* Jason comes to taunt her about his infidelity. The story has to do with Medea seeking justice. But a different play might first have Jason appear to tell Medea of his love for another and *then* Kreon tell Medea she has to leave the kingdom. Now the story would suggest something about the disasters of marriage. Euripides was not writing of a mere husband-wife struggle but was instead working on a larger concept regarding justice versus revenge. He introduces the larger theme by bringing Kreon on first, and he lets the smaller issue (a husband-wife fight) arrive second. Plot, then, puts the events into an order which will best serve the playwright's intent. Plot forces the audience's attention upon the issue the author wishes to emphasize.

6. Plot Develops Suspense.   The last act of *Wait Until Dark* contains one of the most frenzied half hours the theatre can offer: Look out! The villian has cornered the blind lady! No, she's free; she has gotten all the lights off so he's as blind as she! No, wait . . . he's opening the refrigerator and the light shows him where she's hiding and she doesn't know! *Look Out!* The tensions continue to mount, so much so that even a sophisticated New York audience was yelping in fear when *Wait Until Dark* played on Broadway.

Magnificent craftsmanship makes *Wait Until Dark* a thrilling melodrama. We care about the blind lady, who is a nicely sympathetic character in sharp contrast against the cruel killers. But the plot machinations create doubt that even this nice person will survive, and that is indeed a job of fine writing.

Arthur Miller's strong play *The Crucible* emphasizes thought and character. But there is certainly as much excitement in *The Crucible*'s last act as in *Wait*

Until Dark, and for much the same reason. The plot at work makes John Proctor go through existentialistic agonies of decision-making as the play moves him toward his fate. Proctor is prodded to his decisions by plot techniques quite similar to those used in *Wait Until Dark.*

The Crucible is strongly a thesis play, seeking to evoke in the viewer questions regarding personal morality. *Wait Until Dark* has little thesis, if any, and instead seeks to be a suspense thriller. Yet in both plays the playwrights' techniques are remarkably similar, and in the last acts of the two plays there are well-plotted twists and turns, reversals and discoveries. The difference between the two is that one play brings the audience into physical suspense and the other forces the audience to become involved with mental and moral processes.

The point here is that plot develops suspense. Often, as in *The Crucible,* plot develops character and illustrates the play's meanings. For plays such as *Wait Until Dark* and *The Crucible,* it is the well-crafted plot that communicates to the audience. Remember, suspense is not unique to melodramas!

7. Plot Is Active.   Plot can be considered a series of actions that might be explained by the stimulus-response diagram so often found in psychology books:

Stimulus causes response, which itself becomes a stimulus, which causes a response, which. . . . For instance, person A insults person B; B responds by slapping A; A responds by slugging B; B responds by punching A; A draws a pistol; B hides behind a chair; A slinks around to the side to get a clean shot at B; and so on.

The stimulus-response is the major conflict at work in *Who's Afraid of Virginia Woolf?* There is a prod-prod-prod quality to the two major characters. The major conflict elevates the play above mere petty bickering; the stimulus-response cycle stops the play from being dully repetitive because each new cycle is more dynamic. Plot creates actions.

8. Plot Provides Surprise.   Plot provides sudden turns, new events, and unexpected twists. The new event strikes the character, and new aspects of the person may be seen as a result. Consider, for example, Macbeth's response when the frightened Murderer has to report that Fleance managed to escape: to that surprise, Macbeth jumps and twists and begins turning in the wind. There are vital changes in the big man's character; we in the audience will be surprised that he can behave in such petty ways. Plot brings forth the twists that show the steps of his destruction.

Birthday Party ends with a surprise: The landlady and her husband go back to their old ways as if absolutely nothing had happened. *The Dumb Waiter* ends with a surprise: Gus, the hired killer, stumbles in to be the victim. And of course *Wait Until Dark* is filled with surprises. They bring to the audience a sense of newness, of freshness, of constant change. For that reason, the surprises are highly valuable. The play appears to be more dynamic, more vital, more interesting.

9. Plot Creates Building Blocks. A play can be considered a series of buildings toward a final height (or climax). A sense of the dramatic requires rising action, that is, increases in suspense and tensions. Each new event hurls the play forward.

Plot carries the action toward that climax. If there is inadequate plot, the building blocks collapse and lie flat and tired. If the plot does not hold up the play, then all the playwright has left is character. All too frequently such heavy burdens break the backs of purely character plays. The result can be an unfortunately dull evening in theatre.

10. Plot Shows the Play's Thought. The playwright uses plot to lead the audience to conclusions. Plot selects and emphasizes points, thereby stressing the play's basic meaning, and it leads to an ultimate climax that helps the playwright draw the audience's attention to the play's subject and theme. Via plot, the playwright *shows* actions that communicate the intellectual quality of the whole; without plot, the playwright can only *tell* the play's meaning in one of those well-known tiresome curtain speeches in which a poor character has to deliver The Message. Obviously, *showing* is the better approach.

11. Plot Awakens Audience Responses. Plot can bring the audience to tears, to laughter, or to cries of fright. For example, as director of *Carousel* I marveled each production night at how Billy Bigelow's death—a quick surprise—made the audience gasp in shock. The plot then called for the entrance of Julie, Billy's new-made widow. The audience cried openly as Julie mourned over Billy, and there were even more tears when the plot introduced the song that follows Billy's death, "You'll Never Walk Alone." Plot next brings on stage the Heavenly Friend who has Billy rise in order to go to Judgment, a process that evokes some laughter. In the space of only a few minutes, due to the plot's movements of action, audiences had gasped in shock, cried, and smiled or laughed. It is neat craftsmanship.

I also marveled, as director of *The Dumb Waiter* and *The Birthday Party*—two plays by Harold Pinter—at how audiences responded to the way the plot slowly disclosed a basic evil and fear. In both plays the playwright expertly hides information from the audience, slowly disclosing small hints in a way that forces the audience to piece the whole together. At first, audiences tend to be withdrawn from these plays because of style, but the plots draw them in. Suspense grows.

For romantic and perhaps somewhat melodramatic scripts such as *Carousel*, or for avant-garde suprarealism such as *Dumb Waiter* and *Birthday Party*, plot is used to create audience response, drawing them into the action of the play. Without plot, a great deal of audience attention would be permanently lost.

Summation

Plot organizes the action. It helps the playwright to force changes in characters, making them react and grow. Plot creates suspense and holds audience attention. It is the basic structure of the whole.

Chapter Fifteen

Plot: Part Two

Introduction

A play's plot is constructed with a series of interlocking and sometimes inter-changeable portions; the playwright fashions these into a welded invisible whole that will bring forth the basic conflict, develop the story line, give the characters a dynamic growth in a suitable environment, and illuminate the subject and theme. The *portions* of plot provide the topic of this chapter.

There is no one construction approach. A great deal of individuality is found in play constructions. There *is* a system of dramatic construction found in drama's mainstream, but within that system are a number of major and minor variations. A chess master must choose between a small number of possible strategies, but he or she has millions of different combinations of moves to achieve that basic plan. So does the playwright find that there are only a re-stricted number of construction frameworks but that there are many variations in approaches.

It is a mistake to think that one approach is "good" and others therefore "bad." In art there can be, and must be, a number of voices. No one has freedom to close off a voice simply because of personal preference or ignorance, and the playwright must not allow the theoreticians to dictate the "best" approach or framework. Such dangers are real: One can find an "expert" who attempts to force all writers into the avant-garde and to avoid all conventional devices, and another can find an "expert" who permits only the conventional. It is rather as if we should all wear the same brand, color, style, and even size of shoe because the salesman happens to like only that one.

Some playwrights achieve great success with largely shapeless works. For example, William Saroyan's plays typically are wandering, loosely put together, and sprawling; his plays such as *The Time of Your Life* show the author's insouciant disregard for tight construction. In contrast are the playwrights whose fondness for tightly woven fabrics can be seen in their works such as *Ghosts* (Henrik Ibsen), *The Little Foxes* (Lillian Hellman), or *Death of a Salesman* (Arthur Miller). For some authors, then, a looseness is necessary, and for others the tight construction is equally important. Let no one like the shoe salesman persuade the playwright that one or the other is "good" or "bad."

On the other hand, let no playwright conclude there is absolute freedom. Certain truisms exist concerning plot, which have been proved during western theatre's two thousand years; the playwright denies these at peril of the health of his or her playscript. This chapter intends to describe the various portions of plot, and in some cases it will recommend certain approaches. The playwright's attention will be called to the truisms. The astute reader will think of exceptions, often brilliant, to the premises, but the playwright should not conclude that the exceptions become the rule.

The Pieces of Plot

1. The Standard Diagram. The following "diagram of plot," which shows preparation, rising action, climax, falling action, and denouement, may be very familiar to you. It has appeared on blackboards in every high school and college in the country:

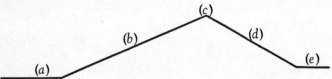

In such a diagram, (a) is *preparation,* which establishes background and current situation and hints at coming problems (exposition and foreshadowing); (b) is *rising action,* starting with the point of attack the moment the upswing begins and consisting of discoveries and complications; (c) is the *climax,* the highest point of all tension; (d) is *falling action* with few, if any, complications and with a decrease in tension; and (e) is *denouement,* possibly including catharsis, when loose pieces are wrapped up.

The problem with this diagram is that it lies: No play follows such a pattern. The diagram's chief advantage rests only in its easy convenience for sketching on a blackboard. Unfortunately, however, it is too easy. Such a simple-minded diagram can lead to misunderstandings about the way in which plays are structured.

The diagram's first error is its indication that rising action consists of nonstop increase in tension. The diagram shows a consistent rise in tension, but the opposite is true: Often a playwright will deliberately relax the tensions in order to be able to start up again. The diagram needs a jagged line instead of the smooth increase.

The rising action line also is inaccurate because it suggests that a play always moves toward its goal. Such a "straight-line play" would be boring for its creator and for its audience. Instead, plays are less obvious. And some plays contain scenes which move laterally: The porter scene in *Macbeth* appears to relax tensions but instead moves laterally from the line of action and thereby makes the audience become even more tense, waiting for the discovery of the murder. Such a device became popular with movie-maker Alfred Hitchcock.

The diagram also indicates a one-complication play: There is the first complication to change the movement from preparation (line *a*) to rising action (line *b*), but not another complication thereafter. Therefore, the diagram shows a play that has no action to make the rise; there are no complications to continue that rising action. The diagram is of a no-incident and boring play.

Finally, the diagram seems to suggest that a lengthy preparation (line *a*) is typical. It is not, nor is it necessarily "good." There also is quite a long ending: The diagram indicates that after a play's climax it ends . . . and ends . . . and ends.

Drama exists in its time and space. A one-dimensional drawing limits that understanding. Instead, one needs to construct a three- or four-dimensional model. The blackboard is ill-suited for diagrams about an art which takes place in time and space. If one *must* sketch the structure of a play, then its complexities in complications should be suggested. In the diagram below, each new line represents a new complication, with some complete within their moments and others started but left to be picked up later. Note the brevity of both preparation and ending:

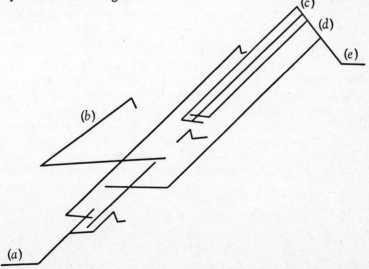

All of the lines in rising action are complications. Some are major—the longest ones—and others are minor. All force the action to continue to rise.

2. Beginning, Middle, and End. The principle sounds unfortuntely all too simplistic. Does a play have to be built with a beginning, a middle, and an end? Of course. How else is it to be built? This dictum from Aristotle's *Poetics* appears to be much too easy: Surely all plays have these three ingredients?

No. Sadly, a play may lack one of the three ingredients. The omission can be frustrating because it is difficult to track down. The author puzzling over revisions or the critic trying to be helpful will instinctively perceive that certainly *something* is wrong, but the mind seldom addresses the matter of problems with a beginning, a middle, or an end. That's just too simple and the mind overlooks the obvious.

The Beginning. A play that has little or no beginning seldom brings the audience around to *care* about the action and the characters; there's just not enough information about the past and the present, about inciting incident, or about characters. There has been no "sense of urgency" established. The play with too much beginning seems to start, and to start, and to start, but it just doesn't *go*. There is a feeling of wheels spinning. Much is promised, repeatedly. The audience's attention fades as it learns that the apparent movement is false. A play such as this is afflicted with two basic causes: First, the playwright is too strongly interested in establishing mood and situation and character but too little focused upon action; second, there is an inadequate or overly-delayed point of attack. The cure for a play with too much beginning may well turn out to be radical surgery: The playwright has to consider cutting away everything that precedes the beginning of the action (that is, removing everything that comes before the point of attack).

The play's beginning is an introduction. No one wants too many or too few prefactory remarks; instead, one expects the beginning to accomplish a number of functions with deft efficiency. The beginning must:

- Hook the audience's interest in the action.
- Imply forthcoming events of interest via foreshadowing.
- Establish the inciting incident that will start the whole problem that will be dramatized.
- Indicate the mood of the play—let the audience feel secure that it knows if this play is a comedy or a tragedy.
- Establish the significant characters (either by bringing them on stage or by implying their presence).
- Establish, as necessary, essential relationships between characters
- Indicate significant information about the time and place.
- Start the action.

Missing from this list is "exposition." Does this mean the beginning should omit exposition? Not exactly. *Some* exposition may be necessary in the opening moments, but it is far better for the play to get the lines of action going first and *then* give the essential details about background material. It is a mistake to list exposition within the beginning because that suggests to the playwright that the whole glob of exposition must be crammed into the initial minutes of the play. Exposition can be disclosed in small pieces as part of the action.

How long should the play's beginning be? No one should answer the question with more than "as long as necessary." The playwright will remember that the core of the play is not found in the beginning which is, after all, primarily only an introduction. A study of a magnificent beginning, such as that which exists in *Macbeth* from the initial witches' chant to Macbeth's reaction to their first three prophecies, will help the playwright better understand how to perceive this part of the play.

The Middle. If the play's beginning is the appetizer, the middle is the main course. Here the action brings forth the characters. The protagonist works to achieve his goal while the antagonist puts up obstacles. There are discoveries and complications, victories and defeats, twists and reversals, and surprise arrivals and departures. Hopes are dashed, then given fresh life. Through it all, the play's basic line of conflict is increased.

The middle of a play contains the richness promised by its beginning. Here is the prime thrust of subject and theme. Here the basic conflict explodes and complications arise to change the course of action.

A play with problems with its middle part is likely to be a play with poor construction of complications. If the middle is dull and inactive, there might be insufficient complications; if the middle is exciting but the actions seem to mean little, there might be illogical complications that do not relate to each other and to the plot; if the middle has characters that seem to grow monotonous, the complications might not be providing enough stimuli for character responses.

The End. After the climax, the play winds down. A few loose ends may need to be tied up, and perhaps a few calm explanations may be needed, but if there are many ends or explanations the ending may feel too awkward. Playwrights ought be very careful with the "author's spokesman's curtain speech" in which a hapless character is forced to speak about the playwright's meaning; such speeches fare poorly with audiences who expect the thematic material to be better crafted into the fabric of the whole.

The ending contains the denouement, the final settlement. All complications are resolved. However, often the playwright will leave questions in the minds of the audience: Nora, ending Ibsen's *A Doll's House*, exits the stage and shuts the door with a famous slam creating a shock that vibrates yet today with its call for just and fair rights. Other plays end by circling back to the beginning:

the end of Ionesco's *The Lesson* brings a pupil to the professor exactly as did the play's beginning, which is the playwright's ironic comment about the continuation of a killing cycle.

Some plays end with remarkably convenient events: A sudden inheritance solves the protagonist's problem; a bolt of lightning kills off the villain; a spectator at one of Perry Mason's trials suddenly rises and suprisingly admits "I did it and I'm not sorry!" although we have not the faintest idea what motivated the person to admit guilt. These are illustrations of *deus ex machina* endings, which means "the god from the machine"; it is a reference to Greek dramas in which cranes lowered gods onto the acting area to resolve the play. For the Greeks, such supernatural activity was part of a cultural concept, and their close relationship with their gods made such events acceptable. Modern times will not permit these solutions.

3. The Inciting Incident. If one is being precise, the inciting incident is not a part of the play. The term refers to an event that has taken place before the play begins, and in that sense it will not happen in the ongoing present-tense action.

The term is self-descriptive. In *Medea* the inciting incident has been Jason's betrayal of his wife Medea by having an adulterous relationship with Kreon's daughter. In *Hamlet* the inciting incident has been the murder (still considered only an ordinary death when the play begins) of Hamlet's father. In *The Glass Menagerie* it has been Tom's decision to leave home in order to survive. The term refers to the event that has lit the fuse we will see explode shortly after the play begins.

Must all plays have an inciting incident? No. One can imagine plays with characters who have no mutual past, nothing that once happened that now brings them together or pulls them apart.

Do most plays have an inciting incident? Yes. There are many obvious advantages for the playwright in having one. The previous action provides a very convenient base of departure for the playwright's construction. Specifically, the inciting incident can spark the point of attack into full fire. It helps build a climate for the actions to come.

4. A Sense of Equilibrium. Plays begin with a certain existing balance of forces. All things are in equilibrium, no matter how precariously balanced; the universe of the play is at rest, even though temporarily. That existing equilibrium may continue for several minutes or it may be broken almost immediately. Its very existence helps create suspense: Audiences note the balance and wait for the change, knowing something is going to happen. In Alfred Hitchcock movies the sense of equilibrium becomes an intense suspense factor as the master plays out the balance. In *Hamlet* the balance is extremely fragile; in *Wait Until Dark* the balance lasts quite long; in *Macbeth* the balance is topsy-turvy and threatening to permeate every living thing in the play's universe.

The sense of equilibrium gives the playwright a moment to "get the house in order," allowing her or him to introduce us to the universe that will be spotlighted during the rest of the play. The feeling of things being in balance suggests a momentary silence. The ticking of a bomb can be louder than normal in that silence.

A play starts with things in balance, but then it jars the balance askew. The play's beginning helps indicate the desired state of things, a rightness of the universe, that makes the disturbances more potent.

5. Exposition. Exposition is one of those "dragons" that a playwright must overcome. Armed with good craftsmanship, the writer can win the battle.

Exposition is for the audience. It simply sets forth necessary background information. It tells the audience who the characters are, where they live, what their current relationships are and why they are that way, and how the past influences their actions. Because exposition deals with *past* actions, it typically does not propel the play forward in its *present* to a sense of future. If a full-length play has time lapses between acts, exposition will be needed to let the audience know of the passage of time.

In some old plays, exposition is handled by a charming jester-narrator who speaks directly to the audience regarding the characters and problems. In other, equally old plays, a pair of servants speak the necessary background information in graceless dialogue. All too typically there will be a butler making minute adjustments to heavy furniture while a maid darts about, ever so cutely, armed with a two-foot device with a wooden handle and a clump of feathers. So typical was the opening that it got a name: "The Feather Duster Scene."

The feather duster scene was so contrived because the characters had no reason to speak about facts that they already knew. It gave way to the stranger-butler situation: A new person arrives and asks questions of the butler. At least here could be some motivation. This situation was replaced by the one with the telegram from Western Union, which was replaced by the one with the radio (turned on just in time to catch the extremely appropriate announcement that relates directly to the play), which was replaced by the one with the telephone call, and so on.

Ibsen suggests a better way to exposition with *Ghosts*. Exposition comes in tiny sections, a bit at a time, during the entire play, and not in a huge clump at the beginning. Each bit of exposition in *Ghosts* is marvelously crafted to be a part of the play's action; instead of being a dull recital of facts that are over and done with, Ibsen shows that exposition can become an active complication to drive the play forward.

Pinter seems to have done away with exposition, although in fact the necessary communications are quietly there. In *The Dumb Waiter* the background information drifts in during the entire play, just as in *Ghosts*, but it often is hidden within other materials. In his play, *The Birthday Party*, the very lack of exposition is a major complication.

Exposition is necessary for most plays, but the playwright will learn that to overcome the problem of stilted conversation the talk that discloses the background facts must be motivated. The subtle approach is more effective than the obvious one.

6. Foreshadowing.   Television soap operas have made foreshadowing one of the best-known of the story-teller's devices: There will be a sharp chord on the organ while the camera zooms in for a closeup reaction shot—Hold—Fade for commercial. Old-time movies have used foreshadowing about as obviously: The doctor holds up a test tube and squints into it against the light: "I don't like that. Not one bit." The doctor's assistant: "Do you mean . . . ?" The doctor: "I'm afraid so." The assistant: "Oh, dear God." The doctor: "If we don't find a cure in the next three hours . . ." The assistant: "That's not enough time to evacuate the state." The doctor: "Exactly." The camera moves to a closeup of the tube. Fadeout.

Examples of the clumsy use of foreshadowing do not prove that the device is worthless. On the contrary, foreshadowing is an important tool for the playwright. It awakens audience interest; it guides attention toward the forthcoming event; it helps the author maintain the play on its correct track; and it opens the door for complications. Foreshadowing also can give characters motivation and depth.

Foreshadowing is commonly discussed as part of a play's beginning. The wise playwright knows that it can be effective throughout the entire action as "road signs" pointing to coming events. As with the case of exposition, the writer must be sure the characters are well motivated in perceiving a forthcoming event as being worrisome.

The *plant* is a close relative of foreshadowing. Plants refer to objects, and foreshadowing normally has to do with events. Imagine a play's resolution that demands that the heroine frantically search for some means to protect herself against the knife-wielding villain. She opens a drawer, pulls out a pistol, and shoots. And the audience probably laughs; the gun is too much of a convenience, too coincidentally available—a *deus ex machina* at its worst. How does one prevent this? With a plant: In Act One someone looking for a stamp for a letter happens to look casually through drawers and in the process comes across the pistol, which after a brief look and an offhand remark about it being awfully old and rusty but perhaps of some dubious antique value, is then returned to the drawer. Now it can be used without being *deus ex machina*. Of course the good writer knows that audiences are sensitive to writing techniques and so the plant should be made subtle, not a screaming indication of a weapon available for Act Three.

7. The Protagonist's Goal and Plan.   The protagonist is the central character of the play who is brought to life by his desire—his passionate *need*—to achieve a certain goal. This desire is an emotional quality: The protagonist is one who *feels* even more than he *thinks*. He will move nonstop to his objective. A protagonist has to have a passionate need to right a wrong, to punish the guilty, to recover the lost child, or to become independent from an insensitive spouse.

The protagonist's goal should be made clear relatively early in the play, because much of the action stems from the protagonist's quest. Macbeth, a classic protagonist, is driven by his passions and greed to achieve the throne and, once there, to preserve it and to protect himself from those enemies he believes secretly share his own secret evil. All actions of the play stem from his striving to achieve his goal, and the play is remarkably unified for that reason.

The protagonist devises plans to achieve his master goal. Hamlet will "revenge his foul and most unnatural murder." To do so he must discover if the Ghost has spoken truthfully—"By indirections find directions out"—and nothing will stop him—"If circumstances lead me, I will find Where truth is hid, though it were hid indeed Within the centre."

Must a play have a protagonist? No The era of the antihero brought dramas without protagonists.

Can a protagonist lack a goal? No. Protagonist and goal are permanently linked.

Can a play have more than one protagonist? Perhaps, but probably awkwardly. One thinks of *The Weavers* with its collective hero/protagonist.

Can the protagonist have more than one major goal? Yes, but it makes for an added writing problem that hardly seems worth the trouble. It would appear easier to have both goals woven in one unified objective.

8. A Sense of Urgency.   Could the play happen yesterday or tomorrow? Might it just as well take place elsewhere? Are these particular individual characters essential or can they be replaced by others without damage to the play? Does it have to be set in this time period or might it be set a decade sooner or later?

A play lacking a potent sense of urgency will meander slowly until it reaches its cul-de-sac, where it will languish away. There must be potent reasons for the play to happen *now,* and *here,* and with *these* very special people. It cannot happen to anyone else, at any other time or place.

Why must *A Streetcar Named Desire* take place at this moment in time? Because right now Blanche needs a haven; she has exhausted all other possible places and has no other place to run for security. Why must *Macbeth* happen *now* instead of last year or next month? Because now Macbeth is flushed with battle, now blood and human life have been made less significant because of war, now he is drunk with the power of leadership, and now the war's end brings Duncan to Macbeth's castle where he can become victim. War already has turned the world upside down; fair is foul and foul is fair. Now is Macbeth's moment: he could not have even considered the possibilities last year, and next week will be too late because he will be calmer then. It *has* to be this moment.

This sense of urgency gives the playwright immediate advantages in characterization and plotting. Without it, the play has no driving force and the people have little need to act. *If the playwright cannot bring a sense of urgency to the play's opening portion, it is time to stop and rethink the entire plan.*

9. The Point of Attack. A play consists of a series of *complications*, each changing the direction of the action and/or extending the dramatic movements. *The first complication is the point of attack.*

When one goes to a football game one first encounters all sorts of color and spectacle. There are the parking lots, the ticket takers, the program sellers, and the pom-poms. There may be a parade on the field; bands and cheerleaders may perform. The teams stream onto the playing field to the accompaniment of cheerleaders' frenzied antics and crowd shouts. There is the ritual flip of the coin. The teams line up and the kicker runs at the ball. *Finally, at the moment of toe-ball contact, the game's point of attack happens.* All events preceding the kickoff are attractive, colorful, ceremonial, and introductory—but the game's action does not begin until the kickoff allows the conflict to take place. For the fans, a delay in the kickoff is simply unacceptable; there are shouts of "let's get on with it." The fans are there for the action, not for the introductory ceremonies.

After the kickoff there will be complications piled on top of complications: interceptions, fumbles, magnificent running sweeps, desperate fourth-down plays, valiant blocking, outstanding tackling, and suspense-ridden goal-line stands. All are a result of the beginning, which was the initial kickoff, the point of attack; all are unified within the basic concept, which is the conflict between two opposing forces.

In a play, the point of attack begins the action. Exposition, mood-setting, identification of forces, establishment of time and place—all are introductory, often colorful and attractive, even ritualistic within conventions of drama. But the play's major action does not begin until the point of attack.

The play with an early point of attack will have more complex action, which will develop rich characters. In *Macbeth* the point of attack is early. There is an uncomfortable equilibrium existing for the first two scenes. Then, in scene three, Macbeth is silent when the witches predict he will be King. The play's action begins there. Events follow with increasing rapidity, making *Macbeth* rich in meaningful activity that illuminates plot and enriches character.

Plays with a delayed point of attack will have inactive introductory passages. Even when the point of attack finally comes, such plays tend to be thin in action. Without the stimuli of action upon characters, the characters often will not be fully drawn.

10. The Complication. The complication is an obstacle, twist, reversal, discovery, or crisis—any new force, physical or psychic, that changes the direction of the play's action. A play with one complication is, by definition, a play with but one change in action and therefore a play that conveys a feeling of "nothing happening." A play with many and frequent complications will be one that generates excitement.

A complication may come from inside the character or from within the universe of the play. The former gives life to Hamlet, Quentin in *After the Fall*, Proctor in the last portion of *The Crucible*, and Macbeth (although it is both internal and external stimuli that makes *Macbeth* such a fast-moving and insightful drama). If the complication is from outside causes, one tends to expect a melodrama (as in *Wait Until Dark* and especially *Raiders of the Lost Ark*).

A play begins in a dynamic equilibrium that is thrown out of balance by the point of attack, which is also the play's first complication. In *Macbeth* the first complication—therefore the play's point of attack—is Macbeth's reactions to the prediction that he will be king, which is a distinct change in the play's direction. He thinks over this prediction as the witches disappear: They cannot be correct because he is not Thane of Cawdor, a title they used to address him. Ross enters to tell Macbeth he now *is* Thane of Cawdor, which is a complication changing the course of the play's action because Macbeth has proof that the witches' predictions will come true. Macbeth murders Duncan, another complication that sharply changes the course of action.

As the play's actions progress, the complications pile up. Macbeth's character takes on added dimensions as he reacts to the various plot devices: the escape of Fleance; the appearance of Banquo's ghost at the banquet; and the sending of killers to find Macduff and his family. The once noble Macbeth soon roars in his castle at Dunsinane—he is a lion whimpering out loud.

A servant enters.

MACBETH

The devil damn thee black, thou cream-faced loon!
Where got'st thou that goose look?

SERVANT

There is ten thousand—

MACBETH

Geese, villain?

SERVANT

Soldiers, sir.

MACBETH

Go prick thy face and over-red thy fear,
Thou lily-liver'd boy. What soldiers, patch?
Death of thy soul! Those linen cheeks of thine
Are counsellors to fear. What soldiers, whey-face?

SERVANT

The English force, so please you.

MACBETH

Take thy face hence.

The proud Macbeth is thus lowered to shouting at a mere servant, and another complication strikes at him: The enemy is coming in force. Macbeth's complications make it an extremely dynamic play, and of course the changes in Macbeth's character—changes that show the play's subject and theme—are results of those complications. Clearly, complications are the spark plugs of a play.

How many complications ought to appear in a full-length play? There can be no stated number, no formula for how many complications ought to appear in a full-length play. But a script containing only a few complications will be static.

Are complications found primarily in melodramatic plays? It is true that complications permeate the melodrama, but they are also an inherent part of non-melodramatic drama.

When is a new complication needed? When the play grows static; when forward motion seems halted; when there is the feeling of dullness; when the characters appear one-dimensional—then a new complication is needed. These answers are risky: It is a mistake to suggest that the complication be considered a cure-all for a static play, a magic elixir of life. But the playwright is encouraged to take full advantage of the complication.

How does the writer plan the play's complications? While constructing the scenario the playwright works out the play's conflict and seeks complications to the protagonist's forward movement. The writer will want complications that can continue for a length of time, in contrast to the small insignificant ones that fade away quickly and provide little change in action.

How long should a complication last? In general, a complication that lasts a page or two is not a complication but likely is a bit of petty bickering unless it deeply affects either action or character. Some complications begin on, say, page fifteen and are pursued until perhaps page twenty-one where they stop and come back to life on page thirty-six and end eight pages later.

How can the playwright learn to build a script rich in complications? First, the author should carefully study several plays that are rich in action. *Macbeth* and *Wait Until Dark* may serve well. Once the writer knows the play extremely well, the next step is to construct the scenario from memory. The scenario will then be checked against the script and corrected as necessary. The writer may also study films—any by Alfred Hitchcock, *Citizen Kane*, *The Searchers*, *High Noon*, *Raiders of the Lost Ark*, *Star Trek II*—and write the scenario, paying careful attention to complications. Certain television programs have established high standards and may be selected—the *Dick Van Dyke Show*, *Mary Tyler Moore*, *M*A*S*H*, *Hill Street Blues*—and again the author should take notes during the show in order to write the treatment in detail. After the playwright has studied a large number of plays, films, and television shows, then the second step is undertaken. Now the author should construct similar treatments, accepting them as imitative, until the approach feels familiar. The goal is to become at ease with the tools. This process ought to involve the detailed writing of three to six different scenario outlines. Then the playwright should turn to his or her own plays that have been written, seeking ways to revise them to make them more active and the characters more dynamic.

The study process given here should occupy the writer's attention for several weeks. It cannot be accomplished in a day or so. The writer may find that continued study will be necessary for longer periods. If so, the writer should approach the additional lessons with a strongly positive mental set. The wise writer knows it is far better to know how to use all available tools in order to be able to select those which are appropriate for a proposed play's content than it is to be missing tools which will force selection from a limited choice of possible plays. Ignorance of a portion of the craft of writing should not be allowed to influence what topics the writer can select or how those topics are to be treated.

11. The Climax.   A play may have more than one climax. Each complication will have some sort of climax—a resolution at the peak of action—but these naturally are of less intensity than the play's major climax or climaxes. The play will contain one final major climax which is the highest point of the whole script; it may have one or two lesser climaxes preceding the final one.

A play with no complications cannot have a climax, for the climax must have the support of those earlier tensions. In *Hamlet* the major climax is the death of the protagonist; a secondary climax is the exit of Claudius during the Players' performance, a moment which gives Hamlet the final proof he needs in his search to discover if the Ghost spoke truly.

The playwright builds the story toward one final moment, a final decision by the protagonist or a final victory in the major conflict. The moment is the highest peak in the play, its greatest intensity. It gives the story its culmination. The playwright usually aims the play at that point before attending to other details. There will be a certain logicality, even if the play is ending showing life's illogicality. The final moment of the buildup is the climax. After it, tensions are evaporating.

12. The Resolution.   All that follows the climax is the play's resolution. Here the play returns to a state of equilibrium. The protagonist is finished now, whether he won or lost; the play now shows its universe in balance, whether it is a comfortable or uncomfortable one. The action, finished with the climax, is shown in its final steps.

Usually the resolution contains a *denouement* which lets the playwright relax the tensions into a comfortable balance. In *Hamlet* the audience is shown there no longer is "something rotten in the state of Denmark" because Fortinbras is to be enthroned and will restore order to the troubled kingdom. In *Macbeth* Malcolm will take the kingdom back to "fair is fair and foul is foul." In *Wait Until Dark* the evil is vanquished and good is permitted to relax.

Resolutions will be brief. They cannot bring in new elements. The play wants to be over. It is hardly the time for the author to force a character to tell the audience what the play meant; if the whole action did not communicate subject and theme, a small summation here cannot correct the problem.

"Look At Cheeta" Endings. The playwright needs be warned away from imitation of the shabby denouements so often seen on countless television shows. There is a popular ending which can be labeled the "Ha, Ha, Ha, Look at Cheeta" device. The label comes from the old *Tarzan* movies which were filled with melodramatic life/death situations that endangered Tarzan, the jungle, and perhaps all civilization until finally Tarzan would triumph. Then the denouement put Jane, Boy, and Tarzan back at their camp watching Cheeta tossing flour into the air to make himself look like a ghost. Tarzan: "Ha, ha, ha. Look at Cheeta." Jane and Boy dutifully look and laugh. There is a closeup of Cheeta, also laughing. Denouement, blackout, and the movie is over; all is happy. Is this too corny to be copied? The *Perry Mason* television show had a standard denouement with Paul, Della, and Perry sitting at a restaurant table and Perry getting off a joke which meant that Paul had to pay the check. "Ha Ha Ha, Look at Paul"; Fade to black. Other examples are easy to find. The playwright should be aware that he or she may have seen so many such denouements that there will be an unconscious assumption that it is "good" to laugh at Cheeta.

13. Unification. *Unity of action* welds all the pieces of plot into a coherent whole. Unity of action also contributes to the artistic impact of the play—we speak positively about the way a playwright fashions an order that unifies the many pieces—but the prime goal is to put the pieces into an order that communicates the author's subject and theme.

Unity of time, place, and action—the so-called "classic unities"—are not classic at all, and the author should freely rebel against critics who protest a play's violation of the sacred unity of time and place.

The play that moves in time and space is as acceptable as the one that tries to keep "stage time" congruent with "real time" and not chance a move in locale. It may be as "good," but of course for reasons other than movement in time and space. There should be a unity of action, however, to hold the whole together. If the playwright seeks to violate this "rule," creating new forms for dramatic writing, *he should do so knowingly.* To go against unification of action by happenstance would likely be a profitless expenditure of time and talent.

Summation

The playwright who knows dramatic literature will recognize this discussion of plot. What is discussed here is nothing more or less than a report of empirical observation: One studies western dramatic literature over its two thousand years and observes certain commonalities. Playwrights over the centuries have certain approaches.

In the next chapter we shall look at some of those plays and note certain structural qualities discussed above. Some abstractions described here will take more concrete life in the following pages.

Chapter Sixteen

Plot: Part Three

Introduction

Previous chapters introduced you to plot terminology and concepts. Now we look at *plot in use*, examining plot in plays. Examples will show how playwrights organize action into a desired pattern to develop the play's salient ideas, and judicious deduction may lead us to understand why the playwrights made particular choices. The goal of these chapters on plot is to help you understand how action is structured so you will be able to better organize your own plays. The questions and illustrations in the following pages will be the ones you can apply to other plays you study.

    In this chapter you will find illustrations of plot treated as a single part of a play. But plot cannot exist in a vacuum, and therefore the illustrations also show other aspects of playwriting. There will be opportunities to note how plot illuminates subject and theme and how the plot's movements increase depth of characterization.

MACBETH, by Shakespeare

A surprisingly large amount of material has been written about Shakespeare, of whom we know but few facts. Born in 1564 (probably in April), he was in his late twenties before history records his involvement with theatre. He was remarkably fortunate in being able to live in an era ruled by a monarch who approved so heartily of theatre—Elizabeth often had to overrule a Parliament intent upon regulating theatre to death in England and in new colonies—and also by falling in with the Lord Chamberlain's Company, which was so dedicated to supporting its playwright.

Macbeth was written around 1606, following *Hamlet*, *Othello*, and *King Lear*. It is an astonishing play in its brevity, strength, and sheer beauty. Of all of his plays, none are shorter except *Comedy of Errors*. For many of us, none are better. I hold that *Macbeth* is as close to perfection as any play we will ever find.

Shakespeare died in 1616 after a comfortable retirement. He was 52. Legend has it he was born on April 23, the date of his death.

THE TRAGEDY OF MACBETH

William Shakespeare

DRAMATIS PERSONAE

DUNCAN, King of Scotland.

MALCOLM,
DONALBAIN, } his sons.

MACBETH,
BANQUO, } Generals in the Scottish Army.

MACDUFF,
LENNOX,
ROSS,
MENTIETH,
ANGUS,
CAITHNESS, } Noblemen of Scotland.

FLEANCE, Son to Banquo.
SIWARD, Earl of Northumberland, General of the English forces.
YOUNG SIWARD, his son.
SEYTON, an Officer attending on Macbeth.
Boy, son to Macduff.
A Sergeant.
A Porter.
An Old Man.
An English Doctor.
A Scottish Doctor.
LADY MACBETH.
LADY MACDUFF.

A Gentlewoman, attending on Lady Macbeth.
Three Witches.
HECATE.
The Ghost of Banquo.
Apparitions.
Lords, Gentlemen, Officers, Soldiers, Murderers, Messengers, Attendants.

SCENE.—SCOTLAND; ENGLAND.

ACT I. SCENE I.
SCOTLAND. AN OPEN PLACE

(*Thunder and lightning. Enter three
  Witches.*)
1. *Witch.* When shall we three meet
    again
  In thunder, lightning, or in rain?
2. *Witch.* When the hurlyburly's done,
    When the battle's lost and won.
3. *Witch.* That will be ere the set of
    sun.   5
1. *Witch.* Where the place?
2. *Witch.*   Upon the heath.
3. *Witch.* There to meet with Macbeth.
1. *Witch.* I come, Graymalkin!
2. *Witch.* Paddock calls.
3. *Witch.*   Anon!
All. Fair is foul, and foul is fair.   10
  Hover through the fog and filthy air.
  (*Exeunt.*)

SCENE II. A CAMP NEAR FORRES.

(*Alarum within. Enter* King Duncan,
  Malcolm, Donalbain, Lennox,
  with Attendants, *meeting a bleeding
  Sergeant.*)
King. What bloody man is that? He can
    report,
  As seemeth by his plight, of the revolt
  The newest state.
Mal.   This is the sergeant
  Who like a good and hardy soldier
    fought
  'Gainst my captivity. Hail, brave
    friend!   5
  Say to the King the knowledge of the
    broil
  As thou didst leave it.

Serg.   Doubtful it stood,
  As two spent swimmers that do cling
    together
  And choke their art. The merciless
    Macdonwald
  (Worthy to be a rebel, for to that   10
  The multiplying villanies of nature
  Do swarm upon him) from the West-
    ern Isles
  Of kerns and gallowglasses is sup-
    plied;
  And Fortune, on his damned quar-
    rel smiling,
  Show'd like a rebel's whore. But all's
    too weak;   15
  For brave Macbeth (well he deserves
    that name),
  Disdaining Fortune, with his bran-
    dish'd steel,
  Which smok'd with bloody execution
    (Like valor's minion), carv'd out
    his passage
  Till he fac'd the slave;   20
  Which ne'er shook hands nor bade
    farewell to him
  Till he unseam'd him from the nave
    to th' chaps
  And fix'd his head upon our battle-
    ments.
King. O valiant cousin! worthy gentle-
    man!
Serg. As whence the sun 'gins his re-
    flection   25
  Shipwracking storms and direful
    thunders break,
  So from that spring whence comfort
    seem'd to come
  Discomfort swells. Mark, King of
    Scotland, mark.

No sooner justice had, with valor
   arm'd,
Compell'd these skipping kerns to
   trust their heels   30
But the Norweyan lord, surveying
   vantage,
With furbish'd arms and new sup-
   plies of men,
Began a fresh assault.
King.   Dismay'd not this
   Our captains, Macbeth and Banquo?
Serg.   Yes,
   As sparrows eagles, or the hare the
     lion.   35
If I say sooth, I must report they were
As cannons overcharg'd with double
   cracks, so they
Doubly redoubled strokes upon the foe.
Except they meant to bathe in reeking
   wounds,
Or memorize another Golgotha,   40
I cannot tell—
But I am faint; my gashes cry for
   help.
King. So well thy words become thee
   as thy wounds;
They smack of honor both. Go get
   him surgeons.
   (*Exit Sergeant, attended.*)
   (*Enter Ross.*)
Who comes here?
Mal. The worthy Thane of Ross.   45
Len. What a haste looks through his
   eyes! So should he look.
That seems to speak things strange.
Ross.   God save the King!
King. Whence cam'st thou, worthy thane?
Ross. From Fife, great King,
   Where the Norweyan banners flout
     the sky
   And fan our people cold. Norway
     himself,   50
     With terrible numbers,
Assisted by that most disloyal traitor,
The Thane of Cawdor, began a
   dismal conflict,
Till that Bellona's bridegroom, lapp'd
   in proof,

Confronted him with self-compari-
   sons,   55
Point against point, rebellious arm
   'gainst arm,
Curbing his lavish spirit; and to con-
   clude,
The victory fell on us.
King.   Great happiness!
Ross.   That now
   Sweno, the Norways' king, craves
     composition;
Nor would we deign him burial of
    * his men   60
Till he disbursed, at Saint Colme's
   Inch,
Ten thousand dollars to our general
   use.
King. No more that Thane of Cawdor
   shall deceive
Our bosom interest. Go pronounce
   his present death
And with his former title greet Mac-
   beth.   65
Ross. I'll see it done.
Dun. What he hath lost noble Macbeth
   hath won.
   (*Exeunt.*)

SCENE III. A BLASTED HEATH.

(*Thunder. Enter the three* Witches.)
1. *Witch.* Where hast thou been, sister?
2. *Witch.* Killing swine.
3. *Witch.* Sister, where thou?
1. *Witch.* A sailor's wife had chestnuts
   in her lap
And munch'd and munch'd and
   munch'd. 'Give me,' quoth I.   5
'Aroint thee, witch!' the rump-fed
   ronyon cries.
Her husband's to Aleppo gone, master o' th' Tiger;
But in a sieve I'll thither sail
And, like a rat without a tail,
I'll do, I'll do, and I'll do.   10
2. *Witch.* I'll give thee a wind.
1. *Witch.* Th' art kind.
3. *Witch.* And I another.

1. Witch. I myself have all the other,
And the very ports they blow,
All the quarters that they know
I' th' shipman's card.
I will drain him dry as hay.
Sleep shall neither night nor day
Hang upon his penthouse lid.   20
He shall live a man forbid.
Weary sev'nights, nine times nine,
Shall he swindle, peak, and pine.
Though his bark cannot be lost,
Yet it shall be tempest-tost.   25
Look what I have.
2. Witch. Show me! show me!
1. Witch. Here I have a pilot's thumb,
Wrack'd as homeward he did come.
(Drum within.)
3. Witch. A drum, a drum!   30
Macbeth doth come.
All. The Weird Sisters, hand in hand,
Posters of the sea and land,
Thus do go about, about,   34
Thrice to thine, and thrice to mine,
And thrice again, to make up nine.
Peace! The charm's wound up.
(Enter Macbeth *and* Banquo.*)*
Macb. So foul and fair a day I have not
seen.
Ban. How far is't call'd to Forres? What
are these,
So wither'd, and so wild in their at-
tire,   40
That look not like th' inhabitants o'
th' earth,
And yet are on't? Live you? or are
you aught
That man may question? You seem to
understand me,
By each at once her choppy finger
laying
Upon her skinny lips. You should be
women,   45
And yet your beards forbid me to
interpret
That you are so.
Macb. Speak, if you can. What are you?
1. Witch. All hail, Macbeth! Hail to
thee, Thane of Glamis!

2. Witch. All hail, Macbeth! Hail to
thee, Thane of Cawdor!
3. Witch. All hail, Macbeth, that shalt
be King hereafter!   50
Ban. Good sir, why do you start and
seem to fear
Things that do sound so fair? I' th'
name of truth,
Are ye fantastical, or that indeed
Which outwardly ye show? My noble
partner
You greet with present grace and
great prediction   55
Of noble having and of royal hope,
That he seems rapt withal. To me
you speak not.
If you can look into the seeds of time
And say which grain will grow and
which will not,
Speak then to me, who neither beg
nor fear   60
Your favors nor your hate.
1. Witch. Hail!
2. Witch. Hail!
3. Witch. Hail!
1. Witch. Lesser than Macbeth, and
greater.   65
2. Witch. Not so happy, yet much hap-
pier.
3. Witch. Thou shalt get kings, though
thou be none.
So all hail, Macbeth and Banquo!
1. Witch. Banquo and Macbeth, all
hail!
Macb. Stay, you imperfect speakers,
tell me more!   70
By Sinel's death I know I am Thane
of Glamis;
But how of Cawdor? The Thane of
Cawdor lives,
A prosperous gentleman; and to be
King
Stands not within the prospect of belief,
No more than to be Cawdor. Say
from whence   75
You owe this strange intelligence, or
why

Upon this blasted heath you stop our
    way
With such prophetic greeting. Speak,
    I charge you.
(Witches *vanish.*)
Ban. The earth hath bubbles, as the
    water has,
And these are of them. Whither are
    they vanish'd?   80
Macb. Into the air, and what seem'd
    corporal melted
  As breath into the wind. Would they
    had stay'd!
Ban. Were such things here as we do
    speak about?
Or have we eaten on the insane root
That takes the reason prisoner?   85
Macb. Your children shall be kings.
Ban.   You shall be King.
Macb. And Thane of Cawdor too. Went
    it not so?
Ban. To th' selfsame tune and words.
    Who's here?
(*Enter* Ross *and* Angus.)
Ross. The King hath happily receiv'd,
    Macbeth,
The news of thy success; and when
    he reads   90
Thy personal venture in the rebels'
    fight,
His wonders and his praises do con-
    tend
Which should be thine or his. Silenc'd
    with that,
In viewing o'er the rest o' th' self-
    same day,
He finds thee in the stout Norweyan
    ranks,   95
Nothing afeard of what thyself didst
    make,
Strange images of death. As thick
    as hail
Came post with post, and every one
    did bear
Thy praises in his kingdom's great
    defense
And pour'd them down before him.

Ang.   We are sent 100
To give thee from our royal master
    thanks;
Only to herald thee into his sight,
Not pay thee.
Ross. And for an earnest of a greater
    honor,
He bade me, from him, call thee
    Thane of Cawdor;   105
In which addition, hail, most worthy
    Thane!
For it is thine.
Ban. What, can the devil speak true?
Macb. The Thane of Cawdor lives. Why
    do you dress me
In borrowed robes?
Ang. Who was the Thane lives yet,
But under heavy judgment bears
    that life   110
Which he deserves to lose. Whether
    he was combin'd
With those of Norway, or did line
    the rebel
With hidden help and vantage, or
    that with both
He labor'd in his country's wrack, I
    know not;
But treasons capital, confess'd and
    prov'd,   115
Have overthrown him.
Macb. (*aside*) Glamis, and Thane of
    Cawdor!
The greatest is behind.—(*To* Ross
    and Angus) Thanks for your pains.
(*Aside to* Banquo) Do you not hope
    your children shall be kings,
When those that gave the Thane of
    Cawdor to me
Promis'd no less to them?
Ban. (*aside to* Macbeth) That, trusted
    home,   120
Might yet enkindle you unto the
    crown,
Besides the Thane of Cawdor. But 'tis
    strange!
And oftentimes, to win us to our
    harm,

The instruments of darkness tell us
truths,   124
Win us with honest trifles, to be-
tray's
In deepest consequence.—
Cousins, a word, I pray you.
Macb. (aside) Two truths are told,
As happy prologues to the swelling
act
Of the imperial theme.—I thank you,
gentlemen.—   129
(Aside) This supernatural soliciting
Cannot be ill; cannot be good. If ill,
Why had it given me earnest of suc-
cess,
Commencing in a truth? I am Thane
of Cawdor.
If good, why do I yield to that sug-
gestion
Whose horrid image doth unfix my
hair   135
And make my seated heart knock at my
ribs
Against the use of nature? Present fears
Are less than horrible imaginings.
My thought, whose murder yet is but
fantastical,
Shakes so my single state of man that
function   140
Is smother'd in surmise and nothing
is
But what is not.
Ban. Look how our partner's rapt.
Macb. (aside) If chance will have me
King, why, chance may crown me,
Without my stir.
Ban.   New honors come upon him,
Like our strange garments, cleave
not to their mold   145
But with the aid of use.
Macb. (aside) Come what come may,
Time and the hour runs through the
roughest day.
Ban. Worthy Macbeth, we stay upon
your leisure.
Macb. Give me your favor. My dull
brain was wrought

With things forgotten. Kind gentle-
men, your pains   150
Are regist'red where every day I turn
The leaf to read them. Let us to-
ward the King.
(Aside to Banquo*)* Think upon what
hath chanc'd; and, at more time,
The interim having weigh'd it, let
us speak
Our free hearts each to other.
Ban. (aside to Macbeth*)* Very gladly.
Macb. (aside to Banquo*)* Till then,
enough.—Come, friends.   156
(Exeunt.)

SCENE IV. FORRES. THE PALACE.

(Flourish. Enter King Duncan, Len-
nox, Malcolm, Donalbain, *and* At-
tendants.*)*
King. Is execution done on Cawdor?
Are not
Those in commission yet return'd?
Mal.   My liege,
They are not yet come back. But I
have spoke
With one that saw him die; who did
report
That very frankly he confess'd his
treasons,   5
Implor'd your Highness' pardon, and
set forth
A deep repentance. Nothing in his
life
Became him like the leaving it. He
died
As one that had been studied in his
death
To throw away the dearest thing he
ow'd   10
As 'twere a careless trifle.
King.   There's no art
To find the mind's construction in
the face.
He was a gentleman on whom I built
An absolute trust.
(Enter Macbeth, Banquo, *and* An-
gus.*)*

O worthiest cousin,
The sin of my ingratitude even now
Was heavy on me! Thou art so far
before   16
That swiftest wing of recompense is
slow
To overtake thee. Would thou hadst
less deserv'd,
That the proportion both of thanks
and payment
Might have been mine! Only I have
left to say,   20
More is thy due than more than all
can pay.
Macb. The service and the loyalty I
owe,
In doing it pays itself. Your High-
ness' part
Is to receive our duties; and our
duties
Are to your throne and state children
and servants,   25
Which do but what they should by
doing everything
Safe toward your love and honor.
King.   Welcome hither.
I have begun to plant thee and will
labor
To make thee full of growing. Noble
Banquo,
That hast no less deserv'd, nor must
be known   30
No less to have done so, let me infold
thee
And hold thee to my heart.
Ban.   There if I grow,
The harvest is your own.
King.   My plenteous joys,
Wanton in fulness, seek to hide them
selves
In drops of sorrow. Sons, kinsmen,
thanes,   35

And you whose places are the near-
est, know
We will establish our estate upon
Our eldest, Malcolm, whom we name
hereafter
The Prince of Cumberland; which
honor must   39
Not unaccompanied invest him only,
But signs of nobleness, like stars, shall
shine
On all deservers. From hence to In-
verness,
And bind us further to you.
Macb. The rest is labor, which is not
us'd for you!
I'll be myself the harbinger, and
make joyful   45
The hearing of my wife with your
approach;
So, humbly take my leave.
King.   My worthy Cawdor!
Macb. (aside) The Prince of Cumber-
land! That is a step
On which I must fall down, or else
o'erleap,
For in my way it lies. Stars, hide your
fires!   50
Let not light see my black and deep
desires.
The eye wink at the hand; yet let
that be,
Which the eye fears, when it is done,
to see.
(Exit.)
King. True, worthy Banquo: he is full
so valiant,   54
And in his commendations I am fed;
It is a banquet to me. Let's after him,
Whose care is gone before to bid us
welcome.
It is a peerless kinsman.
(Flourish. Exeunt.)

A Discussion
of Plot in MACBETH

With the remarkable smoothness that is part of his genius, Shakespeare has
efficiently accomplished a tremendous amount in just a few minutes: He has
introduced the major characters; deftly implied that Macbeth is a noble warrior

and a good man; identified the protagonist and given him a goal, even started plans to achieve that goal; created Duncan as a kindly person so the King's death will be more shocking; and shown Banquo to be a loyal man, which will make even more powerful the moment when Macbeth turns on him. With a poet's power, Shakespeare has used metaphors that express indirectly the play's subject and theme, "Fair is foul and foul is fair." The play is in forward progress already. It is a magnificent beginning.

Where Is the Point of Attack?   Which of the following is the play's point of attack?

1.   Scene One, when Third Witch says they will meet Macbeth?
2.   Scene Two, the Sergeant's description of the battle?
3.   Scene Two, Duncan ordering Ross to tell Macbeth he is promoted to Thane of Cawdor?
4.   Scene Three, Banquo's request that the Witches tell him a prophecy?
5.   Scene Three, Macbeth's reactions when the Witches tell his fortune?
6.   Scene Four, when the King says he will visit Macbeth's castle?

Answer 1 is not valid; that is foreshadowing but not a complication because it does not change the direction of the action. It also foreshadows the play's subject and theme. Do you see how? Answer 2 also is not valid; this tells of past actions and therefore is exposition. Answer 3 is not valid; that does not change the course of the action, although it will later provide a complication in Scene Three. Trace the line of the plot for your own knowledge. Answer 4 is not correct; here we receive foreshadowing for future movements of the plot; later in the play, Macbeth will decide he has to kill Banquo and Banquo's heirs because of this prophecy, which means that this moment is foreshadowing. Answer 5 is correct: it is not so much that the Witches *tell* him he will be King as it is his own reactions that change the course of the action. Answer 6 is the beginning of a complication; once Duncan gets to Macbeth's castle, he will be murdered.

Note how the playwright emphasizes Macbeth's reactions with Banquo's descriptions on lines 51–52, 54–56, and 142. Here indeed is the point of attack. It changes the course of the action, it hints directly at the play's basic intellectual content ("Things that do sound so fair" relates to what we already have heard about "fair is foul. . . ."), it strongly involves the protagonist, and Macbeth's silence draws audience attention into his mind and soul where the battles of this play will roar. It is a marvelously strong point of attack. It is remarkably early in the play! If you want a model, here is a perfect one of the way a point of attack works.

What Alternatives Did Shakespeare Have?   The play works so smoothly that everything seems just right. Of course, we say, the point of attack must come here. Where else? But it could have come later. Imagine the author stating his goals. "Let's see. First I have to establish mood because the play depends upon mood and darkness, so I'll write some scenes for that. And I have to introduce the characters so the audience will know them under one set of conditions to see them change under developing plot action, so I'll construct scenes with Macbeth, Duncan, Lady Macbeth, and Banquo. And I have to insert exposition about the war." That playwright might fashion a scenario as outlined briefly below:

- Scene One. Battlefield. Show Macbeth fighting valiantly. Outnumbered, he wins anyhow. Establish (a) war, (b) Macbeth as warrior, (c) Macbeth as brave and good man.
- Scene Two. Camp. Night. Macbeth binds wounds of his men. Banquo and Macbeth chat about the nature of war. Good moment to express philosophy about war and valor.
- Scene Three. Camp. Later. Night. King Duncan and Macbeth. Show goodness of the King and the respect Macbeth has for the man and the office. Show relationships: warmth, respect.
- Scene Four. The heath. The witches. Although audience cannot see Macbeth and Duncan, apparently the witches can. Shows their magic. They laugh sardonically about the men. Foreshadowing.
- Scene Five. Macbeth's castle. Lady Macbeth and Macbeth. Show their relationship. She is sharp, cold, ambitious. Foreshadowing.
- Scene Six. Macbeth sleeping. Camp. Witches appear to him as in a dream. He shouts in fear. Banquo awakens him, comforts him. Macbeth: "Methinks I saw a dagger." Foreshadowing.
- Scene Seven. As Scene Four. Exposition, foreshadowing.

An entire act with yet no forward motion, no point of attack: does this strike you as absurd? But of course. We have, after all, the model that Shakespeare wrote, and anything else appears horribly out of key. But if you had not read Macbeth, might this scenario appear effective?

I Hope You Note the Dramatic Effects Achieved so Strongly with the Early Point of Attack. For your writing, I strongly urge you to consider a structure that puts the point of attack early in the play, adequately amplified.

Can the Modern Playwright Achieve as Much with an Early Point of Attack? Of course. For evidence of this, examine the plays of Harold Pinter. Many Arthur Miller and Tennessee Williams plays have early and strong beginnings with the point of attack sharply etched.

When Does the Plot Move Again? Shakespeare puts the plot in full motion almost immediately after that initial complication. In the same scene Ross tells Macbeth that he now is Thane of Cawdor; the witches have made three predictions and immediately two of them are proven correct. This movement of the plot provides a sharp stimulus to Macbeth. He becomes preoccupied with the hunger of ambition. The movement of the plot forces him to consider the morality of his actions and desires: In lines 130 through 141 he begins examining problems of right and wrong which come with wanting to be king. *Plot, then, stimulates character and thought.* Plot is not simply a contrived outside device but instead is intricately married to character and thought.

How Much Exposition Does Shakespeare Insert into the Play? Precious little. It is true that there is some brief discussion about the war, but that is merely a third cousin to the play. Shakespeare wastes no time on exposition but instead implies a great deal and lets the rest handle itself. Could *Macbeth* have been written with large beats of exposition? If so, what effect would that have had upon the play? Remember your answer when you construct your own plays' openings.

THE DESPERATE HOURS, by Joseph Hayes*

The Desperate Hours brings us up to modern drama. This strongly-plotted suspense drama first played on Broadway in the mid-1950s and was made into an exciting motion picture with Humphrey Bogart as the chief hoodlum (the last hoodlum role he played) and Frederick March as the father. The play's basic situation of a good and wholesome family being terrorized by thugs is the stuff of good melodrama, and conflicts grow easily from the clash of the extremes. Since the play opened it has been followed by countless dramas and movies in the same vein—the family out camping, hunting, boating, or simply driving down the deserted highway, at the beach or mountain, in a small town or large, always set upon by hoodlums, with one who is wildly vicious, one who struggles against his internal concerns of good against evil, and a leader who tries to keep his gang in line. The family almost always contains a young girl ready for womanhood, a younger son, and a harried father. After you have read *The Desperate Hours* you will recall its many spinoffs seen later.

The Desperate Hours has the craftsmanship one expects from a professional. The pace is controlled by the author, starting slowly so it can build; the characters are studies in contrasts, each in relief against the others; and the plot is strong and effective. The play is valuable for you to study. Its parts show up well and the machinery can be examined.

Numbers in the margins refer to notes that appear on the pages following the play.

As you read the play for the first time, ask yourself these questions:

1. Why does the playwright set the play's opening early in the morning?
2. Do you see how the author controls the tempo, even from the first lines?

*My thanks are due to Joseph Hayes for his personal permission to quote extracts from his play, *The Desperate Hours*.

3. Earlier there was a discussion of the professional playwright's "rule of three." Where do you find the repetitive triad in this play? What does it achieve?

4. What is the author trying to accomplish with the first scene?

5. Identify foreshadowing, exposition, and the play's point of attack.

6. By the time the father and children have left the house you have a clear vision of a large number of characters. How did the playwright achieve that?

THE DESPERATE HOURS

Joseph Hayes

Time: *The present*
Scene: *The City of Indianapolis*
Act One: *A day in autumn*
Act Two: *Later*
Act Three: *Later*

CHARACTERS

TOM WINSTON
JESSE BARD
HARRY CARSON
ELEANOR HILLIARD
RALPHIE HILLIARD
DAN HILLIARD
CINDY HILLIARD
GLENN GRIFFIN
HANK GRIFFIN
ROBISH
CHUCK WRIGHT
MR. PATTERSON
LT. CARL FREDERICKS
MISS SWIFT

SCENE

The action throughout the play alternates between two sets on stage. In the first two acts, the Hilliard home is at stage-right and the Sheriff's office is at stage-left. In Act Three, the Hilliard home is at stage-right, and at stage-left is a corner of an attic room. The action shifts back and forth between the two sets by the use of blackouts and sliding black curtains which mask the set that is not in focus.

The Hilliard home is the principal set. This consists of various rooms, all blended together by fluid action; lights focus the attention in the various rooms, as the action of the play requires.

On the ground-floor level of the house, there are two rooms in view at all times: the living room and a back hall or pantry. In the living room, there is an outside door in the rear wall; next to this door are stairs rising to the upstairs level. At right a door gives access to a den or library, off-stage. At left, facing downstage, there is another door; this door, presumably, leads into a dining room; the dining room is adjacent to a kitchen; the kitchen door opens into the pantry or back hall. In this manner, a character leaving the living room exits through the dining-room door and in a moment reappears in the pantry. This pantry is a small room in itself. In addition to the kitchen door, there is an exterior side door of the house itself opening off the pantry at stage-left. Back stairs descend along the exterior wall at left: a narrow passageway gives access to the upper floor. The entire ground floor, then, consists of a living room with front stairs curving up, a front door, a door to the den and a door to the dining room; a pantry with a door to the kitchen, an exterior side door, shelves, and a narrow stairway going up. In addition, a portion of the side yard is visible at left.

The upper level—constructed above the ground-floor level described above—consists of two bedrooms and an upstairs hall between; this hall gives access to the downward flow of the front stairway. The bedroom at stage-right is the master bedroom, containing twin beds, windows right and up-center, and a bureau. The bedroom at stage-left is a boy's bedroom, with a bunk, various shelves with toys, and a window overlooking the side yard. Between the two bedrooms is a small hall: downstage is a small table with a telephone.

At far left stage, during the first two acts, is the Sheriff's office on ground level, a bare sort of room with a wall-clock, a desk, various files, and radio and intercom apparatus. In the last act, a corner of an attic appears at stage-left; this is constructed above the Sheriff's office, and in Act Three the office is completely masked.

ACT ONE

SHERIFF'S OFFICE: The curtain rises, morning light fades in on the Sheriff's office. Winston, a deputy sheriff inclined to matter-of-fact laziness, sits at desk, speaking on the telephone. On the desk are an intercom, radio apparatus, sheafs of papers, and so forth. #1 The wall-clock reads 8:10.

WINSTON. [*Plaintively.*] Baby . . . didn't I just tell you? I can't leave till Bard gets here. [*He listens.*] Listen, baby—this night shift gets my goat as much as it does yours. You think I wouldn't like to be in that nice warm bed? [*There is a buzz from the intercom on the desk.*] Hold it. [*He speaks into the intercom.*] Yeah, Dutch?

DUTCH'S VOICE. Winston . . . Bard's going to want those Terre Haute reports right away.

WINSTON. [*Irascibly, into intercom.*] What do you think I'm gonna do with 'em . . . eat 'em for breakfast? [*He flips off the intercom, returns to the phone.*] Hello, baby . . . [*Listens.*] Yeah, that's what I said, isn't it? In that nice warm

bed *with you*. Who'd you think I . . . [*Listens.*] Okay, okay, baby . . . go back to sleep and wait for Papa. [*Hangs up, shakes head, pleased; speaks with gusto.*] Give me a jealous woman every time! [*Bard enters. Winston is sleepy and glad to be relieved. Bard takes off jacket, removes gun from shoulder-holster through* #2 *the following. All very casual and commonplace at first.*]

BARD. [*As he enters.*] Morning, Tom.

WINSTON. [*Stretching.*] Well! About time.

BARD. [*Stows gun in drawer of file.*] Overslept. Sorry. #1

WINSTON. [*Rising slowly.*] You got a lovely excuse.

BARD. I'll tell her you think so. [*Above desk, riffles reports.*] Quiet night?

WINSTON. [*Preparing to go.*] If kids'd stay out of cars and off motorcycles, we'd soon be out of jobs around here.

BARD. Not another burglary in Speedway City? [*Laughs.*] This guy's getting tiresome.

WINSTON. A real sex-nut, that one.

Same old story . . . all he took was diamonds and women's panties. What the hell's the connection.

BARD. You figure it out, Tom. [*Then tensing . . . so that from now on the pace and tone change.*] What's this?

#3 WINSTON. [*Yawns, looking over* Bard's *shoulder.*] Federal prison break . . . Terre Haute. None of our concern.

BARD. When'd it come in?

#3 WINSTON. [*Ready to leave.*] Hours ago. The three of 'em busted out some time before dawn. . . .

BARD. [*Sits at desk, snaps button on intercom.*] Why didn't you call me?

#3 WINSTON. Call you? Why?

DUTCH'S VOICE. Yes, Jesse?

BARD. [*Into intercom.*] Dutch . . . get me Lieutenant Fredericks, State Police.

WINSTON. Jesse . . . remember what your Irish wife threatened last time I routed you out of the nest. . . .

BARD. Terre Haute's only seventy miles away. They could've *walked* here by now!

#3 FREDERICKS' VOICE. [*On intercom— crisp, middle-aged, cynical.*] I wondered when you'd start yipping, Bard.

BARD. [*Quickly.*] Fredericks . . . anybody sitting on anything?

#4 FREDERICKS' VOICE. I'm sitting on just what you're sitting on, Deputy. Only mine ain't sweatin'.

#5 BARD. Griffin's woman . . . Helen Laski . . . any dope on her?

FREDERICK'S VOICE. Not a trace. Chicago . . . Cleveland . . . St. Louie. All we know is she was here in town three weeks ago.

BARD. Just don't let any cop touch her. She's the beacon'll lead us straight . . .

FREDERICK'S VOICE. Bard . . . it's an FBI case anyway. The city police've ripped whole buildings apart. We got the highways blocked. We're working through all the dives. . . .

BARD. If Glen Griffin wants to come #5 here, no roadblock's gonna stop him. And he's too sharp to hole up any place you'd think of looking.

FREDERICK'S VOICE. Look, lad . . . get that chip off your shoulder. [*Shortly.*] You want Griffin so bad, go get him! #5 [Bard *flips off the intercom.* Winston *reluctantly removes his coat.*]

WINSTON. Glen Griffin . . . is he the #5 one you . . . ?

BARD. [*Thoughtfully.*] Yeah . . . he's the one. [*Studying reports.*] Glenn Griffin #5 . . . his brother, Hank . . . and . . . who's this third one? Samuel Robish.

WINSTON. Life-termer. A three-time loser. And nasty. [*As Bard* picks up the phone and dials, Winston *returns his coat to the hanger.*] You're not going to get any sleep today, are you, Winston? No, I'm not going to get any sleep today. I'm going to sit on the teletype machine like a good little boy scout. . . . [*Bard smiles a bit as* Winston *exits. Then he speaks into the telephone in contrasting gentle tones.*]

BARD. Hello, Katie. Did I wake you? . . . #6 I've just had an idea . . . why don't you go over to my mother's for the day? [*Laughs—but the urgency comes through.*] Oh, stop groaning . . . how often do I ask you to *let* her talk your arm and leg off? . . . No, not this afternoon. *Now!* . . . And Katie . . . don't mention where you're going, huh? . . . To the neighbors, anyone . . . Good. . . . Right away. Take a taxi. . . . Sure, splurge. [Bard *hangs up, sits thinking, with the smile fading.* Winston *enters, with* Carson, *who is youthful, businesslike, rather studious-looking.* Winston *places a teletype message on desk before* Bard.]

WINSTON. It had to break, Jesse. [*Then* #7 *with a touch of sarcasm as* Bard *reads.*] Oh—this is Mr. Carson, FBI.

BARD. [*Briskly.*] How are you? Look, it says they beat up a farmer south of the prison before daybreak. How come we're just getting it?

CARSON. They left him in his barn, out cold . . . ripped out his phone. He just staggered into a general store and reported his car stolen. . . . [*With a touch of good-natured irony.*] How are *you*?

BARD. Have you put this on the air?

CARSON. Deputy, I've been in touch with Sheriff Masters by telephone.

BARD. I hope he's enjoying his extended vacation . . . he sure picked a fine time to leave me in charge here. . . .

CARSON. The way I understand it, you know this Glenn Griffin fellow better than any police officer in the area. How about your taking over this section? [*Pause. The whole weight falls on Bard. He accepts it . . . slowly. Then:*]

BARD. Okay . . . Okay . . . Let's find that car! [*He goes into action—hands tele-type to Winston.*] Tom, put this description on the air. Tell 'em to repeat it every half hour.

WINSTON. [*Protesting.*] We'll be flooded with calls. Every crackpot in five states . . .

BARD. [*Sitting at desk.*] We'll follow up every tip!

WINSTON. [*To Carson—groaning.*] I hope you know what you just did! [*Winston exits. Carson moves to desk and offers Bard a cigarette.*]

CARSON. Any ideas where they might dig in?

BARD. [*Shaking his head.*] All I know is . . . just as long's Glenn Griffin's running around free and safe—with that prison guard's .38 in his paw—well, it's not free or safe for anyone else. No decent people anywhere—whether they've ever . . . [*The lights begin to dim.*] heard of Glenn Griffin or not . . .

#8

HILLIARD HOME: *Lights rise slowly. We see the complete outline of a typical house in the suburbs: pleasant, comfortable, undistinguished. Eleanor Hilliard, an attractive women in her early forties, enters from the dining room, moves to front door, opens it and looks out. The morning light outside is bright and cheerful. Not finding the morning paper, she closes the door as Ralphie enters from dining room. Ralphie, aged ten, is dressed for school and carries a half-empty glass of milk, which he stares at balefully as he sits. Eleanor, who is extremely neat, is arranging pillows on the sofa.*]

#9

ELEANOR. [*Gently.*] Ralphie, you left your bike outside all night again.

RALPHIE. [*As though this answers her.*] It didn't rain.

ELEANOR. Well it's not going to rain today, either. But you're going to put it in the garage before you go to school. [*Dan Hilliard enters from dining room and crosses to front door to look out. He is a typical, undistinguished but immediately likable man in his forties.*]

DAN. [*Calling up the stairs as he passes.*] Cindy! It's eight-thirty.

CINDY. [*Off, in her room upstairs.*] Can't a girl straighten her girdle in peace?

#10

DAN. [*Surprised.*] Girdle?. . . Girdle! [*Goes to Eleanor.*] Ellie, can a twenty-year-old child with a figure like Cindy's . . .

#10

ELEANOR. [*Smiling.*] It's a joke, Dan.

DAN. Oh. Thank the Lord. She has to have a solid hour for primping and then she complains all the way downtown because we don't live in the city limits.

RALPHIE. Ain't love disgusting?

ELEANOR. Don't say "ain't."

DAN. [*To Ralphie—firmly.*] Don't say "love," either. [*There is a thud of a newspaper thrown against the front door. Dan steps swiftly to the door. He and Eleanor have a slight collision. She moves downstage and he opens the door and goes off onto the porch.*] Hey! Hey!

ELEANOR. [*Teasing.*] Try holding your nose and gulping it, Ralphie.

RALPHIE. It tastes sour.

ELEANOR. [*Picking up her small pad and pencil from coffee table.*] Yesterday it tasted like chalk. [*She sits and starts making her shopping list. Dan returns, picks up the* Indianapolis Star, *and enters the room, closing the door.*]

DAN. [*A suggestion of grouchiness.*] Some day I'm going to catch up with that paper boy and we're going to have a lawsuit on our hands.

ELEANOR. Dan, you have time for a second cup of coffee.

DAN. [*Glances at his watch and then up the stairs.*] In half a minute she'll come prancing down those stairs and start urging me to hurry. [*Dan exits into the dining room. Ralphie takes a long drink of the milk but cannot finish it. Cindy comes down the stairs in time to see him.*]

CINDY. Well, *today* you are a man! [*She goes to the closet, gets her coat and bag.*]

RALPHIE. If cows only knew how I hated 'em!

ELEANOR. What would they do?

CINDY. [*To Eleanor.*] Where's Dad? What was he shouting at me?

ELEANOR. What does he shout every morning at eight-thirty?

CINDY. He shouts it's eight-thirty.

ELEANOR. You win the kewpie-doll. [*Cindy moves swiftly toward the dining room as Dan appears in the door with a cup of coffee.*]

CINDY. [*To Dan as she swings past him.*] Say, you'd better hurry!

DAN. [*Looks after Cindy, then to Eleanor as he sits on sofa.*] What'd I tell you? [*Dan sets his cup of coffee on the table and picks up the newspaper and reads.*]

RALPHIE. Dad . . . Why did the moron lock his father in the refrigerator?

DAN. [*His attention on the newspaper.*] Ralphie, do I have to answer that one?

RALPHIE. [*Brightly.*] Because he liked cold pop! [*There is an escape of breath from Dan which might or might not pass for a laugh.*] Well, why don't you laugh?

DAN. I laughed. What do you want me to do . . . roll on the floor?

RALPHIE. You *almost* rolled on the floor last night when I told you why the moron ate dynamite.

ELEANOR. [*Shakes her head warningly but continues writing.*] Ralphie . . .

RALPHIE. My name is Ralph. R-a-l-p-h. There's no Y on the end of it. I looked up my birth certificate.

ELEANOR. Sorry. [*Through the following, Ralphie rises and, with glass in hand, moves to the chair by front door to pick up his jacket and football; he rather elaborately manages to conceal the half-glass of milk on the floor out of sight in the process.*]

RALPHIE. Big game after school today. Fourth grade versus fifth grade. [*Having achieved his purpose; with a sigh of relief.*] We'll slaughter 'em! [*Kisses Eleanor.*]

ELEANOR. 'Bye, darling. [*Dan leans back to be kissed, but Ralphie brushes past him and goes to dining-room door, where Dan's voice stops him.*]

DAN. Hey! Aren't you forgetting something?

RALPHIE. [*Embarrassed and uncertain.*] Oh. [*He then returns to Dan, who leans for a kiss; instead, Ralphie extends his hand and shakes Dan's hand with grave formality.*] So long, Dad. I hope you have a very pleasant day at the office. [*He turns and goes into the dining room, leaving Dan staring after him, then reappears in the pantry on his way to the side door.*] So long, dream-witch. I hope Chuck Wright doesn't even notice your new dress.

CINDY. [*Steps into pantry with glass of*

orange juice in her hand.] 'Bye. Flunk geography, will you, pest?

RALPHIE. [*As he goes out the side door.*] Mister Pest to you.

ELEANOR. [*Calling from living room.*] Ralphie! Your bicycle!

DAN. What do you suppose that was all about?

ELEANOR. [*Toying with her pad and pencil.*] Our son Ralph . . . spelled R-a-l-p-h . . . considers himself too old to kiss a man . . . that's you . . . goodbye or good-night.

DAN. [*Covering his hurt.*] Oh.

ELEANOR. He said last night he hoped you'd understand.

DAN. [*With an empty smile.*] I was hoping maybe he just didn't like my shave-lotion. [*As Eleanor unconsciously touches his hair.*] Ellie, what's happening to both of them lately? This . . . this young lawyer Cindy works for . . . she can't be *serious*, can she?

ELEANOR. [*Sits.*] She hasn't confided in me, Dan . . . which could mean she is.

DAN. She's only twenty years old!

ELEANOR. I was nineteen.

DAN. You had some sense.

ELEANOR. Sure. I married you.

DAN. [*As though he has proved a point.*] Well, I didn't drive a Jaguar! [*Cindy enters from the dining room and goes to put on her coat.*]

CINDY. Chuck and I find his Jaguar a very comfortable little surrey. Come climb into my Ford coupé, Dad . . . and don't whisper when I'm in the next room. It's not polite.

DAN. [*As he rises and moves to closet.*] Now she'll speed.

ELEANOR. [*Automatically.*] Careful now, Dan.

CINDY. [*Satirically—chidingly.*] Mother . . . you say that every morning of the world. What could possibly happen to a man in the personnel office of a de-

partment store? [*She exits, closing the door.*]

DAN. [*Pointing at closed door.*] That's what I mean! That's not Cindy. Those are Chuck Wright's ideas. Last night on the way home, she asked me point-blank if I didn't think I led a pretty dull life.

ELEANOR. What'd you say?

DAN. [*Firmly.*] I said I didn't like Chuck Wright, either. [*Dan goes to the door, and Eleanor follows him.*]

ELEANOR. Dan . . . at Chuck's age . . . you were going to be another Richard Halliburton, remember? Climb the Matterhorn . . . swim at midnight in the Taj Mahal. My father threatened to throw you . . . [*Outside, Cindy taps horn impatiently.*]

DAN. I'm going to be late. [*They kiss: casual, without meaning, habit.*] If you're going to use the car today, buy some gas first. *Before* you have to walk a mile for it this time. [*Dan exits. Eleanor closes the door. Eleanor leans against the door a second, utters an almost silent "Whew," puts her shopping list and pencil on the telephone table, pushes her hair back from her forehead, pushes up her sleeves and prepares to begin the day. She moves to sofa, folds the newspaper and straightens the cushions. Then she goes upstairs, casually humming, and into Ralphie's room. She shakes her head and begins to gather up the soiled clothes. She flips on a small portable radio and takes the clothes down the hall, presumably to the bathroom, disappears.*]

NEWSCASTER'S VOICE. . . . five-state alarm. Police authorities have requested all citizens to be on the lookout for a 1941 Dodge sedan . . . gray . . . mud-spattered . . . bearing Indiana license plates number HL6827 . . . that is HL6827. . . . One of the convicts is wearing a pair of faded blue farmer's

#11

overalls which were . . . [Eleanor has returned and flips the radio to music. The music plays through the scene. Eleanor starts to make Ralphie's bed. The door chimes sound.]

ELEANOR. Wouldn't you know it . . . every time . . . [The chimes sound again, insistently. She comes down the stairs, but before she reaches the last step the chimes are heard for the third time. She crosses to the door and opens it.] Yes? [The young man who stands there . . . still out of sight . . . is in mid-twenties and wears faded blue farmer's overalls. He is tall with—at the moment—a rather appealing boyish expression on his handsome face.]

GLENN. Sorry to bother you, ma'am, but it looks like I lost my way. [As he speaks, Robish and Hank Griffin appear outside and enter the house by the side door, stealthily.] Could you kindly direct me to the Bowden Dairy? I know it's somewhere in the neighborhood, but I must have the wrong . . . [Hank Griffin— who is younger than Glenn, shorter, not so handsome, with a confused, hard but somehow rather sensitive face—remains in the pantry, looking out the window of the #12 side door. Robish is large, bull-like, slow, with a huge head sunk between two bulky upthrust shoulders. He goes into the kitchen at once and reappears in the dining-room door. Both wear prison garb. The following action has a cold, machine-like precision about it.]

ELEANOR. [Her back to the room.] Let me see. I've seen that sign. But there are no dairies very close. You see, this is a residential . . . [Robish now stands in the room. Eleanor becomes conscious of his presence. She breaks off and turns. In that moment Glenn whips out the gun, forces his way into the room, pushing Eleanor. He slams the door and locks it, then moves down to Eleanor.]

GLENN. Take it easy, lady. [As her mouth trembles open.] Easy, I said. You scream, the kid owns that bike out there'll come home an' find you in a pool of blood. [Glenn only nods to Robish, who stumps up the stairs and through . the following looks into Cindy's room, Ralphie's room, then enters the master bedroom and searches.] You there, Hank?

HANK. [Speaking as he moves into the living room.] All clear out back. Lincoln in garage . . . almost new. Garage lock broken. [Eleanor looks at Hank, who returns her state boldly. A shudder goes through her. Through the following, Glenn's swagger suggests a deep insecurity. Above, Robish is examining and discarding various of Dan's clothes in the bedroom . . . creating havoc. Glenn steps to Eleanor.]

GLENN. I'll take the keys to the Lincoln now, lady . . .

ELEANOR. Keys? . . . [Conquering shudders.] Keys? . . .

GLENN. Lady, when I talk, you snap. Snap fast!

ELEANOR. Top of . . . top of refrigerator . . . I think . . . I always misplace the . . . [As Glenn nods to Hank, who goes into dining room then into pantry with the keys and out the side door and off.] Take it . . . you only want the car . . . take it and go. . . .

GLENN. [Shouts toward the stairs.] What're you doin' up there, Robish—takin' a #13 bath?

ROBISH. Nobody home but the missus. [He goes into upstairs hall, with Dan's clothes.]

GLENN. I figured it. [He examines the house . . . looks into the den.] Good-lookin' family you got, lady. I seen 'em leavin'. [As Robish descends.] How many bedrooms up there, Robish?

ROBISH. Four. An' two complete cans, for Chrissake. . . . [The sound of a car door being slammed startles Eleanor.]

GLENN. Don't be so jumpy, lady. Only the kid brother takin' care of the cars.

ROBISH. [*Holding up Dan's suit.*] Th' sonofabitch's got five suits up there. [*He tosses the suit over the back of chair and goes into the dining room . . . to reappear a few moments later searching the shelves in the pantry.*]

GLENN. Class, all the way. . . . [*To Eleanor.*] I guess you're tumbling to the idea, ain't you, lady?

ELEANOR. [*Picks up her purse from sofa.*] You want money . . . here . . . take it . . . anything . . .

GLENN. [*Takes purse and dumps contents on sofa.*] Pretty. [*Holds up a locket.*] Gold? [*As Eleanor nods wordlessly, he slips it into his pocket.*] I got a gal with a yen for gold a mile wide. [*Picks up the money.*] This all the dough you got in the house?

ELEANOR. [*With difficulty.*] Yes . . . yes . . . my husband always says . . . too much cash in . . .

GLENN. [*Grins.*] Old man's right. Ain't ever safe to have too much cash layin' around. [*He pockets the money.*] Gives people ideas. [*Robish returns, disgruntled.*]

ROBISH. [*To Glenn.*] My gut's growlin'.

GLENN. We heard it.

ROBISH. [*To Eleanor.*] Missus, where you keep th' liquor?

ELEANOR. [*Backing away from him to chair, sits.*] We don't have . . . I don't think we . . . [*Hank enters the side door, locks it.*]

GLENN. [*Gesturing to den.*] Robish . . . park your butt'n there'n keep your eyes peeled that side-a th' house.

ROBISH. [*Aggressively; to Eleanor.*] I ain't had me a drink'n eighteen years.

GLENN. Robish, you don't hear so good. It's a kinda library. Improve your mind. [*Hank enters from dining room.*]

HANK. Gray job's in the garage, outta sight. Lincoln's ready in the driveway . . . headin' out. But she's low on gas.

[*He hands the car keys to Glenn, who pockets them.*]

ROBISH. [*Stolidly.*] I need me a gun. [*Glenn nods to Hank, who turns and runs upstairs. Through the following, he looks into Cindy's room, Ralphie's room, and enters the master bedroom, where he searches through the top bureau drawer, tossing out handkerchiefs and other odds and ends of clothing.*] I don't like none of it.

GLENN. [*Calling up the stairs.*] Hey, Hank, Robish, don't like it. After them hard bunks . . . them concrete floors!

HANK. Tell 'im to lump it.

GLENN. Lump it. Robish. [*Gestures to den.*] In there.

ROBISH. I don't feel right without a gun.

GLENN. Tell you what, Robish . . . Let's you'n me go out an' stick up a hardware store!

ROBISH. Now you're talkin'!

GLENN. [*Sardonically.*] Sure . . . Come'n, Robish. Every copper'n the state's waitin' for us to pull a job like that! [*Moves to door.*] What're you stallin' for? [*Hank finds an automatic in the drawer and pockets it and starts back downstairs.*] Come on!

ROBISH. [*Turning away—growling, inwardly seething.*] Awwww . . . don't do me no favors. [*For the first time, Glenn laughs. Hank, watching Robish, joins in. Eleanor stares. Robish's face hardens* #14 *and, scowling he makes a sudden movement toward Hank.*] What're you yakkin' at, yuh . . . [*But Glenn moves. The laughter dies. He grabs Robish, whips him about.*]

GLENN. [*In low hard tones.*] Lissen! How many times I gotta tell you? Keep your mitts off the kid, you don't wanna get your skull laid open. [*Pause. Robish and Glenn face each other. Then Robish turns sullenly and grabs suit of clothes, growling. Glenn, having asserted his total control, laughs, takes cigar from humidor on coffee* table and tosses it to Robish.] Here . . . make yourself sick on a good cigar. [Robish, seething, doesn't attempt to catch it; it falls to the floor. Then, defiantly, Robish steps on it, grinding it into the carpet.]

GLENN. Robish, you gonna give the lady the idea we ain't neat.
ROBISH. [He picks up the humidor.] Coupla brothers! Shoulda knowed better. Ain't neither one dry back-a the ears yet. [Robish exits into the den.]

<h1 style="text-align:center">First Discussion of
THE DESPERATE HOURS</h1>

The numbers refer to marginal notations.

1. Why does the playwright begin with this air of sleepiness? Does the slow pace shift gears when Bard hears of the break?

2. The stage directions say that this scene takes place in a sheriff's office, but note the way the playwright establishes the scene in many other ways. The routine way Bard removes the gun from his shoulder holster suggests a great deal. What other actions and lines show this is a police office?

3. What are these strokes, in plot terms?

4. Note the professional at work: Here is more foreshadowing, but Hayes wisely shifts the style to comedy.

5. Professional playwrights work on a "rule of three" to communicate important information. How many times does Hayes establish the name of Glenn Griffin? Write the various sentences that identify Griffin: Do you see how the information is communicated in subtle ways without repetition?

6. This is smooth writing. Why does Hayes have Bard call Katie? The playwright neatly increases foreshadowing, here using a different technique. The result is increased suspense.

7. Even the FBI is involved. This heightens concern about the Griffin personality. Notice how Hayes makes each stroke larger than the previous one: Here is, in a neat nutshell, the "building block" premise at work.

Scene One efficiently conveys an air of immediate danger. With a professional playwright's smooth craftsmanship, Hayes lets us know that Bard is only the Deputy and that the sheriff is out of town, that Griffin has a grudge against Bard, and that all the forces of the police will be concentrated upon finding these criminals who are a major threat.

Scene Two starts languidly. The very serenity itself is a suspense-creating quality because it contrasts so sharply with the tensions that were building in Scene One. Hayes again shows writing skill in the way he neatly shows, rather than tells, the normalcy of the Hilliard household. These people live placidly with troubles no larger than the newspaper boy's delivery technique.

8. Do you see the effect of foreshadowing? Notice how the playwright lets us know that we will see "decent people."

9. Ralph is being established as a bright, clever, full-of-being-a-boy, ten-year-old. The author will need that bright-eyed intensity in the latter parts of the play. He is shown, not described, in a number of clever ways.

10. Why does Hayes refer to Cindy's girdle? Yes, it is a way of mentioning her age; more importantly it leads to a comment about her figure and her blossoming from girl to woman. The play, written in the mid-1950s remember, will set up Cindy as a potential victim.

11. First, what is this in terms of plot? Second, what is wrong with the newscaster device? If you saw it as foreshadowing, you are correct; if you feel the device is awkward because its strains plausibility/probability, again you are correct. It is too convenient that the radio would be talking of the convicts just as Eleanor turns it on.

12. This entrance is what, in plot terms? It is clear, certainly, and you ought to be able to identify this well. If you are not certain, ask yourself about the play's balance: Has it shifted? No doubt of it, this entrance changes the course of the action. It stands out as a strong complication, and already you know that the rest of the play is set up to follow this moment. Has there been an earlier complication? No. What is this, then?

13. *Contrast* helps move this play forward. The contrast in the sheriff's office, between sleepiness and tension; the contrast between the sheriff's office with the officers worried and concerned versus the placid Hilliard home; and the contrast between normal suburban life and the tough, violent life of the criminals, all combine to keep the play's balance shifting rapidly. The play is crisp and alive with sparks from contrasts.

14. The building-block theory continues. As if it weren't enough that the criminals are tough and threatening, now Hayes creates an even greater sense of terror: One of the criminals worries the other.

THE DESPERATE HOURS (continued)

ELEANOR. [*Who has been watching in horror.*] What . . . what do you . . . ?

GLENN. [*Ignoring her, crosses to Hank.*] What'd you find? [Hank, *keeping his eyes on Eleanor, takes the automatic out of his pocket and hands it to Glenn, who examines it.* Glenn, *to Eleanor.*] Lady, now I ask you . . . is that a nice thing to keep aroun' the house? [*He hands the automatic to Hank, whispering.*] Put it in your pocket and keep it there. Family secret, huh? What Robish don't know, don't hurt nobody . . . okay? [Glenn *laughs, gives Hank a playful push and goes to chair in high spirits.*] Let 'em comb the dives!

HANK. [*Sits on sofa; jubilantly.*] You foxed 'em good, Glenn.

GLENN. Came aroun' their roadblocks

#15

like we was flyin' a airplane! Everything's chimin'! [*He sits in the armchair, becomes conscious of the comfort. He raises himself by the arms and sinks again into the chair, delighted.*] Foam rubber, I betcha. Foam rubber, lady? [*Eleanor nods.*] I seen the ads. [*He squirms in the seat, enjoying it.*] Melts right into your tail!

#16

HANK. [*Takes a cigarette from the box on the coffee table, lights it with the table lighter and, rising, hands it to* Glenn.] Christ, what a place to take the stir-taste outta your mouth! Freezer full-a meat! Carpet makes you want to take your shoes off!

ELEANOR. How long do you intend to
. . .

GLENN. [*Casually.*] Be outta here by midnight, lady.

HANK. Midnight? I thought you said Helen was waiting . . .

GLENN. Not in town, Hank. We don't make it so easy for 'em. She left three weeks ago.

HANK. [*Laughs, rises, grabs a fistful of cigarettes from the box on the coffee table, picks up the lighter, and flips it several times in her face.*] I don't care if we never leave. [*He exits into the dining room and reappears in the pantry, where he stands looking out the window of the side door.*]

GLENN. [*Rises.*] Now, lady . . . you think you can talk on the phone without bustin' into tears?

Character!

ELEANOR. [*Rises with great difficulty, takes a feeble step, then gets control of herself, straightens, and walks with dignity and determination to the phone table, turns to face* Glenn.] Whom do you want me to call? [*Glenn laughs.*]

GLENN. I always go for a gal with guts! That's *whom* we're gonna call—a gal with real guts! Person to person . . . Mr. James calling Mrs. James . . . Atlantic 6-3389 . . . in Pittsburgh. Pittsburgh, P.A. [*Blackout.*]

SHERIFF'S OFFICE: *Lights rise swiftly.* Carson *sits near desk, writing on small notepad. The clock reads 5:32.* Bard *is finishing a telephone conversation, a note of exultation in his voice.*

BARD. [*Into phone.*] Year . . . okay . . . good deal! [*He replaces the phone.*] Pittsburgh! They've located Helen Laski. Avalon Hotel, Pittsburgh. We'll have a record of any calls to or from . . . in a few minutes now.

CARSON. Bard . . . stop me if I'm out of line . . . but what's this thing to you? You, personally? **#3**

BARD. [*Slowly rubbing his chin.*] You've heard of that first law of the jungle . . . haven't you, Carson? [*The light on the radio flashes.* Bard *presses the button, snaps.*] Deputy Bard! **#3**

WINSTON'S VOICE. Jess . . . this is Winston. Car three.

BARD. What've you got Tom?

WINSTON'S VOICE. That hardware store holdup on the south side . . .

BARD. [*Eagerly.*] Yeah? Yeah?

WINSTON'S VOICE. [*Wearily.*] No guns stolen. All they took was fishing rods. [Bard *presses the button and looks at* Carson.]

CARSON. They'd be too shrewd to pull a stunt like that.

BARD. Look, Carson . . . do me a favor. It's almost time for supper. All I've heard since morning is how damn wise those rats are. I'm up to here with it.

CARSON. Where're they getting their clothes?

BARD. My theory is they're running around naked so nobody'll notice 'em. [*The telephone rings.* Bard *picks it up.*] Deputy Bard . . . Yeah . . . [*Disappointment.*] Yeah. Okay. [*Hangs up.*] Helen Laski checked out of the Avalon Hotel last night. No phone calls, no messages of any kind received today . . . [Carson *rises and with a look at* Bard *goes to the window.* Bard *bursts out.*] I **#4** know! *I* know! They'd be too smart to make a call to a hotel. They used somebody in between!

CARSON. [*At the window.*] I didn't say a word.

BARD. You know where that leaves us, don't you? Beating our tails ragged over nothing around here.

CARSON. Only you don't believe it.

BARD. Sure I believe it. I'm a trained police officer. I go by the facts, not crazy hunches. I reckon they're not here.

CARSON. [*Turns.*] Why don't you put some more patrol cars on the streets, anyway? Just in case?

Car.

BARD. [*Rises and paces.*] That damn jalopy's been reported in every state in the union . . . sixty times in Indiana alone! The earth won't open up and swallow it! Okay, let's try anything! [*He picks up phone, dials . . . as the lights

again.

dim.*] Where is that beat-up gray car?

HILLIARD HOME: *It is dark outside and dim throughout the house, except for the living room which is brilliantly lighted. Eleanor sits on the sofa, staring ahead. Hank is in the pantry sitting in a chair which is obviously from the breakfast nook; he holds the portable radio from Ralphie's room in his lap with the music playing—a*

#17

loud jazzy tune, in contrast to the soft gentleness of the morning music. Hank wears a dark red shirt with a cardigan sweater over it and the prison trousers. He smokes fairly steadily.

#17

The ravages of the afternoon are everywhere apparent; the atmosphere of invasion hangs over the entire house. There is an open box of cigars on the coffee table with some of the cigars scattered on the table. There is a carton of cigarettes, with the top ripped back, on the table. A coffee cup is also on the table and another is on the table beside the armchair. There are odds and ends of food. The ashtrays are filled to overflowing.

In the living room, Glenn, at window, is filled with a sense of triumph; he is almost gay, and his enjoyment of what follows is clear. Glenn wears a pair of Dan's slacks and a sport shirt. Eleanor, alert in every fiber, is pale, haggard, stiff. Robish is entering from the den; he is wearing a full suit including shirt and tie—Dan's best, and it does not quite fit. A cigar is jammed in the corner of his mouth.

ROBISH. What if this joker gets suspicious . . . that gray car parked right in his own garage?

The car
#5

GLENN. [*Casually.*] Can it, Robish.

ROBISH. [*To Eleanor.*] Why ain't he here? You said quarter to six.

#18

ELEANOR. The traffic may be heavy . . . or Cindy may have had to work late . . . or . . . anything *anything*! [*Hank suddenly rises and looks out the window in the side door. He moves up toward the kitchen door and calls:*]

HANK. Glenn! Black coop just turned in the driveway.

GLENN. Turn off the clatter back there. Hank. [*Hank turns off the radio and places it on the back stairs.*]

HANK. [*Looking out the side door.*] You want me to grab 'em?

GLENN. Not with all them cars goin' by out there.

HANK. Woman comin' around to the front door, Glenn. [*Eleanor places her hand at her mouth. Glenn unlocks the door.*]

GLENN. [*To Eleanor.*] You don't have to do nothin' but keep your trap shut. [*He turns the gun to cover the front door. There is a brief pause. The front door opens and Cindy enters, casually, swiftly, a trifle breathless. She stops dead when she sees Glenn.*] Come right in, redhead. [*Cindy backs away, pulling the door closed, but she suddenly stops, frozen in the door. The reason she stops is simply that Glenn has turned the gun toward Eleanor's head.*] We still got the old

#19

lady, Sis. [Robish *is standing at den door . . . dull, brutish . . . with his little eyes roving over* Cindy. Cindy *closes the door and stands in front of it.* Glenn *grins.*] That's bein' real sensible.

CINDY. [*Planting her feet slightly.*] Mother Character! . . . how long have these animals been here? [Eleanor *starts, as though she would warn* Cindy. Glenn's *grin flickers, fades and a hardness comes into his face . . . but not into his tone.*]

#20

GLENN. Spitfire, too. You watch out, redhead.

HANK. [*At side door, calls.*] Glenn! He's lookin' in the garage.

GLENN. [*Calling to* Hank—*confident, knowing.*] He'll come in. [*He grabs* Cindy *and pushes her toward chair.*] Sit down now, sweetie . . . and no talking. Not a goddam word.

HANK. [*In pantry.*] He's coming around now—fast. [Glenn *moves into position near front door. Pause. Then the door opens, and* Dan *enters, evening paper in hand.*]

DAN. Ellie, whose car is that in the . . . [Glenn *slams door shut behind* Dan, *and* Dan *breaks off, staring in bewilderment at* Glenn, *then at the gun.*]

GLENN. [*In flat cold tones.*] It's loaded. Now lock the door. . . . [*Sardonically.*] Please. [*Unable to speak yet, his eyes on* Glenn, Dan *turns and locks the door. Then:*]

DAN. [*Baffled; softly.*] What're you . . . why . . . I don't . . .

GLENN. You never know what's comin', do you, Pop? [Dan *then turns to* Eleanor.]

DAN. Ellie? . . .

ELEANOR. I'm all right, Dan.

DAN. [*Looking about the room, glances toward stairs.*] Where's Ralphie?

ELEANOR. Not home yet.

HANK. [*Calls from pantry.*] Driveway ain't blocked, Glenn.

CINDY. The house is crawling with them, Dad.

GLENN. [*Sizing her up.*] Don't get me jumpy, redhead, this thing's liable to explode.

#20

DAN. [*Flatly, glancing at newspaper in his hand.*] Glenn Griffin.

#21

GLENN. [*Laughs; takes paper.*] Lotsa people heard-a me, didn't they? [*In satisfaction.*] Front page. [*Disgusted.*] They always gotta use the same goddam picture. [*He tosses the paper to the floor.*]

DAN. Griffin . . . you fire that thing . . . and you'll have the whole neighborhood in here in two minutes.

GLENN. I don't want to take that chance, Hilliard . . . any more'n you want me to.

ROBISH. You dumb, mister?

GLENN. [*Sizing up* Dan.] Naw, he ain't dumb, Robish. He's a smart-eyed bastard, this guy. . . .

#21

DAN. What're you . . . I don't understand . . . what do you *want?*

GLENN. Take it easy, Pop.

DAN. [*Controlling himself with effort.*] What do you want here?

GLENN. [*Takes a step toward* Dan.] I don't want nobody to get hurt. . . . What do *you* want, Pop?

DAN. That's . . . what I want, too. [*Then, shrewdly.*] That's what you're depending on, isn't it?

#21

GLENN. You got it, Buster. First try.

DAN. But . . . why *here?* Why *my* house?

GLENN. Your break, Pop. I like the location. Those empty lots'n both sides. The bike parked on the nice lawn. I like suckers with kids . . . they don't take no chances.

DAN. Anyone who could think up a scheme like that is . . .

GLENN. [*Cutting in.*] . . . is smart, Pop.

ELEANOR. [*Quickly.*] Dan! They've done nothing.

GLENN. Now I'm gonna explain the facts-a-life to you, Hilliard. You listen, too, redhead . . . listen good. You can get brave . . . and one of you . . . just might any time you feel up to it. Might even get away with it. *But . . .* that ain't sayin' what'll happen to the others . . . the old lady here . . . the redhead . . . the little guy owns the bike. . . . [*Slight pause.*] Okay, Pop, you got it all the way now. [*Another pause. Dan moves to sofa and drops his hat on it. Eleanor's hand and his meet, briefly clasping. Dan turns to Glenn.*]

DAN. [*Taking a deep breath.*] How long?

GLENN. [*Grinning.*] Now that's the kinda sensible talk a guy likes to hear.

#21 DAN. [*Firmly.*] How long?

GLENN. Matter of hours . . . before midnight . . . maybe sooner. Meantime, everything goes on just like normal.

DAN. Why midnight?

GLENN. [*Almost politely.*] None-a your goddam business.

ELEANOR. They have a friend coming . . . with money.

DAN. What if . . .

GLENN. [*Speaking at the same time; stops Dan*] Lady, you speak when I tell you.

DAN. The police are looking everywhere for you. What if . . .

GLENN. They ain't looking here, Pop. They show here, it ain't gonna be pretty.

DAN. They could trail your friend . . .

GLENN. Let's get one thing straight, Pop. [*Gesturing to the window.*] Any red lights show out there . . . you folks get it first. [*There is a slight pause. Dan crosses to the window and peeks out between the drawn curtains. Glenn laughs.*] Gives you a funny feelin', don't it? You don't know what's happenin' . . . or where . . . or what it adds up to . . . for you. Ever had that feelin' before, Pop? Me, I get it all the time. Even kinda like it. But you and me . . . we ain't much alike, are we, Pop?

CINDY. [*A breath.*] Thank God.

DAN. [*Turns from window.*] Griffin . . . if you . . . what if I could get you the same amount of money you're waiting for? Now. Before midnight.

ROBISH. Hey, that don't sound like a bad . . .

GLENN. Hilliard, you maybe think you're a big shot . . . fifteen thousand a year. But I had me a look at your bankbooks. Two hundred lousy bucks in the kitty. Hell, I had more'n fifteen grand in my hands at one time, Pop . . . and I ain't twenty-five yet.

CINDY. I hope it helped pass your time in jail . . . counting it.

DAN. I could raise more. I could . . .

ROBISH. What about that? We could blow outta here right away! This joker's usin' his brain.

GLENN. [*Sharply.*] Use yours, Robish. Helen's on her way *here*.

ROBISH. To hell with that! Why should me and the kid risk our necks . . . just so you can get some copper knocked off.

GLENN. [*Dangerously now—low and intense.*] Go spill your guts somewhere else! #22

ROBISH. [*Shouting.*] What do I care who busted your goddam jawbone? #22

GLENN. [*Topping him.*] I'll bust yours if . . . [*They are now shouting at each other across Dan.*]

ROBISH. This guy talks sense! Don't I have nothin' to say? . . .

GLENN. NO! You ain't got a goddam stinkin' thing to say! [*Robish retreats slightly. Glenn turns on Dan more quietly but with force.*] You, Hilliard . . . I seen #21 what you been up to. Robish here, he ain't got a brain. *But . . .* he ain't got a gun, either. Don't try to get in between, you smart-eyed sonofabitch. Clickety-clickety-click. [*He makes a gesture at Dan's temple.*] I can see them wheels goin' around in there, Pop. *Don't ever try that again!* [*He backs away, eyes on Dan; speaks softly now—to Eleanor.*] Now, lady . . . serve us up that chicken you been thawin' out.

DAN. My wife's not your servant.

GLENN. [*Thinly . . . daring Dan to protest.*] I always wanted me a servant. . . .

ELEANOR. [*Begins to rise.*] I don't mind, Dan.

#21 DAN. [*Firmly.*] I do. Sit down, Ellie.

GLENN. [*Exploding wildly.*] Lissen, Hilliard! I . . . [*Then he stops; sizing Dan up, forcing control . . . almost quietly at first, building in intensity.*] I had a old man like you. Always callin' the tune. Outside his house, nobody. Inside, Mister God! Little punk went to church every Sunday . . . took it from every-

#23 body . . . licked their shoes . . . tried to beat it into Hank'n me . . . be a punk, be a nobody . . . take it from you shiny-shoed, down-your-noses sonsabitches with white handkerchiefs in your pockets! [*He snatches the handkerchief from Dan's breast pocket, spits into it, and throws it on the floor.*] You remember, Pop . . . I could kill you just for kicks. [*Pause. Without taking his eyes off Dan he again gestures to Eleanor, speaks coldly again.*] Now, lady . . . get out there'n cook it. [*Eleanor starts to rise, but Hank's voice stops her.*]

HANK. [*Turning from window in side door.*] Kid comin' up the driveway . . . walkin' . . . [*Glenn starts for the front door.*]

DAN. Griffin . . . you've got to let me explain to Ralphie first. . . . [*Robish grabs Dan by the shoulders and shoves him against the window.*]

GLENN. I don't got to do nothin'. You pull anything now, you can sit'n watch me kick the kid's face in.

HANK. [*Calling again from the side door.*] Comin' to the front door . . .

GLENN. [*At front door, unlocks it.*] You got to learn to take orders from other people now, Pop. . . . [*The front door opens and Ralphie enters, whistling. Glenn slams the door behind him and locks it. Ralphie stops.*]

RALPHIE. [*Bewildered.*] Hey . . . what is . . . [*Robish takes a single step.*] Who are you? [*He turns to the door, and runs to the dining room . . . as Hank appears in the dining-room door.*] Get out of . . . [*Ralphie whirls and dashes to the front door, evading Glenn.*]

DAN. [*Quickly.*] Ralphie, it's all right! It's . . . [*Robish grabs Ralphie at the door.* #24 *He shakes him by the shoulders roughly, venting on the child the spleen that Glenn has stirred in him.*]

ROBISH. Where ya think you're goin? Don't you know who's boss 'roun' here? Ya gotta take orders from Griffin. Griffin's the big shot 'round' here. . . . [*As Ralphie's head snaps back and forth, Dan moves. He grabs Robish, whips him around. Ralphie breaks away and runs,* #24 *fighting tears, to Eleanor on the sofa. She takes him in her arms as he sits, clutching her. Dan slams Robish against the window and draws back for a blow, his mind gone blank; he is propelled blindly by jungle atavistic urges beyond his control. But Glenn steps in.*]

GLENN. It ain't gonna be like this! Not like this, see! [*In the scuffle the table near the chair is overturned. Eleanor stifles a scream as Glenn brings the gun down on* #24 *Dan's shoulder. Dan goes down. Robish recovers and starts toward Dan, but Glenn steps in between.*] You hear me, Robish? *Nothin's gonnna screw this up!*

ROBISH. [*Blinking owlishly at the gun in* #24 *Glenn's hand.*] You think I'm gonna let that . . .

GLENN. [*An order—low, intense.*] Get outta here!

ROBISH. [*Glaring, goes to dining room door.*] My gut's growlin' again. [*Robish kicks open the dining-room door and exits. Dan, his tie askew, manages to sit in chair, holding his shoulder. Glenn regains his familiar swagger.*]

GLENN. Give the old lady a hand, redhead. Out there . . . if you please. [*Cindy and Eleanor rise, Eleanor going into dining room.*]

CINDY. Where do we keep the rat poison? [*As Cindy follows Eleanor, Hank steps into her path, blocking her way. Glenn laughs and crosses to foot of stairs; Cindy is trapped between them.*]

#19 GLENN. [*Goading Dan.*] She's a honey, ain't she, Hank?

HANK. [*Arrogantly.*] I don't go for redheads.

DAN. [*Sensing danger for Cindy.*] Griffin . . .

CINDY. [*With a sharpness, to Hank.*] For God's small favors, make me eternally grateful. [*Hank drops his arm and Cindy exits into the dining room. Hank follows her with his eyes and gives a low whistle. Glenn turns to Dan.*]

#19

GLENN. Kid's been in stir for three years, Pop. Don't cost nothin' to look.

#21 DAN. [*His eyes still on Hank.*] Just don't try

changing your mind, young fellow.

GLENN. Hilliard, you're a funny gink. You don't know when you're licked, do you? . . . Now just one thing—you got a gun in the house?

RALPHIE. [*Too quickly, as he kneels on sofa.*] No . . . we don't.

GLENN. [*Enjoying himself.*] Well, Pop?

DAN. You heard the boy. I don't have a gun.

GLENN. That's right. You don't. Show him, Hank. [*After Hank displays the automatic.*] There for a minute I thought you was gonna lie to me, Pop.

DAN. Griffin . . . listen to me . . .

GLENN. I'll do the talkin'. You listen, Hilliard! That dough's halfway here now and nothin's gonna foul this up, see. You pull any of that muscle-stuff again . . .

Continued Discussion of THE DESPERATE HOURS

15. Here is a fine example of a "plant."

16. Here Hayes cleverly implies exposition. He shows the audience that these men have been in prison a long time.

17. Here is contrast again.

18. The professional writer is at work here. Instead of having someone refer directly to the time, Robish communicates what time it is by addressing an entirely different matter. The passage of time is smoothly implied.

19. Now it begins to be clear why Hayes earlier made reference to Cindy's attractive figure. Of course this will be the beginning of a long series of complications.

20. The use of "redhead" suggests a different relationship than would the use of "kid." Hayes implies a great deal with subtle word choice.

21. Dan is alert, quick. The man who earlier seemed unable to cope with his children now is shifting to a fast-thinking cool man who will stand up to protect his family.

22. Hayes has used almost no exposition. When he does (as here when he gives Glenn a goal), it is part of something else (Robish's anger here).

23. The plot now draws background materials from Glenn, giving him some motivational factors.

24. Violence continues. Again, there is a building-block concept, with each new complication full of fire.

The Desperate Hours illustrates smooth Broadway craftsmanship at work. The playwright has deftly put together contrasting pieces that will lead into future explosions. It is a strongly crafted work, and you would do well to notice the areas of strength in this play.

Plot, Summation

Here you have seen examples of plot in action. You have seen that there are strongly different approaches to crafting a play, leading you to conclude that no one perfect way to structure the plot of a play exists but instead there must be a structure designed particularly for the playwright's intent. The examples illustrate the need for a strong plot, and you have seen how the playwrights did not merely insert plot elements but also made each element adequately sustained. You notice the building-block concept in action, the effect of complications upon characterization, unification of point of attack with the protagonist and with the play's thought, and the strength that comes with an early point of attack.

It is difficult to make strong recommendations without sounding formulaistic, and I have no intention of returning to the French Academy rules, but from my experience I suggest that you consider several points when you construct your own plays. First, start with an early point of attack. Ignore your desire to establish mood and character and all of that: Get the plot in motion as strongly as you can as early in the play as possible. The more delayed the point of attack, the more likely the beginning will be crammed full of nongripping materials.

Second, be sure the point of attack—and each complication and plot turn—has sufficient strength and amplification. A complication deserves to be perceived. It must be prepared, struck hard, emphasized, and perhaps repeated. Foreshadowing is extremely helpful.

If you are in earnest about playwriting, your next step will be to follow this same investigative process with a number of other plays. Look for foreshadowing, exposition, plants; see where the point of attack comes; observe how the playwright sustains and amplifies the complications; get a feel of the pace of the play from the rhythm of complications; and look at the structure leading to the final climax. You should make your own marginal notes in a number of plays, discovering the craftsman in action.

Use the same analysis technique on your own plays. Having worked on other plays, you will have developed a certain dispassionate observation technique; use that on your works and be as objective as you can. Once you have studied your own plays, you may better perceive your strengths and weaknesses.

Exercises

1. Find a copy of *Macbeth* and read further into the play. Label each new complication. Make an action scenario of the first several acts of the play, noting every French scene and complication.

2. Read *The Crucible* by Arthur Miller and make an action scenario of at least the first half of the play. Note every French scene and complication. Where is the play's point of attack? How does Miller sustain that moment?

3. Read *Streamers* by David Rabe and make an action scenario of at least the first half of the play. Identify the point of attack.

4. Read *Night Must Fall* by Emlyn Williams and note how the playwright achieves suspense. Note the way foreshadowing creates the chilling effects. Make an action scenario that emphasizes the foreshadowing strokes.

5. Read *Adrienne Lecouvreur*, by Eugene Scribe with Earnest Legouve (1849), to discover what is meant by a "well-made play." Diagram the conflicts and the entanglements.

Chapter Seventeen

Character:
Part One

Introduction

Playwright and performer become collaborators in their mutual efforts to bring to artistic life a dramatic character strong enough to exist with apparent independence yet always part of the overall fabric of the play. Writer and performer share a number of common goals. The playwright creates a being who will be appropriate for the play's needs; the performer gives that character a life force on the stage. The writer fashions a human being where none existed before, shaping a new entity from remembered sensory fragments much as a sculptor creates a form by freeing it from the block of granite; the actor wears that human form like a head-to-toe body stocking, adapting his own self to make it a better fit.

Modern theatre—that which started a century ago with Ibsen—has been sharply affected by the formal study of human personality. Freud, James-Lange, and a host of followers are intently studied by current playwrights who are necessarily more concerned about psychological truth than were past playwrights. Most contemporary dramatists appear to want audiences to thoroughly understand the characters of the play, even if some writers seem unconcerned if the audiences also will like the characters.

Performers are equally affected by the search for psychological integrity. Today's actors, unlike their ancestors, continually dig into characters' inner beings. The search is so intense that they may find motivations and other qualities where the playwright intended none. For performers, creating a character is the single most important aspect of the whole of acting. Many base their work on a system established by Constantin Stanislavsky (1865–1938) who is so significant to theatre that you would be wise to study *My Life in Art, An Actor Prepares,* and *Building a Character* in order to understand better how actors go about their work. In those books are rich materials that will help you to create multidimensional dramatic characters.

Neither playwright nor performer will seek to present "real people"— theatre practitioners always remember that drama is not life but instead is an artistic interpretive representation of life—but both *must* start their work from life. A number of qualities of dramatic characters are listed below. Some of the discussions will appear dogmatic and inflexible as if the "qualities" are "rules." I do not intend them as rules or laws, but the playwright who strays far from these qualities runs the risk of losing the riches that can come from well-drawn multidimensional characters. As with every aspect of an art, rules can be broken provided good reasons exist.

Qualities of Dramatic Characters

1. For the Writer, as Well as for the Performer, Perhaps Nothing Is More Crucial for the Creation of Well-Drawn Characters than the Concept of Taking Directly from Life. Writers can too easily fall into a trap of imitating other imitators: This writer may draw a character as did Tennessee Williams, or that writer may create a scene in the style of Arthur Miller. The trap is there for actors, too: That actress may seek to imitate Judith Anderson, or that performer may play the role as would a Marlon Brando. Too quickly truth will be lost. There will be an imitation of an imitation of an imitation. The source—life— fades in the distance.

Dramatic characters are built of pieces of memory, sections from relatives, traits of enemies, hopes and failures the inner self holds secret, and fantasies and daydreams. These little pieces are welded by the imagination into one coherent entity. Often the process is helped by a mystic self-determination on the part of the character who participates in the creation of itself.

Writers must observe carefully their own reactions, emotions, and inner drives. In themselves they find the raw materials for the characters they will invent to participate in the play's universe. The writer's first source always must be the self. The lives of close friends and strangers, people who live next door or people featured in news stories, family members and those who live in distant places—these are the people who come from life as sources for dramatic characters. The writer who merely imitates an imitation has none of those riches.

The writer must continually observe and note traits, eccentricities, and emotions with all the insight and sensitivity he or she can bring to focus. *All of these notes and observations are written in the writer's journal.* There the characters are saved until needed. Notes and observations accumulate. Soon many notes begin to mesh together and a fully-drawn multidimensional character begins to emerge. The process of looking at life and recording human qualities will make the character more dimensional than would be the character if she were simply lifted from another playwright's script. The process of writing the observations and characters into the journal directly helps the writer increase his or her insight and sensitivity.

2. Second to the Concept That the Writer Must Draw from Life Is the Understanding that Character Is Action.   Novels can describe. Essays will tell. *Drama is the art of showing.* All that can be known of a character will stem from actions and reactions; all that makes a character interesting and vital is action, direct or indirect; relationships of characters on stage are shown by actions. Conflict, which gives characters more dimension, is action. A character without action is dull, pale, lifeless; a character who is in motion is far more interesting.

A *character is the sum part of his actions during the play,* including to some degree those actions that take place outside the stage area or which are reported to have happened prior to the beginning of the play. There is necessarily a limit how many actions can be reported because of the premise that drama must show, not tell. Finding ways to bring action onto the stage is part of the playwright's task, and it often demands great ingenuity.

3. Characters Are Constructed of Playable Emotions.   Certainly it is true that characters may also be intellectual beings, but emotions come first and must dominate. Beginning playwrights frequently populate their plays with characters who espouse philosophical views as if quoting from text books but not caring about the topic. Often such characters seem to engage in a debate, point and counterpoint; one telltale sign of the debate is the sentence beginning with the word "but." "But I tell you man has virtues." "Ah? But what of his wars?" "But what of his ability for love?" Such characters lack plausibility. Characters who are built on a series of intellectual precepts are likely to be the playwright's spokespeople, present in the play simply to speak for the author. Such characters need to be removed from the play; substituted for them should be characters who have an emotional need and hunger to be involved with the topic areas.

4. Strong and Often Contrasting Emotions Will Build Strong Characters. Weak characters have weak emotions. The strength of emotion gives the character a vitality, a meaning in life, a hunger. Even "lost souls" can have these strong emotions—indeed, they *must* have emotional involvement with the sense of being lost or having no direction—if they are to be significant figures in the drama. Major characters go through extremes of emotion—from hope to despair, for example—and those movements give the play added motion and impact.

A performer who fails to bring the playwright's emotions to life will be letting slip the richness of the character. The result will be a dull production even though the script may be crisp with sparkling emotional movements, and if the production does not maintain the emotions the audience may well think the flaw is in the script. Quite often this problem is found in productions of plays with weighty themes: For example, an amateur production of a play such as *Waiting for Godot* may get so concerned about the theme that the emotions will be overlooked, thereby taking an exciting script and turning it to mush. The process also loses the thematic thrust of the play: If the characters are not projected with emotional involvement, the audience will not become involved and so the play's meaning will appear insignificant.

5. Drama Shows Characters from Life in Emotional Actions and Reactions in Often Explosive Situations, which Can be Comic or Tragic. The playwright looks at life and finds humans in their emotional conditions, then interprets and emphasizes certain of those emotions for the needs of the play. The emotional characters are drawn from life but with necessary readjustments and fine tunings to make them viable dramatic characters; people in life do not lead such ordered lives as do dramatic characters with actions related to a theme and made part of a progressive whole that builds to a climax.

6. Characters Are Selected to Bring Out the Playwright's Subject and Theme. Every character is in the play for a reason that will relate directly to the subject and theme. The relationship is kept artistically subtle—writers do not wish to write allegorical medieval dramas such as *Everyman*—but it must be present to unify the play. Each character may have an appropriate tragic flaw, so significant for tragedy; or each character may have a spirit of fortune, so important for comedy, that helps express the author's views as stated in the play.

Characters' life-styles mirror the meaning of the play, either directly or indirectly, and their actions portray the essences of the play's thematic concepts. Even minor characters are selected because they relate to the play's meaning; often they help the primary characters move within the play's thought.

Characters' *emotions* are selected because they illuminate the play's meaning. The characters' *intelligence* seldom knows the play's meaning. The writer is careful never to create characters who know the play's meaning and therefore verbalize it, turning the play into a lecture or essay.

7. Emotions Need Be of Sufficient Size for the Play. Characters with emotions too large for the play's basic concept will turn it into a farcical melodrama, because exaggeration creates comedy and exaggerated emotions seem totally unlike life. Characters with emotions too small for the play will shrink the basic concept and make it seem dull..

Performers must carefully measure the emotional ranges of the roles they play, being quite sure to play the correct size. If the actor is unsure of how large the emotions should be, she or he will need consultations with the director until the question is resolved.

Playwrights must be certain that they give adequate keys to performers and directors about the size of the emotions. A writer may believe his play contains all the necessary answers, but someone who does not know the play may not see those answers. Because the playwright writes for interpretive artists, special care is needed to be sure communications from script to actor are ample.

8. Emotions Are Necessary for Audience Identification.   The audience responds to characters' emotions. If the playwright (or the performer) wants the audience to relate to the character, emotional action is essential. The audience will empathize with emotional qualities, thereby becoming more deeply involved with the overall actions of the play. *That involvement will cause the audience to be concerned with the intellectual concept of the play.* Without the emotional keys, audience concerns about the play's subject and theme will be considerably lessened.

Playwrights often create characters and situations to display related emotions. There can be a step-by-step progression: A given character may start by feeling timid, move to apprehension and then fear, and at the climactic moments of the play be experiencing panic and terror. Another character may move from casual knowledge to close friendship to love to a willingness to give up all. These movements through ranges of emotions will create multidimensional characters who can stimulate others in the play to feel comparable depth of emotions, thereby adding color to the entire drama.

For the performer, such emotions are rich in opportunity. To be able to portray a character who has many emotional responses gives the performer a set of challenges which will pull his or her entire being into the role. The performer is stimulated by the artistic challenge, and the result will be enhanced concentration upon the role and more effort to create it with correct intensities. Such involvement on the performer's part can only benefit the playwright. Due to the nature of "empathic responses," audiences will have feelings that echo those of the stage personnel: If the actors are deeply involved with the characters, the audience will subconsciously feel the same sort of interest in the characters.

9. Primary Characters Must Face Crucial, Pivotal Decisions that Will Affect the Rest of Their Lives and Possibly also the Lives of Others.   Plays put characters at a pivotal point in their lives, give the characters intense motivation to choose one or the other of the directions, and make the stakes high for the decision. The playwright may give the characters one or more such pivotal moments—in plot terminology, such moments are *complications*—in which the character has to make a crucial decision. The moments may come early in the play—again in plot terms during *the point of attack*—in which case the rest of the play will show the effects of that decision; or the moment may be late and be the climax of the play.

All of us face many decisions in life. The choices we made yesterday create the world we live in today. We now live the product of the many decisions made over years of choices, and the path we follow today is a result of a choice made yesterday. We often make such choices without knowing the long-term significances, or perhaps without an awareness there is a decision being made.

Drama takes such moments from life and builds them to a larger size. For the characters they are genuine moments of truth with much significance. The play will present a character with a mandatory choice between Path A or Path B. The nonchoice—"I won't take either path"—is itself a choice, of no less importance to the character than either Path A or Path B.

Drama puts the character into the situation and then increases the stakes. There *must* be a decision, and the results of that decision will be extremely important for the character. The character has to decide *now*—there is a powerful *sense of urgency* that propels the character and the play—and there will be accelerated results accumulating from that decision.

The performer's task is to find the character's moments of truth and then to judge how strongly they are to be played. Overplaying the decisions can turn a subtle play into a coarse melodrama; underplaying the moments can prevent the audience from perceiving any change at all in the character's path; ignoring the need to find the moments will turn a dimensional character into a flat and rather uninteresting role. With the aid of a sensitive director, the performer will be able to establish the correct level of intensity for the single or many pivotal decisions in the play.

10. The Most Important Pivotal Decisions Belong to the Protagonist (or Central Character).   The writer establishes the focus of the play by ensuring that the most significant pivotal moments are faced by the play's protagonist or central character. If other characters also experience such moments of truth, the crisis necessarily must be smaller than that of the protagonist.

11. Pivotal Decisions Must Be Directly Related to the Play's Plot and Its Subject/Theme.   Pivotal decisions that are of no importance to the plot or thought of the play will be jarringly out of focus. The actions of the characters, most certainly the primary characters, must be unified with the plot's action, or else there will seem to be several different lines of unrelated action. Indeed, if decision points are not related to the basic plot and thought, the playwright probably will discover that there are really two plays being forced into one shell.

12. Often the Primary Character Will Become Aware of the Significance of the Decision Point.   The idea of "discovery," first formulated by Aristotle, suggests that the play's protagonist will come to grips with the meaning of his or her decisions and actions. This sober sense of awareness adds great weight to the play's meaning. It gives the protagonist a concept of the meaning of his actions, and it also contributes to the audience's understandings. Most often the protagonist is the one who will come to a realization (for example, Macbeth in his "Tomorrow and tomorrow and tomorrow" speech), but sometimes the discovery is made by a secondary character (such as Biff in *Death of a Salesman* during his short speech about Willy having all the wrong dreams). Playwrights guard against letting the discovery become too blatant; there is a great temptation for the discovery to become all-insightful and all-wise curtain speeches.

13. Dramatic Characters Are Not Able to Act except When Motivated, and Their Reactions Will Be of Equal Size to the Motivating Forces. A stimulus-response cycle keeps dramatic characters moving and changing, with each stimulus provoking a response that is a stimulus for another response. Characters are motivated to react. If motivation does not exist, the character's reactions will appear artificial and without plausibility. If the characters react in large terms to small motivations, that too will appear artificial. The reverse also holds true: Small reactions to large stimuli appear to lack plausibility.

14. The Playwright Thinks of Dramatic Characters not as Separate Entities in the Play but as Parts of a Whole that Consists of Plot-Character-Thought. "Character" cannot exist by itself in the play. For unification to occur, plot, character, and thought should be so closely intertwined that often it is impossible to distinguish one from the other. Plot causes character to respond; character provides the plot with complications. The actions from both character and plot give the play its intellectual concept. The play's thought is responsible for the creation of initial plot and character movements.

15. Dramatic Characters Must Be Plausible. Their Actions Must Be Plausible. The sharpest rebuke possible for a performer is the sentence, "I cannot *believe* you." So, too, the playwright might be sure that characters can be *believed.* It matters not a bit that this or that action might be *possible*—in our world we see every day the impossible being made possible—but every action must be *plausible.* If the audience cannot believe the character or the actions, the playwright has missed the target.

16. In a Gestalt Sense, Characters—Especially Primary Characters—Add Up to Being More than the Sum of Their Parts. Dramatic characters are constructed of many components that perhaps might be isolated, but the totality must always seem to be larger than the components suggest. Much of that added dimension derives from the characters' placement within the overall action of the play—the action happening around them adds to their character—and also from the audience's subconscious perception of them, adding qualities to characters in response to subtle cues. The wise playwright draws the dramatic characters in a way to enhance, not distract, the gestalt reactions.

17. Actions Speak Louder than Words.   The truism needs little explanation. What a dramatic character *does* provides the sharpest clues to the nature of the character. Much of what is known about a character comes from the following:

1.   What actions the character takes.
2.   What actions the character does not take (such as, action through inaction).
3.   What emotions the character displays and feels.
4.   What emotions are markedly absent from the character.
5.   What the character says; sometimes, from what the character does not say.
6.   What responses (usually emotional) the character elicits from others in the play.
7.   What descriptions the character prompts from others in the play.

Of these clues, the strongest is the first: What actions one takes are far "louder" than whatever ringing speeches one may make. A *character is made up of actions during the play.*

18. Finally, a Dramatic Character Is Interesting and Usually Likable.   If the character is not *interesting* the playwright should remove him or her from the play. The playwright who finds the character boring to write is facing a hint that ought not be ignored.

The character also may be *likable.* Not all plays present likable characters, but most plays achieve a greater impact with likable characters because audiences are drawn to care about the characters, to be concerned about them, and to be involved in the character's fate or destiny. Respect and admiration for characters also are possible audience responses, but the factor of caring and liking is highly significant.

I think it helps the writer to like and respect the characters he or she creates. If the writer does not, will the audience?

Summation

Presented here are a number of concepts regarding dramatic characters. For the beginning playwright, these will serve as a start toward writing characters to fit within the play. The more advanced playwright will use the guidelines as a checklist to measure his or her characters. Of course, all guidelines are subject to change and modification, and these are no exception.

Also discussed was the performer's work with the writer's character. The playwright must always keep in mind that the play is intended for the stage and audiences, not for a solitary reader. The production process of bringing a play to life is complex and involved. Of all the steps in that process, few touch the playwright more closely than the performers' processes of interpretation and re-creation. The wise playwright makes the play stageworthy by keeping the performer in mind. This chapter indicates some areas where the work of playwright and performer make close contact.

The following chapter gives specifics and illustrations of the concepts discussed here; there, character will be treated in terms of concrete writing techniques and character types. Taken together, these two chapters are intended to help the playwright bring dramatic characters to life as the play's needs indicate.

Chapter Eighteen

Character:
Part Two

Introduction

What is a protagonist, and must the play have one? Are characters autobiographical creations of the playwright? What is meant by "playable objectives"? What devices does the author use to communicate aspects of character to performer and audience? Why is the confidant a shallow and one-dimensional character, and what can be done to change that? Why are utilitarian characters considered poor choices for a play? Should a play have an antagonist?

Here we discuss these and similar questions regarding dramatic characters. The discussions will lead to examinations of techniques of writing dramatic characters and to details about the types of characters commonly found in the plays. When possible, concrete examples will support the discussions. The goal is to give the writer answers to questions that so often concern hurdles in the writing process. You recognize, I hope, that the following examples will not indicate *laws* but instead will suggest strong possibilities for consideration. These are guidelines to learn the easier way of writing characters.

Characters of the Play

The following paragraphs examine some character "types" that a playwright may consider putting into a play. Of the options, some are considerably less viable than others. But *it is crucial for the writer to select and create dramatic characters that are appropriate for the needs of the play.* As the playwright creates characters their relationship to the overall play must always be kept in mind. *It is essential to invent characters who are motivated to act as the play's plot and thought will demand.*

Listed below are some but not all of the characters the playwright is likely to consider. Because they are listed does not mean that you should reduce characters to formula. But plays are fashioned of certain conventional qualities, which include some character inclinations, and these can be discussed and evaluated. With these descriptions will be notes regarding how performers approach such characters. You will keep the performer's needs and working techniques in mind, thereby increasing the play's chances of succeeding.

The Protagonist. It is hard to understand why so much confusion befogs playwrights' understanding of the protagonist. Some dramatic experts dismiss the protagonist along with the melodrama, saying both are dead—which is a premature obituary. Some playwrights simply do not wish to understand the protagonist because they have the mistaken idea that a protagonist is out of date, that he is an antiquated creature found only in old-time movies who is noted primarily for a strange fondness for white hats plus a kinky habit of kissing horses. *The truth is, the protagonist* (a) *makes the play easier to write, and* (b) *makes the play's intellectual content more clear.*

The playwright must have a working knowledge of the various aspects of the protagonist. First, the writer must understand what makes a protagonist:

- *A protagonist actively pursues a goal that is highly important to him or her. The pursuit will encounter severe obstacles and difficulties that the protagonist must struggle to overcome, and the goal will have deep emotional significance for the protagonist and, indeed, others in the play.*
- *The protagonist will be single-minded about the pursuit and the goal, driving hard to achieve the desired result.*
- *In most cases the protagonist will have a master plan to achieve the goal—one perhaps modified during the action of the play because of the antagonist's obstacles. A definite plan is sharper than casual extemporaneous wanderings. The plan will be stated or implied early in the action.*
- *Almost always the goal will be one that is commonly considered meretorious—protagonists seldom go after goals that are merely selfish or cruel.*
- *Most often the protagonist's personality will have qualities commonly considered worthy. The protagonist will likely be one with admirable qualities.*
- *The protagonist's pursuit of the goal will be the significant issue, not whether he or she achieves that goal.*
- *Usually the protagonist will be liked and respected by most others within the play.*

The protagonist must care, deeply and possibly desperately, about the goal. For example, Blanche in *A Streetcar Named Desire* absolutely must find a refuge or die. Hamlet's soul demands that he do everything possible to discover if the Ghost spoke truthfully and, if so, that he avenge his father so the poor, troubled spirit can finally rest. Medea must have her final revenge in a world in which all powers of right have ignored her pleas for justice, and so no matter what the cost—even if it means the lives of her own children—she *will* get revenge.

The protagonist is a unifying force in the play. Action and characters relate to the protagonist. Furthermore, the protagonist begins the action, which means that he or she necessarily will be involved with the play's point of attack. Of course, the protagonist ends the action, which in turn means that the climax of the play will relate to the protagonist's final victory or failure in the pursuit of the goal.

The protagonist is the one around whom all action spins. The protagonist both causes the play's action and is the recipient of it; that action is the central thread of the play's plot. The process of that action and its outcome will convey the play's subject and theme, and the manner in which the action takes place will fix the play as dramatic, comic, or tragic. *The protagonist, in sum, unifies the play's action.*

Is it possible for a play to have more than one protagonist?

Yes. Such plays are written when social issues are important, for example. In an era in which groups are set against groups, drama may respond with plays that illustrate such conflicts, such as Hauptmann's *The Weavers,* which is a drama of labor versus management with a group of faceless weavers as the protagonist. *Waiting for Lefty,* by Clifford Odets, is the American version of that struggle, telling of a group of taxi drivers. In these plays the protagonist is a group, not an individual, and the social issues provoke the action.

It also is possible for a play to have two individual protagonists. Both, however, will need to be in movement at the same time, actively working for the single goal. For example, in *Romeo and Juliet* both lovers are protagonists, and each is in conflict with different antagonists as well as with the same objectors to their union.

Despite these examples, however, it should be pointed out that plays with double or collective protagonists are exceptions. Most drama has focused upon a single protagonist. After all, if the protagonist unifies the action, there is danger that two or more protagonists will "muddy the waters," by having each unifying a different action. For that reason, many playwrights prefer one major protagonist.

What of a play with person A as the protagonist for the first half of the action and person B taking over as protagonist for the rest of the play?

The proposal sounds disturbingly like a play with little unification. Whatever stopped person A from continuing would be a climax at the half-way point. There would then be a second climax for person B at the end of the play. Undoubtedly such a play might be written successfully, but it has all the earmarks of being two separate plays that the author is trying to force into one.

Is is possible for the protagonist not to care? Is is possible for her or him to grow weary or bored with the pursuit or the goal?

No. The protagonist cannot be bored and still serve as a protagonist. Imagine a John Proctor in *The Crucible* becoming indifferent to the persecution of his neighbors and himself and what those acts would mean to mankind. Imagine Cyrano de Bergerac deciding he simply does not care any longer and he will sit out this fight, thank you. A protagonist may wear many coats, but the dramatic values are lost if this key character is bored or indifferent.

Must the protagonist be "the good guy"?

Not necessarily. One thinks of Regina Gibbons in *The Little Foxes,* who is a villain without ethics or morality in a world of villains, but who is a strong protagonist. In *Medea* the playwright has valid arguments for her actions, but she sets her hand so sharply against her children that she cannot be considered "good." Most often the protagonist will have more "good" qualities than "bad," but only simplistic thinking will have the character purely good. In old melodrama, with its simple morality of good and evil, the protagonist was often amazingly "good," but today, after the antihero movements in literature, the climate does not favor the superhuman protagonist. Motion pictures undoubtedly will continue having the traditional hero, and one may assume that plays may return to larger-than-life characters.

Does the playwright have to draw a protagonist that the audience will like?

It is not essential that the audience like the protagonist, although it is common. Nevertheless, the audience must be involved with and have an emotional response to the protagonist. The audience may dislike a Regina, for example, and there is probably audience opposition to a Medea as the play progresses. The essential factor is that the audience must *care* about the protagonist's struggle and goal. If the audience does not care, quite likely it is because the protagonist does not, and that denies the role the protagonist must serve. In most plays the playwright draws a protagonist with qualities that the audience will find likeable, sympathetic, and enjoyable.

Do all plays require a protagonist?

No. Effective drama exists without a protagonist. Usually there will then be at least a strong central character to tie actions together and to give the author a focal point, but often that too is not present.

Given the advantages of a protagonist, why would a playwright not wish to structure a play around this character?

Some playwrights wish to avoid the protagonist structure on the premise that it is an antiquated convention that tends to force a play into a simple conflict between two forces, almost in melodramatic terms.

Does the protagonist need a plan?

Assuredly, yes. The protagonist must know, first, what he or she wants and, second, how he or she intends to go about satisfying that intense desire. Perhaps elements of the plan will change, as obstacles crop up, but the protagonist must have a concept of direction.

Must the protagonist verbalize the plan?

Not necessarily. If the protagonist does not speak the plan, there ought to be enough hints for the audience to be able to perceive something of the goals. The playwright may wish to write the plan and stick it on the bulletin board above his or her typewriter in order to keep the play going in that correct direction.

Playwrights may avoid having the plan stated for fear it will be too blatant. However, it can be done quite effectively. For example, in *Macbeth* Duncan announces that his son Malcolm will be Prince of Cumberland and therefore next in line. Macbeth cannot accept that if he is to be king, and so he speaks an aside that indicates his plan:

The Prince of Cumberland! That is a step
On which I must fall down, or else o'erleap,
For in my way it lies.

The protagonist may speak indirectly of a *need*, from which a plan can be deduced. In *A Streetcar Named Desire*, Blanche speaks often of her need for a refuge. To Mitch she says, "I need kindness now." The implication of Blanche's goal and plan is clear.

One convenient way for the playwright to force the protagonist to indicate the plan is to have a second character insist upon that information. Person A may demand to know, "Just what do you want from me, anyhow?" Or, "Why did you come home? You aren't acting like yourself: what are you trying to do?" To such questions, person B will have the opportunity to indicate goal and plan.

For the performer, the protagonist is a delight. Of course an actor enjoys playing the lead role, and he or she responds to challenges found in any significant character. But the actor's primary enjoyment with the protagonist results from playing a character that is deeply involved emotionally, responsive to stimuli, totally committed to a goal, and quite active throughout. The playwright is wise to invest those sorts of qualities into other characters, as well as in the protagonist, in order to draw out the performers' abilities and thus help create a better production.

The Antagonist. The protagonist has a single-minded drive to achieve a goal. If there are no obstacles or counterforces, then the protagonist will quickly win. The play is over. The antagonist provides the necessary countermovement.

Without the antagonist's opposition, there would be no testing of the protagonist's will, no opportunity for the protagonist to display depth of interest in the goal, and no chance to overcome obstacles and thereby show other aspects of the personality.

The antagonist must be strong. The battle must be equal, or victory will be swift. The protagonist's intense desire must be matched by an antagonist that is equally determined. An unequal conflict cannot sustain itself. Without the struggle, little will be shown of the characters' strengths, weaknesses, cleverness, and determination. The struggle gives characters the chance to react to various stimuli, thereby causing more dimensionality to be shown.

Suspense is maintained by the struggle. In a match between two top prize fighters, power and strategy are employed to keep the outcome in question until the final round. First one fighter appears to be winning, then the other. Victory may go to either. So, too, goes the match between protagonist and antagonist. In *The Crucible*, John Proctor goes through a series of choices and fights the antagonists; not until the last moments is the final decision clear. In *Streetcar*, Blanche moves toward her goal in many different ways, winning and losing, and she employs all of her weapons in her battle, but ultimately the antagonist proves the stronger and she loses. The struggles keep the final outcome in doubt.

As the name implies, the antagonist tends to be the antithesis of the protagonist. Often the antagonist is something of a mirror opposite to the protagonist: The goodness of an Othello is matched by the evil of an Iago. The protagonist will establish a direction, and the antagonist will move contrarily. *Each contrary movement of the antagonist will be an obstacle—in plot terms, a complication—to the protagonist's design.* Therefore, the antagonist is a major contributor to the play's plot.

Must the antagonist be a "bad guy"?

Not necessarily. In tragedy the antagonist typically is more "evil" than "good." The classic antagonist is found in *Othello:* Iago is totally evil, motivated by evil. In serious drama the antagonist is apt to be a bleaker human than he will be in lighter plays. Usually the protagonist dictates the antagonist: To the extent that the protagonist represents good, so will the antagonist show evil.

Is an antagonist required in a play with no protagonist?
No.

Is an antagonist required in the play with a protagonist?
No. It helps to think of the antagonist as "embodiment of the obstacles" in the protagonist's path. If the play does not have an antagonist but there are sufficient obstacles from other sources, the desired effect can be achieved. However, it is more typical to find an antagonist in a play with a protagonist: They rather go together like, as the song says, love and marriage. In modern drama the

characters may not be so sharply drawn as simply the antagonist or protagonist, but they may serve these roles.

Assuming that a play has a single protagonist, does it follow that there should be but one antagonist?

A highly important function of the single protagonist is to focus the plot and all of the other characters into a cohesive whole. No other character unifies the action, and so the number of antagonists is of little importance except according to the play's needs in other aspects. The protagonist may be so strong that several antagonists are necessary to provide an adequate opposition, as in *Cyrano de Bergerac*.

Is it possible for a single character to serve as both protagonist and antagonist simultaneously? In other words, can the chief obstacle to the protagonist be herself or himself?

Few topics are discussed as often in my playwriting classes as this question about the protagonist who is torn between internal choices. Quite often there are arguments that Hamlet the protagonist is opposed by Hamlet the antagonist. Hamlet, the argument goes, does not take the action the protagonist wants because of the vast indecision of the antagonist. It makes an interesting argument, but this is a misreading of Hamlet's reasons for not taking action. He is not indecisive. Instead he is attempting to determine if Claudius and Gertrude are truly guilty. For Hamlet the Ghost's testimony alone cannot suffice: If one assumes that spirits can exist and communicate, then one must also be prepared to assume that the ghosts may be sent by a devil demon and may be the devil in disguise. Therefore, Hamlet has to accumulate additional evidence about the Ghost's testimony. He does not oppose his own quest, and therefore he is not his own antagonist. It is true that Hamlet has doubts, uncertainties, and insecurities, but these are not the qualities of an antagonist.

Shakespeare's *Hamlet* is not a play about a young man who cannot make up his own mind and thereby foils himself. On the contrary, Hamlet is shown to be quite active. And the playwright did design a definite antagonist into the play—Claudius. Just because the play presents Hamlet's interior concerns, it doesn't mean that we should ignore the playwright's careful use of exterior forces.

A playwright who wishes to write about a protagonist agonizing over a mighty choice is advised to present on stage the forces embodying the sides of the dilemma. Interior quandaries must be externalized by the action. Interior qualities seldom can be shown but must instead be told.

It is possible for a playwright to construct an effective drama that embodies both the protagonist and antagonist in one person—one thinks of interesting expressionistic plays, for example—but plays often are better told within the more standard protagonist-antagonist structure because that form expresses the conflicts more clearly. Obstacles and complications are also sharper when externalized. The protagonist-antagonist structure allows better communication of the play's subject and theme.

For the performer, the antagonist is often as exciting to perform as is the protagonist, and for many of the same reasons. Dramatic literature is rich in well-written antagonists that give artistic challenges to performers—Stanley in *A Streetcar Named Desire*, Iago in *Othello*, Yang Sun in *The Good Woman of Setzuan*—and performers meeting those challenges have created exciting theatre. The playwright should be careful not to overstate the antagonist—performers often tend to magnify the antagonist's negative force—and in production the character should be controlled.

Protagonist and Antagonist: A Short Summation. Protagonist and antagonist are the chief characters in the play. They will be the first to come to the author's invention, and they will provide the play with conflict and dramatic action. The active desire to achieve a goal will create a plot, and the antagonist's counter-movements will enrich the plot with complications. The characters are attractive to audiences and help stimulate interest in the play.

> *A NOTE TO BEGINNING PLAYWRIGHTS. I can offer you no better advice than this: Your early plays simply should be based around protagonist–antagonist conflicts so you can learn how to develop these two characters. You will find that the plays will move more easily in their dramatic lines with this structure that, you should remember, has been a constant in all recorded Western dramatic history. The system makes writing much easier. Once you have proven an ability to work with these characters, then freely experiment with other approaches.*

Other Dramatic Characters

The Utilitarian Character. In older dramas the butler and maid were typical utilitarian characters that existed only to make announcements such as, "Dinner is served," or "Lord Carrington has arrived, mum." Often they began the play with the infamous "feather duster scene," with the maid flipping a feather duster over the furniture while the two spoke the exposition: "Detective Hanley, you know, believes that the murderer had to be someone inside the castle, which you realize means we know the person." "Yes. Unless, as you remember, it might've been a ghost."

In more recent plays the utilitarian character may be the mailman, delivery boy, or landlady. The have lightweight speeches: "Here's the letter you've been waiting for these past six months, hoping it will be good news," or "Is this the party that ordered the large pizza for one?"

Such characters tend to be flat and one-dimensional. If the playwright invests more in them, there is a danger that they will grow cute. For the performer, they are thankless roles. "There's no such thing as a small role, only small actors" is a phrase invented to cheer up performers stuck with these characters. Too many nondimensional characters in a play will give the whole play a flat appearance, much the same as two off-key chorus members can "flatten" the whole musical.

The Confidant. The confidant is easily recognized by the large question mark always etched on his or her forehead: "But, Sally, why do you want to leave Bill? Hasn't he been good to you and the kids?" or "Jimbo, do you want to tell me what's wrong?" The playwright uses the confidant in order to get to the answers—the questions are simply a ploy—with the result that the confidant has no opportunity to become a developed character.

The performer unaware of the reason the character has been written into the play will go to inventive lengths to give depth and meaning to the lines. Often that effort will magnify the role out of proportion and pull the play subtly out of shape. It also is possible that audience attention will fade during the confidant's speeches.

Does it follow that the confidant cannot be a viable dramatic character? No. The playwright can give the confidant characters more dimensionality by increasing their reason for existing in the play. A stronger motivation for concern will make the confidant stronger. A good first step to take is to revise the confidant so that he or she has an emotional stake. It might be as easy as simply rewriting the lines from questions to emotional statements: "Damn it, Bud, I'm not gonna let you run away! Not again! No friend of mine gets pushed out of town!"

The Raissonneur. The *raissonneur*, the "voice of reason," illustrated neatly by the character of Philinte in Molière's sharp-witted comedy, *The Misanthrope*, typically is the author's mouthpiece. In *The Misanthrope* the playwright's theme is given life by Philinte in his recommendations for moderation and against extremes in behavior. The *raissonneur* sometimes is present during the entire play and often seems to speak most tellingly at the final moments. The device has grown out of favor in contemporary drama. Today's writers think it is too obvious to have one character charged with the responsibility of speaking for the author. They think it is better that the totality of the play communicate the playwright's concepts.

What does the playwright do if certain concepts should be expressed directly? Rather than have one character who exists simply to state the author's concepts, today's writers tend to spread those concepts over a number of characters. Alternatively, the *raisonneur* figure is given a series of additional traits so that she or he will no longer be obviously the author's voice. The *raisonneur* in many ways resembles the Greek chorus in that there are tendencies to comment on the action and to suggest ideal audience responses. Contemporary writers, however, usually seek to lead audience responses with indirection. The whole of the play, not one character, is expected to carry the weight of meaning.

The Narrator.   The narrator is an unpopular device with experienced playwrights and theatre producers. The basic idea of a narrator violates the concept of drama as an art to show and not to tell. A narrator is simply too easy, too convenient: Once the writer permits the narrator into the script, it follows that the narrator will increasingly *tell* of the action with the playwright *showing* less.

The concept of the narrator, however, has supporters. It is popular with playwrights who (*a*) are beginning; (*b*) have seen one or two Shakespearean productions with highly effective opening monologues from narrators; (*c*) are enchanted with "breaking down the walls of the stage" by having a character directly address the audience; and (*d*) are making the transition from novel writing and still want to be able to speak at the audience/readers.

The performer finds the narrator role easy enough to play. There is little challenge and little work to create the role. The narrator often needs a good voice, rather like a radio announcer, and a winning way.

But what of the exceptions? It certainly is true that the narrator has been used to good effect. The narrator brings a New England morality to *Our Town*, an insouciant charm to *The Teahouse of the August Moon*, and a bittersweet tenderness to *The Glass Menagerie*. The narrator can be effective when lecturing in didactic drama, as in *The Good Woman of Setzuan*. Often narrators are popular in the large outdoor dramas, especially to make transitions between the many episodic scenes. However, even though examples can be cited of effective use of the narrator, all too often the device fails.

Are there secrets to making the narrator more effective? If the playwright finds that the play absolutely demands a narrator, perhaps a good first step to using the role effectively is to prevent the narrator from speaking about plot. In particular, the narrator should be kept from stating exposition if at all possible. For example, Tom in *The Glass Menagerie* is a narrator who nicely expands the universe of the play without being a mere tool to tell the audience about story elements. Also, the narrator can become a more rounded character with direct participation within the play, as does Tom, instead of being an outside observer.

The "Typical" Personages.   Let's imagine a "typical" play with the characters of Mommy, a typical thirty-one-year-old housewife; Daddy, a typical thirty-five-year-old salesman; Sissy, a typical eleven-year-old going on twenty-four; and Bud, a typical seven-year-old who is practicing to be a sports announcer like

Howard Cosell. Visiting them this week will be Granny, a typical visiting grandmother. The play will take place in the typical American living room in the suburbs of a typical midsize American city. Mommy will be cooking dinner (hamburgers, hot dogs, and apple pie); Granny will be knitting an American flag.

Of course such a play would lack artistic dignity and it would quickly become boring unless the author intended a trenchant satire as Albee did with *The American Dream.* The wise playwright avoids any idea of writing about "typical" people involved in "typical" activities. Instead, the playwright looks upon "typical" as a red-flag warning of a potentially dull play.

What steps should the writer take to avoid this problem? The playwright must fix strongly in mind the idea that all humans are different. So, too, should dramatic characters be different: The same individuality that creative spirits enjoy proudly should be part of the characterization in the play. Characters ought have distinctive qualities to move them from "typical" lives.

The Delightful Eccentric.   Plays derive a remarkable brilliance from delightfully eccentric characters that are colorful, unusual, and huge. In a world full of sparrows, the eccentrics are the exotic rain-forest birds with sweeping rainbow-colored plumage. Plays such as *Harvey, Arsenic and Old Lace,* and *The Odd Couple* sparkle to life with the offbeats. Normal people populate the real world, but it is the eccentrics who give us a glimpse of a different life-style and who are the ones we treasure. Such is the case with the characters in *You Can't Take it With You* and *The Time of Your Life.*

Of course the eccentric will make a comedy roll briskly, but the playwright must remember that the character can also be well-placed in straight dramatic works. The Porter in *Macbeth* is a delightful nonconformist when he explains that drink will cause three things:

Marry, sir, nose-painting, sleep, and urine. Lechery, sir, it
provokes and unprovokes: it provokes the desire, but it takes away
the performance . . . it makes him, and it mars him; it sets him
on, and it takes him off, it persuades him, and disheartens him;
makes him stand to, and not stand to. . . .

"Nose-painting," by the way, refers to the red veins one sees in a drinker's nose.

Eccentrics may be tinged with a sort of insanity that is remarkably clear-headed. Sanity and madness create a canny protagonist in *The Madwoman of Chaillot.* The "madwoman" is the only one capable of perceiving the insanity of the world.

Playwrights find that the delightful, eccentric characters can bring sunshine where dull darkness had existed, and often such fey souls will have a brisk vitality that will extend the play's subject and theme. The lovable eccentric's individuality rubs off on other characters, making them sharper. No one would suggest that every play should have an eccentric, but such an unusual bird of paradise may be just the solution for playwrights who find that their characters are dull.

The "Law of Contrast." A playwright may feel that the characters are in a slump and missing sparkle. Contrast can bring them back to life. If the play seems to have taken on a deadly evenness, contrast may spark changes. When conflict seems to have worn itself out, contrast may give new fire to the clash.

How can contrast add so much to a play? By providing colorful and dynamic opposites. For illustration, consider the strong man at the circus. The barker promises amazing feats while the strong man flexes his muscles, takes a deep breath, then bends over the awesome-looking weights and with a mighty grunt lifts the bar over his head. Is he strong? Well, perhaps.

But suppose a ceremony is inserted before the Strong Man does his act. From the audience two burly men are selected to come up on the platform and together lift the weight. They tug, red-faced with effort, but cannot raise it more than knee-high. Now the strong man does the lift: With no help he swings the weight over his head and holds it there while the barker leads the crowd in counting the seconds for a full minute. Is he strong? Indeed, yes. He has been shown in contrast to the others. His strength is twice that of other men. Without contrast, however, his strength could not be displayed; contrast shows the qualities more clearly.

Without a "down" there can be no "up." Mutt and Jeff, good and evil, Abbott and Costello, Martin and Lewis: They go together because contrast helps one emphasize the other. Indeed, contrast makes one invent the other: There could be no Sluggo without Mister Bill, and without Sluggo, Mister Bill would not be a total victim.

Contrast gives dimension to character. In *The Odd Couple* and *The Sunshine Boys* it is contrast that creates character qualties and, indeed, creates the play. The delicacy of Blanche is brilliantly etched by the brutish Stanley, and her poetic flights rise higher in contrast to Mitch's clumsy fumblings for words. So, too, contrast makes *Desire Under the Elms* supercharged with vibrant conflict: The coldness of Ephraim's age makes Abbie's youth warmer. In Garcia-Lorca's *Yerma* the contrast is between desires: Yerma's single-minded desire for a child is set against her husband's single-minded preoccupation with keeping the land fertile. Inez, Estelle, and Garcin bring intense conflict to Sartre's *No Exit* because each one is a perfect antithesis to the other in a powerful display of contrasts. Indeed, *No Exit* seeks to say that "Hell is other people," but it really states that "Hell exists when people of such contrasting values are set together."

Contrast between characters puts each in better focus. The goodness of an Othello and the evil of an Iago complement one another. Neither would be as strong without the other, and *Othello* would lose its drama without those contrasts. This suggests that the playwright who wants to draw a protagonist markedly full of compassion may want to add to the play a character sternly lacking in forgiveness in order to make a contrast that will enhance the quality of compassion. A gentle person needs a savage one, or a morally concerned one needs one with no morality. Many plays can be cited to illustrate the values of sharp contrast.

Contrast within a character is equally dynamic. The "live or die, action or delay" contrasts within *Hamlet;* the dependence versus independence of Nora in *A Doll's House;* or the weaknesses and easy fears contrasted with the confidence and authoritativeness of the captain in Strindberg's *The Father;* these contrasts bring tensions to the plays and force the action. Contrast makes the character appear to be more dimensional, more interesting. Contrast makes the character come alive.

There is no "law" that says that contrast must be part of the play, but playwrights will find that the benefits of contrast are worth their attention. For the audience, contrast provides interest factors. Often, too, contrast gives the play greater clarity.

Do Characters Change During the Play?

As the play progresses, do the characters change? Do they grow, develop, or become different in outlook and behavior? Or do they remain the same through-out the action from beginning to end? Theories about this subject abound, and scholarly arguments about it become intense. One side suggests that characters change as a natural response to stimuli of action and other characters. The other argues that characters are incapable of changing: Once the writer puts the pieces together, the character remains fixed. What may be perceived as change is merely an illumination of additional aspects of the same unchanged character.

The question appears destined to become a constant in theatre studies. It seems to me to be denying the force that theatre creates. Isn't *A Doll's House* about the extreme changes in Nora that lead to the magnificent slamming of the door as she leaves her husband at the end of the play? Is the Nora we meet at the beginning of the play capable of making that exit at the end, or does she evolve? Doesn't *A Doll's House* show how Nora changes and how, in contrast, her husband is too rigid to be able to cope with changes? Hasn't Macbeth's greed for power changed him from a noble and honorable warrior we see at the beginning of the play into a man frenzied over petty details, a murderer, and a killer of women and children? Isn't *Macbeth* written precisely to show the changes? Is Blanche the same at the end of *A Streetcar Named Desire* as she was at the beginning? In the opening moments she still had wispy hopes. At the end she has fallen over the edge of despair. Isn't that change?

I believe that dramatic characters are capable of change and that the process of change is precisely what has to take place in response to stimuli.

Characters are representatives of life, interpretive symbols of our own selves. Why must we take the position that they lack the capability for change that marks mankind's development?

But much more importantly than this, I believe that the notion of non-changing characters is a dangerous one for playwrights (and also for actors and directors). The playwright benefits from thinking that the character can change, develop, or grow in appropriate circumstances. The opposite view presents characters as mere static blocks, immune to stimulus-response cycles. That view may be popular with those who do not create drama, but it cannot be viable for playwrights.

There must be appropriate motivation for changes, of course. At one time it was fashionable to write temperance melodramas that featured miraculous changes in characters, from evil to good, from drunken sots to pious nondrinkers, that were usually caused by a waif's tear. Today's theatre will not accept such implausible character changes. But just as adequate motivation must be present, so also should there be appropriate responses to the motivating forces. If it is not plausible for characters to change without motivation, it is equally implausible for characters to remain static in the face of motivational forces.

Characters as Autobiographical Symbols

In a very real sense, all dramatic characters have distinct autobiographical qualities. All are, after all, born of the writer's personal dreams and frustrations. They have breathed the same angers, cried the same defeats, and laughed the same excitements. Major characters and often minor ones are pieces of the writer's rib.

But that does not imply that playwrights create autobiographical dramas every time they write a play. Instead what is suggested here is that the nature of the creative process stems from the self. The playwright has no better source for characters than his or her private self. It must be emphasized that *inside the writer are all the emotions ever needed for any drama.* It is all there inside of you. You have felt love, hate, anger, pride, despair, rejection, and every other emotion you could wish for your dramatic characters. You have swung from the heights of joy to the depths of defeat. You know the sweetness of earned victory, the coldness of loneliness, and that mysterious breathlessness that comes from a loving caress. Your job—the writer's task—is to bring out those emotions and make them part of the characters who need them. To do that, you must go first to your inner self, to your memories, and there you must unlock secrets that you've held distant even from yourself. The writer is a reflective person, absorbed in the wonders of humanity as shown in the self.

Assume for a moment that you wish to write a play about a person who will take steps toward self-destruction. To bring that character to life, do you draw from television or movies? No. That would be imitating another writer's imitation, with the added confusions of an actor's interpretation. There would be too many barriers between your view and life. Truth would be lost. Well, then, do you draw from psychology textbooks and articles about suicide? No. These are fine resources, and many of the details drawn here might later be helpful as you put finishing touches to the character, but these are abstractions, often examinations of a "mean" profile, and distant from flesh and blood.

Well, then, where do you start? You start from yourself. But you've not attempted suicide? You can write of murder without having killed, male writers can write of female characters and females of males, and we can all write of characters older than ourselves. To bring the character to life you will dig into your private sensory banks. Recall your moments of greatest despair. What caused you to feel so badly? What did you do? Could you hear words of hope or did you reject them? What changed in the way you moved, walked, spoke, or sat? How did you treat casual friends, or close relatives? Did you want others to know of your despair? Did you wall yourself in? Did you think of suicide, consider the options, plan the methods? Did you have religious concerns about suicide? Think of metaphors and images that best describe the way you acted and felt.

Your observations of others when they were in their greatest despair add color and details. Think of how they looked and moved, what they said, and the manner in which they said it. Did they refuse to hear those who would help? Did they grow more unhappy because of other's attempts to give aid or, conversely, because they felt ignored?

Your imagination adds more depth. Where did the character go to school? What books influenced her? Were her parents loving? cold? rich? Was it a close-knit family? What image does she have of herself? What does she love? What does she reject? What music and colors would she select?

You may wish to add artistic elements—say, a flash of humor or a self-mocking laugh or a tender hope. You will wish to make the despair forthcoming, not internalized, so it can live on the stage. Now you add qualities gleaned from psychology textbooks. Certainly your writer's journal is receiving details, and you will be bringing the character to the play where she can speak and move. A self-building process makes the character begin to take on dimensions, almost as an independent agent. For instance, she can do this but not that, she wants to say the other but not this.

The final product will resemble none of the contributors, yet will carry parts of each. As the playwright pushes forward, it is likely that the script's needs will create more changes. Yet the character's original roots are taken from the writer's own soul, and those connections make a special relationship between author and creation. That closeness is quite unlike any that actors or directors may experience, and for the playwright the character's successes and failures in production will be felt in a way that only fellow playwrights can understand.

The playwright finds that the character's self-definitions are helpful in expressing the protagonist's goal, in giving the essence of the character's mental set, or in letting the character express her entire being. These self-definitions may be direct or indirect.

Henrik Ibsen uses self-definition often with his primary characters. For example, in *Hedda Gabler*, Hedda herself states what she wants. Ibsen does not have her make the statement until Act Two, perhaps because it is not needed earlier. Note that Ibsen turns Mrs. Elvsted into a temporary confidant to get at Hedda's reply:

MRS. ELVSTED
There is something behind this, Hedda. Some hidden purpose.
HEDDA
Yes, there is! For once in my life I want to have power over a
human destiny.

Ibsen *shows* Hedda's character in many ways but the playwright needed her to say this crucial aspect of self.

The playwright may have the character express himself in a particular manner that is itself a self-definition. Into the quiet Wingfield home arrives self-confident and vibrant Jim O'Conner. Tennessee Williams has Jim speak of his goal. It is not a specific career goal but a broader concept of keeping himself ahead of the world. Jim is in sharp *contrast* to the others in *The Glass Menagerie*, and he makes the air crackle as he speaks to Laura:

JIM
. . . I believe in the future of television!

(He turns to her.)

I wish to be ready to go right along with it. Therefore I'm
planning to get in on the ground floor. In fact I've already made
the right connections and all that remains is for the industry itself
to get under way. Full steam—

(His eyes are starry.)

Knowledge—Zzzzzp! Money—Zzzzzp! Power! That's the cycle
democracy is built on!

Jim's character is neatly shown. His vitality defines himself, and it is the antithesis of Laura and thus defines her: Jim is confident in his ability to move forward, and Laura never will share that secure feeling.

Playwrights use dialogue to express character. For example, when Macbeth is told that the Queen is dead his speech starts with a reference to her and then shifts to show his mood:

MACBETH

She should have died hereafter;
There would have been time for such a word.
To-morrow, and to-morrow, and to-morrow
Creeps in this petty pace from day to day
To the last syllable of recorded time;
And all our yesterdays have lighted fools
The way to dusty death. Out, out brief candle!
Life's but a walking shadow, a poor player,
That struts and frets his hour upon the stage
And then is heard no more. It is a tale
Told by an idiot, full of sound and fury,
Signifying nothing.

It is the first time that Macbeth is shown in such despair. In the reflective moment, Macbeth's character is shown as it begins to change.

Note, please, that this also is use of plot to stimulate response: Shakespeare carefully times the death of Lady Macbeth to come when he needs to expose Macbeth's inner decays. The playwright's goal here is to change the character, to cause him to be more inner-directed and philosophical. The Queen's death helps bring about that evolution from bold warrior to somber despairer. It is the simulus-response cycle at work.

Efficiency

The playwright seeks to use every word and every pause with telling efficiency. A piece of character should be shown in every speech; deft strokes should continue until the character is shown in full flesh and total coloration. Often it is the accumulation of the little pieces that will give a character great dimension.

No idle chit-chat and no laid back conversational wanderings will achieve this goal. If your scenario describes scenes in which "characters discuss" this point or "talk about" that, possibly you may be thinking of an inefficient scene. Your characters have few moments of life on the stage. Efficient use of that time can create memorable people who live with audiences for years.

One modern master of characterization is Tennessee Williams. He deftly uses every word. Read the first time that Stanley meets Blanche in *A Streetcar Named Desire* and you will find that the man is being hospitable, Kowalski style, to the unexpected guest, but that his first concern—after only three words to Blanche—is his wife: He immediately asks for Stella (he calls her, tellingly, the "little woman") and the audience is quickly aware that he is deeply protective. That quality, of course, will later dominate. In the introductory moments, however, he is relaxed and as polite as Stanley is likely to be. Blanche, too, is shown with quick effectiveness: She lies about drinking, she is timid, and she is frightened. Williams even gives Blanche some motivation, if such is needed, for her poetic flights, when he has her say she is an English teacher.

Read carefully that opening scene in this modern classic and you will see finely-honed efficient writing: In but a few moments, Williams has sharply set forth the characters. Stanley later will become enraged at the attacks upon his nest and with atavistic destructiveness he will remove the threat, but in the beginning Williams draws Stanley differently. As you read the dialogue (out loud is best), see how many words or speeches you might eliminate. I suspect you will discover that there is no excess baggage.

Descriptions of One Character by Others

Edmond Rostand's beautiful *Cyranò de Bergerac* is set in France of 1640. Act One takes place in the Hotel de Bourgogne. Dozens of colorful characters are milling about, waiting for a performance. Rostand uses the large cast to keep the stage active and to build Cyrano's entrance. Almost two dozen references are made about Cyrano before his first appearance.

". . . he is the lad with the long sword."
"Noble."
". . . an extraordinary man."
"The best friend and the bravest soul alive!"
"Poet—"
"Swordsman—"
"Musician—"
"Philosopher—"
"His sword is one half of the Shears of Fate!"

Cyrano is the tragic clown with the disfiguring nose. Again, Rostand has others describe the protagonist in order to make the point more vividly.

Such a nose!—Mv lords, there is no such nose as that
nose—You cannot look upon it without crying: "Oh no,
impossible! Exaggerated!" Then you smile and say: "Of course—I
might have known; presently he will take it off." But that
Monsieur de Bergerac will never do.

What others may say about a character can be a fine descriptive tool for the playwright. Physical descriptions, as of Cyrano's nose, come to the playwright easily. There also may be descriptions of the character's basic strengths or flaws.

The last moment of *Death of a Salesman*—the "requiem" scene—gives one final look at Willy Loman with a surgical cleanliness. Willy is dead. Linda, his widow, stands with Biff and Happy, the two sons. There is talk about the funeral, about the man. Then Biff speaks the crucial lines about Willy Loman:

"He had the wrong dreams. All, all wrong." And again: "He never knew who he was." Miller's writing genius deftly and quickly opens the character's core.

It also is possible for the playwright to strike twice with one blow. A speech may describe one character and at the same time give new insight into the speaker. In the fourth scene of *A Streetcar Named Desire* Blanche angrily describes Stanley as a brute, an animal, the missing link. She reminds Stella of "our bringing up"—that constant concern about their family's status—and says Stanley is like an ape. Blanche is not merely describing Stanley. Unconsciously she shows much of herself. Her motivations are complex. She wants to be "high class," a social lady, above the animals. She works hard to place herself there. She also wants to free her sister from a man she sincerely believes is not good enough. More significantly, Blanche wants to destroy the nest that Stanley and Stella have created for themselves. Why? She wants to make room for herself in a reconstructed secure haven she expects Stella to help build.

One character's description of another can communicate images and significant qualities. The technique is a valid tool for playwrights. There appear to be several ground rules to making the descriptive speech. First, motivation is necessary. Second, the description must fall naturally from the mouth of the speaker. Third, the technique most commonly applies to the major characters, to the protagonist certainly but also perhaps to the antagonist, because it is a wasted effort for less important characters. Finally, the person being described usually is kept offstage, permitting the speaker more freedom of expression.

Playable Objectives

Performers construct character by first searching for the *superobjective,* or the *through line of action.* The two statements mean much the same. The reference is to the character's supreme driving force, a core of being, which gives the character an ultimate destination. It is as if the character is inside a complex maze and must go from start to finish. The "line of action" is the cohesive quality of the movement pattern, pulling the performer-character through the maze.

The superobjective is the master plan. In the maze analogy, the superobjective would be to go successfully from start to finish. That plan consists of a number of *objectives,* which are related moment-by-moment actions in smaller units of the play. For the performer, these are like individual decisions taken at each intersection and corner of the maze. The objectives do not get the character to the finish, but they do lead to it even if they temporarily explore dead ends.

The superobjective and the smaller objectives must all be playable. Generalizations and abstractions are not playable. "To free mankind" is an impossible objective to show, as is "to ascertain the spirit of existentialism within the broad context of latter twentieth-century apathy." Those are essay topics, not objectives for the playwright's characters. The objective must be capable of being played. The playwright must work with concrete objectives for his characters. For instance, instead of having a character plunging forward to preserve democracy—which is too large and too abstract a subject—the playwright will have a character possess goals that the performer can display: This character may want to stop a specific politician from frightening voters away from the polls with the use of threats the week of the election.

Examining Characters after Completing the First Draft: A Technique for Revisions

The playwright will begin revisions after completing the first draft. The enormity of the task ahead may appear overwhelming, and many playwrights become disheartened. Reducing the revision process to a step-by-step approach will permit efficient organization. The key is to examine every character according to a checklist.

The following methodology is suggested to playwrights who have not established a revision process. There are several essential points to this sytem.

1. The author must keep a broad overview of the characters, instead of deeply examining each tiny moment, in order to look at the totality.

2. All notes are made on the script quickly. A quick shorthand or code system is used. For example, plus signs (+) may be used to indicate scenes or moments that are strong and must not get discarded by accident during revisions. A minus sign (−) calls the writer's attention to areas that must be revised. A color system often helps, one that uses red for character and black for diction for instance, or whatever the author finds best.

3. The author must *read aloud* all parts of the script. The playwright is writing for performers to read the script aloud, and so there is no reason to avoid hearing the words now. Besides, and more significantly, the author will find that reading aloud emphasizes problem areas that might be overlooked in a silent reading. ·

The process begins with the establishment of written notes regarding what the author has intended to accomplish.

Preparation

1. Jot down on a sheet of paper the name of the play's protagonist. As you read the script you will keep in mind the qualities a protagonist must have.
2. Next, write the protagonist's superobjective. Ideally, that is stated in only a few words. Then answer these questions, as briefly as seems possible. Why is this objective of crucial importance to the protagonist? What is the protagonist's *emotional* reason to pursue the goal?

3. For all primary characters, write a brief statement (one or two words if possible) for emotional conditions, desires, and goals.

4. Sketch quickly the emotional relationships between characters. Perhaps a diagram or two will help.

5. State the protagonist's *plan*. How will he or she drive to achieve the superobjective?

6. Identify the forces standing in the plan's way.

This preparation step provides the playwright with a "yardstick" to measure the script. These brief notes will help the writer focus upon the essentials of the play. The preparation step holds attention away from petty details.

Readings of the script

1. Read the entire play aloud to yourself with as few stops as possible. For now, ignore problems with diction, and focus instead upon essences of the characters. Use your imagination to see and hear the characters.

2. With a red pencil (or color of your choice), place a check in the margin every time a character seems dull or dead. Place an "M" in the margin each time motivation seems weak. A question mark in the margin will indicate a place where the character is confusing. These sorts of marks will guide you when you return to work on necessary changes.

3. *Read the protagonist—no other character—aloud to yourself from beginning to end.* Ignore the other characters for now. In the margin, label such details as the following: "Statement of goal"; "Statement of plan"; "Statement of need"; "Making movements toward goal"; "An obstacle"; and "Overcoming the obstacle." These notes will force you to be fully conscious of the protagonist's movements during the play.

4. Read aloud just the second-most-important character. Make marginal notes as you did for the protagonist.

5. Read aloud individually each remaining character. If you have utilitarian characters, now is a good time to see if they are too colorless. Here, too, is the opportunity to check the confidant for concern about the protagonist.

These readings should give you a good insight into areas demanding your attention. Plan to revise *major* problems first. Save the smaller problems until later. Some of the smaller ones may disappear as the major difficulties are solved.

Common problems with characters in early drafts.

1. The protagonist
   —has an objective that is not clear.
   —has a motivation that is not adequate.
   —has a plan that is not clear.
   —is not an attractive person.
   —is not adequately active.
   —does not encounter obstacles.

2. The motivation, overall
   —is major, but the characters react in major ways to minor motivations.
   —is minor; characters react without apparent motivation.

3. The dialogue
   —does not pinpoint individuality—all characters sound alike.
   —is too "literary," too artificial.

4. The antagonist
   —is not causing enough difficulties for the protagonist.
   —is not sufficiently motivated.

5. The emotions
   —are unclear in the protagonist.
   —are insufficient; characters do not have sufficient emotional range.
   —are insufficient; characters seem to have little involvement with the situation.
   —are sparked, but last perhaps half a page; the emotions are not sustained long enough.

To repeat for emphasis, the playwright must read aloud to himself the entire script, and then each character individually. For the third or later drafts, the writer may recruit friends or performers to read the play aloud. To hear others read the play is a remarkably illuminating experience. When actors are recruited, the author must refrain from telling them how to read the lines. Instead, the actors should respond as their instincts suggest. There is no reason to feel dismayed if each reading suggests added revision: Plays are not written but are rewritten, and playwrights understand they may need a number of attempts in order to create life.

Biographies

You are the creator and can assign any characteristics you wish to each person in your play. I urge you to list all the details you can: What is the person's favorite food? What is the food least liked? The color the person prefers? What sort of fabrics will the person select for a jacket? Where did the person go to college or, if the person did not attend college, how does he or she feel about school? What was the first fight about and who won? What was the first encounter with drugs/sex/cigarettes/alcohol? What of the person's past does he or she most enjoy replaying? What goals did the person have? Has the person flown a plane, sailed a boat, drifted in a balloon, skied, or been in physical danger? What does the person think of God? What does the person believe follows this life? It often is said that humans become mature when they realize they are mortal after all, when they are thrust into awareness that they will die: Has the character gone through that particular rite of passage? Think of other passages and ask what the person experienced with each.

You will want to think of each person in your play when she is not in your play: You will want to give her life and drive in a universe outside of your play. The added dimensions will make her more attractive. Force yourself to think of the characters busily going through life in a world quite apart from the play.

What makes the person laugh? What makes her cry? When would anger come? Disgust? Fear? What makes her simply want to quit? If the person had magical ability, what single characteristic would she most want to change? If a time-travel device could be available, where in the person's past would she want to go?

Constructing a character is rather like building an iceberg: All that is visible must be supported by a far greater bulk that cannot be seen. Think of it as a one-to-ten ratio: For every piece that is above, there should be ten below.

Will answers to these questions appear in the final draft of your play? Will your characters talk about their balloon flights, favorite beverage, and college life? No. Or probably not, at least; as often as you consider these qualities you may find that more new ideas will follow and may become part of the play. But it is not necessary that they do become part of it; the more you know about the people, the more depth they will take on.

Must you write down all of this material? Of course; you are a writer, aren't you? This material goes directly to the writer's journal. Remember, writing begets writing!

Exercises

1. Positive characteristics.

a. List (in writing) the attributes of someone you *respect*. You may say, for example, you perceive the person to be "loyal" or "honest" or "strong-willed." Try to list *all* of the attributes, including some that may be less positive.

b. List (in writing) the qualities of someone whom you strongly like. You can say the person seems "to have an ability to laugh at self" or "a genuine desire to help others." Again, list all of the qualities in that person.

2. Negative characteristics.

a. List (in writing) all of the attributes of someone for whom you have no respect.

b. List (in writing) the qualities of someone whom you strongly dislike.

3. Write two character sketches, each no less than several pages in length, about two dramatic characters. One is a protagonist, filled with the characteristics you listed for number one, and the second is an antagonist with the characteristics you listed for number two.

4. Write one character sketch, several pages long, about *one* dramatic character who combines characteristics from both number one and number two.

5. Design a scenario for a short play that pits the characters against each other. Find a conflict—perhaps the protagonist wants something that the antagonist refuses to give up—that will bring out the qualities you listed in number one and number two.

Do you find a better understanding of the nature of characters? Do you perceive one way the playwright may seek to invent characters for a play?

6. Examine characters in other plays:

a. Study *Othello*, by William Shakespeare. Describe the antagonist carefully. Iago is considered the classic antagonist: What makes him such a master of evil?

b. Study *Cyrano de Bergerac*, by Edmond Rostand (but only the Hooker translation). Describe the protagonist carefully. What makes him such a supurb hero?

c. Study *The Time of Your Life*, by William Saroyan. Who is the antagonist? Is Blick an evil character? Relate Saroyan's statement about when the time comes to kill with the qualities of the play's evil and good.

7. Examine characters in your plays:

a. Select any one play you have completed. List all of the visible attributes of the protagonist. Is this character one *you* can like and respect?

b. Rewrite the character sketch of the protagonist you discussed above. Try to redesign the character to include more of the characteristics you mentioned in number one.

Chapter Nineteen

Thought

"Thought," one of the significant six elements of drama that Aristotle lists, may be more easily recognized under one of the various names that contemporary theorists use, such as "subject," "theme," "play's message," or "idea." Here we will use the term *thought,* saving other terms for different concepts.

To paraphrase Aristotle, thought is considered to be present in a play that either proves a point or seeks to illustrate a general truth. The play may be either comic or tragic. In a broad sense, thought will be present in all plays, even in the most bewildering or wandering, because the playwright indicates a meaning by the very selection of the incidents, situations, and characters that make up the play.

Thought is a complex part of playwriting. It is difficult to define because thought is expressed in various ways. For the playwright, thought is difficult to refine: plot and character may be revised repeatedly until they finally are shaped correctly, but thought is much more elusive and less responsive to revisions.

The following paragraphs seek to define thought. Examples will follow. When appropriate, some playwriting techniques will be discussed. The playwright will understand that definitions sometimes take on the aspect of rules, but in all cases intelligent variations are possible.

Definitions and Writing Techniques

Thought is the playwright's statement about the way he or she views a personal corner of the world, expressed in dramatic form by the combined effects of the actions of the play and the character's attitudes and emotional involvements, all arranged into a structure that is artistically designed to grow to a final, climactic, and conclusive point. Thought is an intellectual quality that gives a meaning to the universe of the play.

Thought is to the play as the spinal column is to the body. Within it is the central control system that governs all aspects of the organism and makes it move as desired along destined paths. The organism would be a helpless and shapeless blob without it. It is never directly visible, but its presence may be deduced from observations of the visible behavior of the parts. *Thought is, then, the basic linkage that controls all other gears that move the play. Those movements add up to a statement of the thought.*

Thought must be complete and self-contained within the fabric of the play. There can be no set of footnotes for the audience, no "Part Two" to follow later to make the first section's meaning finally clear, and no explanatory speeches before or after the production by a playwright to ensure accurate reception of his communicative attempts. Indeed, most playwrights take pains to avoid speaking about their plays—a request to explain the play usually is met with the play-wright's response, "If I could tell you 'what it means' in a few words, then I wouldn't have needed to write my play."

To draw attention to a play's thought, the strongest method is the action of the protagonist striving for a goal. Frequently the play's thought is encapsulated within the protagonist's goal. For example, the thought of *Medea* has to do with the distinction between justice and revenge. Which is which? When justice falters, is one justified in claiming revenge? The protagonist's actions point at that thought: Medea demands justice, and when justice is not forthcoming, she will have revenge. For a second illustration, the prime thought of *Macbeth* has to do with the deadly results that accumulate as a result of greed for power. What is Macbeth's goal? It is power—and more power—at all costs.

Other methods are found to draw attention to a play's thought. In older drama the *soliloquy* and the *aside* often were road signs that helped indicate thought. The Greek drama used the chorus, a sort of idealized audience response to questions of thought as they appeared during the play. Recent forms of drama often have used *song* and *visual projections* to pinpoint aspects of a play's thought, much as the Greeks used the chorus.

Playwrights do not consider thought to be a lecture or a sermon that is more or less disguised as drama. Playwrights intend audiences to be drawn into the play, to participate sensitively in the play's actions, and to employ mental processes toward working on the questions raised by the play. Playwrights hope audiences will share a thoughtful concern with the play's intended communication.

But plays that present thought all wrapped up like a lecture will offer no challenge to the audience. Plays that are overly explicit simply expect the audience to sit passively while every part of the thought is spelled out with painful clarity. The audience has nothing to do but listen.

Playwrights seldom will permit a character to express the play's thought in so many words. In the 1930s there was in American theatre a wave of plays that came to be known as "agit-prop," or agitation-propaganda. The movement involved American intellectuals concerned that their country was failing, and agit-prop plays were designed to point out social problems and to demand immediate solutions. Popular agit-prop pieces were such strident plays as *Bury the Dead* by Irwin Shaw, a potent shout against war; and *Waiting for Lefty* by Clifford Odets, an indictment of capitalism's failure to provide fairly for labor. As one would expect, agit-prop plays were heavy-handed. After all, to awaken audiences and to convince them to take the action demanded by the play, the propaganda and agitation could not be subtle. Therefore, the play's thought would be pronounced repeatedly. Characters would step downstage to speak a message. Such plays became inartistic sermons until wise playwrights coined a slogan for their agit-prop fellow writers: "If you must write an agit-prop piece, be very sure none of the characters knows what the propaganda is." If the characters do not know the "message," they will be unable to speak it, and therefore the playwrights would be forced to return to showing instead of telling. (The guerrilla and radical theatres of the late 1960s went through the same sort of agit-prop pieces, but without heeding the advice learned thirty years earlier.)

Today's playwrights seldom let a character speak the play's thought in so many words. There is a current distaste for such blatant statements, perhaps caused partly by a rebellion against the excesses of such agit-prop pieces and perhaps also caused by a desire to let the action of the play carry the thrust of the play's thought.

Thought is a basic core of the play, an internal *cohesiveness that binds all portions into one whole. Action often will be organized around the play's thought, thereby creating artistic unity.* Thought must be an internal part of the play. If it is external, the playwright has no choice except to write speeches to express concepts directly, which is a case of telling instead of showing the play's meaning. Thought must be the core of the action, stimulating character and plot. Even didactic drama—plays expressly designed to instruct or exhort—will be based upon a basic thought that becomes the core of the play. From that core, action and characters will grow.

Thought will be unique to each new playwright regardless of the number of plays based upon that thought. The author may write about a general truth that has attracted literally hundreds of playwrights over the years, but the playwright's new view of that common premise will be unlike all views held by those past writers. Each playwright has his or her own voice, personal morality, and private dreams for humanity. The result is that each will bring a new glimpse into the truth that has been stated in the other plays. For example, countless plays have been written about young love that grows rapidly to a maturity because of outside pressures and antagonisms—*Romeo and Juliet* certainly is not the only play about young lovers who defy their elders—but each play differs from the others because each playwright will approach the concept with distinctly individualistic beliefs about people, their needs and hungers, and the morality of their actions.

Theorists and critics serve new playwrights poorly by comparing the new works' thoughts against older plays' thought content. There frequently is an implied criticism—always the older play handled the thought more effectively—which is clearly unfair. The new playwright may be so affected by such commentary that he or she will avoid writing of any thought that already has been the subject of a play. The result will be frantic searching for "originality," most often with disastrous results. Today's playwrights must feel free to write about what they believe is significant, regardless of how many past writers may have worked over the same thought. One of my playwriting students put it quite well: Plagued by critical comments that his play's thought seemed similar to work by Arthur Miller, he simply shrugged and replied, "It isn't my fault that Miller wrote *Death of a Salesman.*" That attitude is perfectly correct: The writer has not time to worry about the existence of the similar thought in others' plays. The writer must speak as his conscience and insight dictates, forgetting that others may have expressed something of the same concerns.

Thought is made interesting because of emotions. Medea cares, deeply, about the injustice done her. Macbeth's entire being is consumed by his ambition. The emotional involvement with the details of existence and the pursuit of the goal creates a fertile ground out of which thought grows. From emotion comes thought.

Universality is in the eye of the beholder; the playwright's focus is upon the specific and concrete. Students in high school and college are told repeatedly that this or that play is a great work because it is "universal." Universality comes to be one of the prime measuring devices to judge the worth of a play, or so it seems to the students. They cannot but conclude that the most successful play will be the one that can be called universal. Those who enter playwriting will, perforce, be tempted to write broadly based universal characters, plots, and thoughts.

But universality is in the eye of the beholder. The playwright must write of a very specific person, involved in quite specific actions. That specificity may lead others to view the work as being universal, but that view likely will not be expressed until the play is fifty or a hundred years old, and so the playwright is not likely to hear the comments anyway. Shakespeare did not intend his works to be "universal"—one advantage he had was a lack of knowledge of the importance of universal writing!—but instead wrote about the efforts of a specific protagonist to achieve concrete goals. The playwright is strongly urged to avoid all temptation to write the universal play.

Subject and Theme

Thought is the governing intellectual substance of the play, its inner core that permeates all other parts and qualities. Clearly, then, thought may be of so much substance that it becomes difficult to analyze. For the playwright, as well as for other theatre practitioners, thought should be subdivided into component parts to permit a more flexible method of looking at the large core of a play.

A play's thought consists of subject and theme. "Subject" refers to the play's basic topic, and "theme" is the author's attitude toward that subject as expressed in this play. Subject is expressed economically, in a word or perhaps two; theme usually is stated in a sentence or so. The subdivision of thought allows the playwright to relate it to plot and character with a greater ease.

Subject is expressed in one or two words, which means there is a danger of oversimplification. The advantages of the limitation, however, are significant: One has to strike the precise essence of the play if only a word or two is permitted, whereas often with longer statements of theme there is a certain amount of meandering.

Theme is expressed in a sentence, perhaps a phrase. The theme indicates the particular slant or point of view that the author is taking toward the subject. Clearly, a given subject may receive widely different treatments from a number of playwrights, each having a different theme or point of view. The theme may point at man's foolishness, or it may find reason to praise man's stature. It may be ironic or dignified. It can look at humanity's errors or at its strengths.

Exercises

State the subject and theme for the following plays. To the extent possible, use only one word for subject and not more than a sentence for theme.

1. *Medea* by Euripides.
   Subject:
   Theme:
2. *The Miser* by Molière.
   Subject:
   Theme:
3. *Macbeth* by Shakespeare.
   Subject:
   Theme:
4. *A Doll's House* by Ibsen.
   Subject:
   Theme:

5. *Death of a Salesman* by Miller.
   Subject:
   Theme:

6. *Our Town* by Wilder.
   Subject:
   Theme:

7. *The Time of Your Life* by Saroyan.
   Subject:
   Theme:

8. *No Exit* by Sartre.
   Subject:
   Theme:

9. *The Dumb Waiter* by Pinter.
   Subject:
   Theme:

10. *A Streetcar Named Desire* by Williams.
    Subject:
    Theme:

Playwrights may spend a creative lifetime to perfect one basic subject and theme. A careful study of the total works of a given author may result in the conclusion that the playwright is repeatedly examining one particular subject. Rather, it is as if the author is attempting to approach the subject from all directions in order to come to grips with its dimensions.

The complete work of Thornton Wilder is a case in point. His one-act and full-length plays suggest that the author was fascinated by a long-range view of mankind from origins to present, seeing always enduring qualities and strengths. In *The Skin of Our Teeth* he makes broad jumps in time from the Ice Age to the present, discovering that in mankind's history there is a remarkable dignity that results from love of family. Family provides the strength for all humanity; there could be no developments, no progress and, unfortunately, no conflicts without family. *The Long Christmas Dinner,* a one-act play, encompasses many generations, their births and deaths, to convey the thought that a family's strength comes from its traditions and ties with the past. *Pullman Car Hiawatha* has the planets speaking, increasing the scope of mankind to the universe. That scope is seen clearly in *Our Town* which in particular affirms the basic dignity and goodness of mankind.

Wilder is not the only playwright whose works appear to focus upon a consistent theme. William Saroyan's plays are hymns to the power of goodness and love. Both Wilder and Saroyan appear to share a respect for "the little people"—Wilder finding a strength in their day-to-day existence and Saroyan finding ordinary people to be extremely unusual and colorful in their intense love of each other and life. Saroyan's plays seem to work on the theme that love overpowers all evil to the point that there is a curious absence of "evil" from his plays. The bleakest character in all of his works is Blick in *The Time of Your Life,* and even this man who has to be killed is hardly a villain when compared to characters found in other writers' plays.

Arthur Miller also seems to pursue a particular subject. His plays appear to be a search for the knowledge of the distinction between good and evil. In that sense, his plays have a moralistic tenor, but of course he is too much a man of the theatre to permit the plays to become sermons. Often Miller's characters will anguish over the distinction between good and evil with such concentration that they are not able to feel other emotions until they have come to grips with the question. In *After the Fall*, which is perhaps Miller's masterpiece and definitely one of the great plays of all American theatre, the protagonist burrows through his life with a desperate need to establish at what point he has been guilty. Finally he has enough knowledge of the differences between good and evil, and then he is able to resume life. It is as if Miller's characters must search out their flaws in order to eliminate them from their future.

That playwrights become deeply involved with a given subject and theme is hardly a weakness. On the contrary, for them the long-term involvement permits greater depth and understanding of the subject area. There also is a possibility of continued growth. As the writer is finishing one play, ideas still flowing may lead to the next play that will look at the subject from yet a different viewpoint. The next play may deny some of the thrust of the present script—the theme may differ that strongly—but when all of the works of the playwright are added together the result may be a surprising depth of study about a given subject. At that time when all of the plays are studied, one is permitted to speak of the playwright's philosophy as expressed in his or her art.

Exercises

The following exercises are designed to force you to examine carefully your own beliefs. You will be asked to suggest your attitudes and concepts about the corner of the world in which you live.

Answer the questions one at a time; do not move to the next question until you have finished answering the first one.

These are *your* responses. There is no right or wrong, no good or bad.

1. Name the subject (one word) that most occupies your attention. It should be the subject about which you have large emotional reactions. It may be a subject such as God, sex, work, future, love, or hypocrisy; any other subject may be chosen from a large list of possibilities. Perhaps you will be able to answer this relatively quickly, or perhaps you may need to stop here for several days to be sure of your answer. *The goal is for you to name the one subject most important to you.*

2. Now state your attitude about the subject. Your statement here will be a sentence in length. The statement expresses your point of view toward the subject; it should indicate a *strength* of feeling. Rework the sentence repeatedly until it perfectly expresses your point of view. Again, this may be accomplished quickly or it may take a long time. Do not rush yourself; this must be a precise and accurate reflection of your view.

3. Your subject and theme undoubtedly are broadly based abstractions. Now move them to specifics. For example, suppose your subject is peace. The theme you have decided on may be something like this: "There can be no peace until there is justice, and justice cannot exist if the damned hypocrites are in power." Move that statement to a concrete: "A neighborhood grows tense and explosive because the company that owns the buildings refuses to listen to tenants' complaints while at the same time it pretends to be a public-service–minded institution." Perhaps you are working on the idea of a church owning slums.

4. Create a protagonist who *cares*, deeply and single-mindedly, about the issue. In the example used in Exercise 3, perhaps she or he will be a lawyer, or a resident who can pull neighbors along, or a member of the church? Give your protagonist a name, a background with social-environmental details, and an age. Then state the protagonist's goal in the play. What obstacles are in the way of that goal? What are the protagonist's plans?

At the risk of oversimplification, you now are in the final stages of preparation. You are ready to begin outlining a play. This process of selection has led, almost automatically, to a play. Many interesting decisions are ahead of you. Will your play be a comedy or drama? Will you name the antagonist or will you be more general? Does the protagonist have allies or is this a solitary battle? Does the protagonist find a fighting friend? Who represents the forces against the protagonist? How can you outline the play to bring the conflicts on stage? Will the play be episodic, with changes of time and place, or will you outline the play to reduce the number of scenes? Will the protagonist win, lose, or face a draw? Will he or she find unwanted allies? Is this to be a play with an angry tone? Is it to be a satire? *To all of these and other questions the answers come from theme.*

5. Make a rough outline of a story from your particular statements of subject, theme, and protagonist. The outline should be two pages long, perhaps more. It will be a step-by-step development of the action—a scenario, in short. *Be sure it reflects your theme in all ways.*

Chapter Twenty

Diction

Introduction: Clear and Distinctive

Diction, the fourth of the six elements of drama, is the playwright's most important tool for communication of the three other elements—plot, character, and thought. Diction refers to the play's words, spoken or sung, expressed in dialogue or monologue. The playwright may elect to use "elevated" diction, which refers to the heightened sensibility of poetic drama; or the writer may decide the play demands "realistic" diction, which is carefully selected everyday usage. In some cases, playwrights mix the two, creating thereby a contrast that gives each style more emphasis.

Good diction, to paraphrase Aristotle, must balance the two extremes. Diction must be clear and distinctive; clarity, he explains, is achieved by use of familiar ordinary words, and distinctive diction is a product of unfamiliar terms, metaphors, and unusual references. An excess of either the ordinary or the unusual is not desired: Too much of the ordinary will make the play dull, and too much of the unusual will be equally disastrous.

"Clarity," or familiar and ordinary words, does not mean that diction must be mundane, banal, or crude. Nor does "distinctive" suggest there should be a search for the unusual and unknown. Some examples can be cited to demonstrate the "clear and distinctive" concept. Here is a passage taken from the concluding moments of William Shakespeare's *King Lear*. You will recall that Lear is holding his dead daughter, Cordelia, to whom he refers in his speech.

LEAR

And my poor fool is hanged. No, no, no life?
Why should a dog, a horse, a rat, have life,
And thou no breath at all? Thou'lt come no more,
Never, never, never, never, never.
Pray you, undo this button. Thank you sir.
Do you see this? Look on her, look her lips—
Look there, look there——

(He dies.)

EDGAR

He faints, My lord, my lord!

KENT

Break heart, I prithee break.

EDGAR

Look up, my lord.

KENT

Vex not his ghost. O let him pass. He hates him,
That would upon the rack of this tough world
Stretch him out longer.

EDGAR

He is gone, indeed.

KENT

The wonder is, he hath endured so long:
He but usurped his life.

"Pray you, undo this button" is one of theatre's most heart-rending speeches. "O let him pass," a cry of anguish from Lear's warmly loyal Kent, raises the tragedy to yet a higher level. The straightforward cleanliness of the diction here makes the scene extremely powerful.

The passage should be examined to see if it is "clear and distinctive," which is Aristotle's definition of "good" diction. The words are simple and ordinary. Indeed, some words are strangely common—dog, horse, rat, and this tough world—for a scene of such poetic intensity. The passage also is distinctive in Aristotle's sense. For example, the last two of Kent's three speeches are something other than normal speech. One does not usually think of "usurping" life, and the plea to let Lear die in peace—"O let him pass"—also is unusual in the reference to the world as a rack which already has punished the old king. Finally, there is Lear's speech. It is clear—quite rich in common words—but it is distinctive, too, because of the repetitions and the effect of the common words at such an uncommon moment.

Diction must perform more tasks than any other single portion of the play, and it must do its job with a quiet efficiency. If diction calls attention to itself, it is pulling attention from thought, character, or plot, thereby damaging the play. Diction must convey information, delineate character, differentiate between the various characters, show each major character's changes in mood and emotion, advance the play's action, control rhythm and tempo, always be clear and communicative to the audience that will hear the words only once, maintain its own aesthetic "rightness," and be written so it can fall comfortably from the performer's lips. Two rules already have been established about diction:

1. Diction must be clear.
2. Diction must be distinctive.

Let us now look at the idea of diction maintaining its own aesthetic "rightness." Diction may be poetic or "realistic."

Poetic Diction

Poetic diction lifts the soul. It rings with bell-like beats and is a music garnered from the universe. The playwrights who have found a way to harness its power have contributed much to the theatre—authors such as Shakespeare, Federico Garcia-Lorca, Maxwell Anderson, Christopher Fry, Archibald MacLeish, and T. S. Eliot. These writers and others have written a number of poetic plays that you can study in order to come to conclusions about the nature of poetic drama. The most significant qualities of theatrical poetry can be stated rather easily:

> *Poetic diction is not merely a matter of word choice, although surely the selection of words is highly important, but instead is more a matter of content. Poetry is used when prose simply is not able to express the intensity and insight that the dramatist brings to bear upon the play's subject. A prose topic, conceived in prose terms, cannot be changed into an elevated poetic drama simply by making the words fancy and pretty, with attention to rhythm and sound. The characters in the play must be capable of speaking in elevated diction, they must be comfortable with the language, and they must Need to speak in poetic terms. Elevated diction will elevate the characters.*

It is interesting that most poetic dramas are "romantic," which is a term that refers to plays that deal with upperclass characters living in distant lands in past times. Even Shakespeare set most of his plays away from his own time and country, as did many of the playwrights of poetic drama cited above. Why would poetic plays require a setting away from the present? Why would poetic dramas be "romantic"?

The answer to these questions further explains the nature of poetic drama. The playwright planning a poetic play will avoid writing of contemporary people because it is difficult to find characters today who speak in elevated diction. One expects the poetic protagonist to be a powerful person in his or her society, a leader, but imagine hearing poetic diction from any of our recent Presidents. The President who showed reporters his belly scar, or the President who was mocked for his smile, or the President who left the office in disgrace: Would any

of them need to speak in poetic diction like King Lear? The kindness of the
passage of time is necessary to make it believable.

There have been exceptions to this generalization. It *is* possible to write
poetic drama that deals with its own time and has less-than-upper-class characters who can express themselves in poetic diction. Maxwell Anderson's poetic
drama *Winterset* deals with contemporary subjects and characters. There are
references to the Sacco-Vanzetti case, and in the play are crude gangsters. It is
hardly romanticism. The play's first speech belongs to one of the gangsters,
Trock. Compare his view of the world—the ugliness of a city—with the pastoral
themes so often found in poetic works. Trock looks at the city, early in a
December morning's cold light:

TROCK

You roost of punks and gulls! Sleep, sleep it off,
whatever you had last night, get down in warm,
one big ham-fat against another—sleep,
cling, sleep and rot! Rot out your pasty guts
with diddling, you had no brain to begin. If you had
there'd be no need for us to sleep on iron
who had too much brains for you.

Another character is Garth, a young man who was involved in a murder.
His father is Esdras, an old rabbi. Garth faces the guilt he carries within and
says, "I'm alone in this." His father replies:

ESDRAS

Yes, if you hold with the world that only
those who die suddenly should be revenged.
But those whose hearts are cancered, drop by drop
in small ways, little by little, till they've borne
all they can bear, and die—these deaths will go
unpunished now as always. When we're young
we have faith in what is seen, but when we're old
we know that what is seen is traced in air
and built on water. There's no guilt under heaven,
just as there's no heaven, till men believe it—
no earth, till men have seen it, and have a word
to say this is the earth.

Garth insists he is guilty. His father tries to make him live quietly with
that fact:

ESDRAS

This thing that men call justice,
this blind snake that strikes men down in the dark,
mindless with fury, keep your hand back from it,
let it be forgotten, forgotten!—

Winterset is one of the few plays that manages to be both poetic and contemporary. Anderson, it should be pointed out, wrote a number of other poetic plays that were romantic, not contemporary, such as *Elizabeth the Queen* and *Mary of Scotland.*

It is interesting to compare the effects of poetry and music in theatre. Music is necessary for the story when mere words no longer suffice: Music elevates the emotions and makes the characters larger than life. For example, Eliza's frustrations and angers grow so large that they cannot be stated in mere words and demand outlet in the song, "Just You Wait," one of the many moments of *My Fair Lady* when song elevates the special qualities of the characters. "If You Could See Her (The Gorilla Song)" brings the shock of the plight of Jews in Nazi Germany to life in *Cabaret* with an impact that mere words could not.

Poetry, like music, also sweeps emotions across the sky. The following passage shows the marvels that poetry brings to an ordinary love scene. This is the famous balcony scene of Edmond Rostand's poetic masterpiece, *Cyrano de Bergerac.* You recall that Cyrano is a disfigured man who desperately loves Roxane who loves (or thinks she loves) Christian, a handsome young cadet in the guards. It is evening. Roxane is above, on the balcony, and Christian is below, stumbling about for words which will win Roxane. Cyrano is hidden in the shadows, feeding Christian words. Finally he pushes Christian aside and speaks to Roxane himself.

CYRANO

It is a crime to fence with life—I tell you,
There comes one moment, once—and God help those
Who pass that moment by!—when Beauty stands
Looking into the soul with grave, sweet eyes
That sicken at pretty words!

ROXANE

If that be true—
And when that moment comes to you and me—
What words will you?

CYRANO

All those, all those, all those
That blossom in my heart, I'll fling to you—
Armfuls of loose bloom! Love, I love beyond
Breath, beyond reason, beyond love's own power
Of loving! Your name is like a golden bell
Hung in my heart; and when I think of you
I tremble, and the bell swings and rings—"Roxane!"—
"Roxane!"—along my veins, "Roxane!"—I know
All small forgotten things that once meant You—
I remember last year, the first of May,
A little before noon, you had your hair
Drawn low, that one time only. Is that strange?

You know how, after looking at the sun,
One sees red suns everywhere—so, for hours
After the flood of sunshine that you are,
My eyes are blinded by your burning hair!
                         ROXANE

   (Very low.)
Yes—that is—Love—
                         CYRANO
Yes, that is Love—that wind
Of terrible and jealous beauty, blowing
Over me—that dark fire, that music—
Love seeketh not his own!
. . . . I never
Look at you, but there's some new virtue born
In me, some new courage. Do you begin
To understand, a little? Can you feel
My soul, there in the darkness, breathe on you?
. . . .

                         ROXANE
Yes, I do tremble—and I weep—
And I love you—and I am yours—and you have made me thus!
                         CYRANO
   (After a pause; quietly.)
What is death like, I wonder?
I know everything else now. . . .

   With rare exceptions, poetry is markedly absent from today's stage. The advent of "realism" and its dependency upon the five senses limits the poetic imagination: Realism writes of people who might live next door, concerned about the small daily events that plague us all. Poetic diction is not necessary for dialogues about sour milk, fried bread, or how to use newspaper to clean the windshield. Poetry enlarges characters—Cyrano, for example, marches off to do battle with one hundred armed men—but characters concerned about fried bread for breakfast cannot be enlarged with poetic power. Hamlet's concern about death—"To be or not to be"—has a size from poetic treatment, quite different from Willy Loman's search for a way to kill himself. The playwright today with the correct eye and ear may be able to tap this rich resource for the theatre.

"Realistic" Diction

Realism began just before the turn of the century as a product of the Industrial Revolution, which did not honor humanity; as a product of studies of the subconscious by the new science of psychology, which suggested man was not in conscious control over his acts; and as a rebellion against the romantic movement, which had grown to excessive proportions with plays about characters of such nobility that they seemed of a different world. Realism aims at truth: It is a lifelike, selective portrayal of the objective world that can be known through the five senses. Realism generally is of its own time and place (in contrast to romanticism which is set in different lands and a past time). Realism almost always is about people who might well live next door. Their diction is reproduced. Hence, it is "realistic" diction.

But realism is no mere tape recording of the way people actually speak. Realism is *selective*. It *represents* contemporary speech. The playwright edits, rearranges, and condenses—in short, the playwright exercises artistic control over the realistic diction. It will sound like contemporary idioms. It will not be a mere stenographic reproduction.

A strong example of the *effect* of colloquial speech is found in *Marty*, a television play (later a movie) by Paddy Chayefsky who was, with Reginald Rose and Rod Serling, responsible for the exciting promises television had in the 1950s. Marty is a short, stout man, balding, thirty-six, and disgusted about being "a fat, ugly little man." He lives with his mother. He is alone, afraid of remaining alone, unable to overcome his own shyness and disgust about himself, and unable to find a girl. (Please remember, this is in a decade of the dating ethic.)

The scene is a neighborhood bar in New York. Marty enters, sits across the table from his friend Angie—"a little wasp of a fellow"—who is reading the sports pages. Marty takes a page. Angie does not look up. You may help bring Marty to life if you think of him as portrayed by Ernest Borgnine who, in fact, played Marty in the movie version:

ANGIE

Well, what do you feel like doing tonight?

MARTY

I don't know, Angie. What do you feel like doing?

ANGIE

Well, we oughtta do something. It's Saturday night. I don't wanna go bowling like last Saturday. How about calling up that big girl we picked up inna movies about a month ago in the RKO Chester?

MARTY

(Not very interested.)

Which one was that?

ANGIE

That big girl that was sitting in front of us with the skinny friend.

MARTY

Oh, yeah.

ANGIE

We took them home alla way out in Brooklyn. Her name was
Mary Feeney. What do you say? You think I oughtta give her a
ring? I'll take the skinny one.

MARTY

It's five o'clock already, Angie. She's probably got a date by
now.

ANGIE

Well, let's call her up. What can we lose?

MARTY

I didn't like her, Angie. I don't feel like calling her up.

ANGIE

Well, what do you feel like doing tonight?

MARTY

I don't know. What do you feel like doing?

ANGIE

Well, we're back to that, huh? I say to you: "What do you feel
like doing tonight?" And you say to me: "I don't know, what do
you feel like doing?" And then we wind up sitting around your
house with a couple of cans of beer, watching Sid Caesar on
television. Well, I tell you what I feel like doing. I feel like calling
up this Mary Feeney. She likes you.

(MARTY looks up quickly at this.)

MARTY

What makes you say that?

ANGIE

I could see she likes you.

MARTY

Yeah, sure.

ANGIE

(Half rising in his seat.)

I'll call her up.

MARTY

You call her up for yourself, Angie. I don't feel like calling her
up.

(ANGIE sits down again. They both return to reading
the paper for a moment. Then ANGIE looks up again.)

ANGIE

Boy, you're getting to be a real drag, you know that?

MARTY

Angie, I'm thirty-six years old. I been looking for a girl every
Saturday night of my life. I'm a little, short, fat fellow, and girls
don't go for me, that's all. I'm not like you. I mean, you joke
around, and they laugh at you, and you get along fine. I just stand
around like a bug. What's the sense of kidding myself? Everybody's
always telling me to get married. Get married. Get married. Don't
you think I wanna get married? I wanna get married. They drive

me crazy. Now, I don't wanna wreck your Saturday night for you, Angie. You wanna go somewhere, you go ahead. I don't wanna go.

ANGIE

Boy, they drive me crazy too. My old lady, every word outta her mouth, when you gonna get married?

MARTY

My mother, boy, she drives me crazy.

(ANGIE leans back in his seat, scowls at the paper-napkin container. MARTY returns to the sports page. For a moment a silence hangs between them. Then . . .)

ANGIE

So what do you feel like doing tonight?

MARTY

(Without looking up.)

I don't know. What do you feel like doing?

(They both just sit, ANGIE frowning at the napkin container, MARTY at the sports page.)

The scene ends. To the untrained observer, Chayefsky merely tape-recorded ordinary discussions. But the scene is carefully structured. It has its own beginning, middle, and end. Chayefsky controls the scene's pace: It opens slowly, both men looking at the newspaper more than at each other, with pauses and gaps. The scene builds to its climax, and Marty's longish speech gives the whole a meaning. From its climax it drops, and the repetition of "what do you want to do" shows the hopelessness they feel. It is a fine example of a beat.

We must never suggest that realism is an examination of the mundane daily events. On the contrary, there can be moments of lightning flashes when the playwright brilliantly illuminates the whole of his theme. Thornton Wilder ends Act One of *Our Town* with the well-known story that Rebecca tells about the letter the minister sent to Jane Crofut; the address includes her name and address, the state, the country, the hemisphere, then the universe, and finally "the Mind of God."

"The Mind of God" shows how realistic diction can extend communication. The imagery fits the stage well, and also it contributes a great deal to Wilder's subject and theme. Note, too, that when small stories are told, they will be constructed with the same detail one expects to see in the script itself: Each story must have its own beginning, middle, and end. Chayefsky ends the story with a twist back to itself: "What do you feel like doing?" Wilder ends his famous envelope's address with a strong conclusion: Says Rebecca, "And the postman brought it just the same." The end has a conclusive effect, rather like slamming shut a book to say, "That's it, there is no more." There can be no doubt that the story is quite completed.

The novelist is not dependent upon dialogue and therefore often makes little attempt to capture the image of conversation. Playwrights are totally dependent upon dialogue and for that reason "realistic conversation" is extremely important. Rules of grammer often will be ignored, and certainly complete sentences are not necessary and often are replaced by phrases—in life people seldom speak in neatly constructed sentences. Characters will interrupt, or perhaps they will pause without interruption. Characters may respond to sentences spoken earlier, or perhaps they seem to hear something not said.

Edward Albee's *Who's Afraid of Virginia Woolf?* brilliantly recaptures the image of conversation. Albee conceived of literate and intelligent characters, and the diction captures those qualities. They also are drunk, or close to it. Martha and George are married and the hosts; Nick and Honey, also married, are the guests and new to the college. Martha and George have been at the college for years; she is fifty-two and he is forty-six. Nick, who is thirty, and Honey, who is twenty-six, have not been in their hosts' home before. The characters are being playful but there are sharp underlying notes of cruelty. The following is taken from Act One:

MARTHA

(Proudly.)

I know better. I been to college like everybody else.

GEORGE

Martha been to college. Martha been to a convent when she were a little twit of a thing, too.

MARTHA

And I was an atheist.

(Uncertainly.)

I still am.

GEORGE

Not an atheist, Martha . . . a pagan.

(To Honey and Nick.)

Martha is the only true pagan on the eastern seaboard.

(MARTHA laughs.)

HONEY

Oh, that's nice. Isn't that nice, dear?

NICK

(Humoring her.)

Yes . . . wonderful.

GEORGE

And Martha paints blue circles around her things.

NICK

You do?

MARTHA

(Defensively, for the joke's sake.)

Sometimes.

(Beckoning.)

You wanna see?

GEORGE

(Admonishing.)

Tut, tut, tut.

MARTHA

Tut, tut yourself . . . you old floozie!

HONEY

He's not a floozie . . . he can't be a floozie . . . you're a floozie.

(Giggles.)

MARTHA

(Shaking a finger at Honey.)

Now you watch yourself!

HONEY

(Cheerfully.)

All right. I'd like a nipper of brandy, please.

NICK

Honey, I think you've had enough, now. . . .

GEORGE

Nonsense! Everybody's ready, I think.

(Takes glasses, etc.)

HONEY

(Echoing George.)

Nonsense.

NICK

(Shrugging.)

Okay.

Albee's dialogue crackles with electricity. The speeches are intricately intertwined and are constructed with stimulus-response cycles. Albee gives his characters a sharp life with dialogue. Honey, for example, is clearly the intellectual lightweight here, and the accumulative effect of alcohol is showing. Albee is preparing her for a scene in which she will have to run from the room. Of the others, George and Martha are made strong, almost performers for Nick and Honey. The scene demonstrates artistic reproduction of real-life dialogue: It would be foolish to write as "people really are" in early-morning-drinking sprees, so Albee interprets and selects such activities to give the *effect* of that dialogue. Theatre is not life but is instead an imitation of life.

Albee's script contains many instructions to the performers (that is, the line is to be read "happily" or "half-heartedly" or "proudly"). Purists might object, claiming that it is the playwright's responsibility to write a line that *is* happy or half-hearted, rather than instruct the performer how to read the line. But to do that requires changing the flavor of the diction or increasing the length of the speech. Far better is Albee's technique of letting the director and performer know what the playwright heard in his mind while writing the dialogue.

Albee is especially talented with word choice, as evidenced by "blew up and went down" here in this brief exchange between Nick and George while Honey and Martha are offstage:

GEORGE

Drink?

NICK

Sure.

>   (With no emotion, except the faintest distaste, as George
>   takes his glass to the bar.)

I married her because she was pregnant.

GEORGE

>   (Pause.)

Oh?

>   (Pause.)

But you said you didn't have any children . . . When I asked you, you said. . . .

NICK

She wasn't . . . really. It was a hysterical pregnancy. She blew up and then she went down.

GEORGE

And while she was up, you married her.

NICK

And then she went down.

Less-talented playwrights would have made the disclosure blunt, less colorful. "I thought Honey was pregnant and I had to marry her." "She told me she was pregnant—she *looked* pregnant—and so . . . we got married. But she wasn't, after all." Albee's word choice, which so well fits the characters, gives a crispness to his play's diction.

Repetition

Accidental repetition accumulates upon itself; the writer lets one slip past and then there are ten. The result is a deadly slowness, and the author usually senses that something has gone wrong but cannot find the cause:

JOHN

Would you mind telling me what you want?

SALLY

What I want?

JOHN

Please. What do you want?

SALLY

I'd think you'd be able to guess what I want.

JOHN

How can I guess? I can't think of a reason.

SALLY

Think harder.

JOHN

I can't guess. Tell me what you want!

SALLY

What I want?

JOHN

Please! What is it you want?

Plays filled with that sort of repetition give one the suspicion the writer expects to be paid by the word. In a few specialized instances, however, deliberate use of repetition can be quite effective. The following is taken from Ionesco's *The Bald Soprano* (translated by Donald M. Allen). Mr. and Mrs. Martin enter, sit, and begin speaking "in voices that are drawling, monotonous, a little singsong, without nuances":

MR. MARTIN

Excuse me, madam, but it seems to me, unless I'm mistaken, that I've met you somewhere before.

MRS. MARTIN

I, too, sir. It seems to me that I've met you somewhere before.

MR. MARTIN

Was it, by any chance, at Manchester that I caught a glimpse of you, madam?

MRS. MARTIN

That is very possible. I am originally from the city of Manchester. But I do not have a good memory, sir. I cannot say whether it was there that I caught a glimpse of you or not!

MR. MARTIN

Good God. that's curious! I, too, am originally from the city of Manchester, madam.

MRS. MARTIN

That is curious!

MR. MARTIN

Isn't that curious! Only, I madam, I left the city of Manchester about five weeks ago.

MRS. MARTIN

That is curious. What a bizarre coincidence! I, too, sir, I left the city of Manchester about five weeks ago.

They continue, discovering that they were in the same coach and the same seat, and that they live in the same house:

MR. MARTIN

I have a little girl, my little daughter, she lives there with me, dear lady. She is two years old, she's blonde, she has a white eye and a red eye, she is very pretty, her name is Alice, dear lady.

MRS. MARTIN

What a bizarre coincidence! I, too, have a little girl. She is two years old, has a white eye and a red eye, she is very pretty, and her name is Alice, too, dear sir.

They discover they are man and wife ("Elizabeth, I have found you again!") and they fall asleep. The repetition is planned, not accidental, and it achieves the playwright's purposes. Life is full of banalities. We also note that the Martins have no individuality; the speeches could be reversed. This, too, is Ionesco's intent. Finally, the complete sentences become soporific. Certainly, they are slow in comparison to the electrically charged lines in *Who's Afraid of Virginia Woolf?* Again, however, that slowness is by design: Ionesco intends a parody in *The Bald Soprano*, and he does not intend the characters to be "like life."

How Long Should a Speech Be?

A play consisting of long speeches will seem wordy and ponderous—a turtle on a philosophical stroll. A play of very short speeches will be choppy and nervous—a butterfly unable to hold itself to a single thought. Both extremes are dangerous to the play's health, but the long speeches are most likely to run the play's batteries down to the point where there is no spark.

"*What is a short speech?*" "*What makes a speech too long?*" The questions are valid. I suggest the following three answers will help the playwright understand the difference between short and long speeches.

An easy first answer is to suggest that the beginning playwright restrict each speech to two or three sentences, preferably less, for the larger part of the play. The writer will remember that dialogue usually consists of phrases, not complete sentences, and that also will help shorten each speech.

Harold Pinter is the master of the economical speech. The following is taken from the opening moments of *The Dumb Waiter*. Ben is reading a newspaper and finds a passage he describes to Gus:

BEN

(He refers to the paper.)

A man of eighty-seven wanted to cross the road. But there was a lot of traffic, see? He couldn't see how he was going to squeeze through. So he crawled under a lorry.

GUS

He what?

BEN

He crawled under a lorry. A stationary lorry.

GUS

No?

BEN

The lorry started and ran over him.

GUS

Go on!

BEN

That's what it says here.

GUS

Get away.

BEN

It's enough to make you want to puke, isn't it?

GUS

Who advised him to do a thing like that?

BEN

A man of eighty-seven crawling under a lorry!

GUS

It's unbelievable.

BEN

It's down here in black and white.

GUS

Incredible.

Silence.

Pinter's dialogue is efficient, clean, precise. The short speeches give the play a forward motion. For the beginning playwright, then, one possible guideline for dialogue is to be sure speeches are limited to two or three sentences, and preferably to only a few phrases.

But assigning a maximum number of sentences or words can be an artificial limitation. Therefore, we turn to a second definition of long speeches versus short speeches. According to some experts, the writer should be sure that a speech contains no more than one idea. As soon as the character wants to change to a second idea, it is time to stop the speech; the second idea will be expressed in a following speech.

When a speech does contain more than one idea, the playwright will be forced to use rather awkward phrases to link them together: "But to change the subject. . . ."; or "However, I don't want to talk about that. . . ."

Yet a third approach for the playwright to consider regarding long and short speeches has to do with the other characters on stage. While character A is speaking, the playwright tilts an ear to the others and listens carefully to hear if any of them has an interruption, a disagreement, a question, an agreement—any response. In a real sense, a playwright must *listen* to the characters. *A speech is too long when it stops another character from speaking.*

It seems to me that there is a major disadvantage of the long speech: The playwright is paying attention to the speaker, working to bring that character to life during the long speech, but all of the other characters on stage will be fading away. Without dialogue, the others die. In these instances the long speeches are injurious to the play.

I do not wish to overstate the case for the short speech. The matter of long speeches versus short speeches may be clarified if the playwright thinks of the long speech as the *exceptional* moment. For example, most of the dialogue in Albee's *Zoo Story* is constructed of short speeches between Peter and Jerry. However, the long speech of "Jerry and the Dog" is a special moment. The length is necessary both for the play's structure and the character's development: It becomes the climax of the play, and for the character it is the final and eager attempt to communicate. Had Albee used long speeches throughout *Zoo Story*, the "Jerry and the Dog" speech would have been merely commonplace. It would have lost impact. The play would have had less of a climactic explosion.

The same structure is found in *Dutchman* by LeRoi Jones: There are primarily short speeches until the play's climax, which is a long speech. For the larger part of the play, Lula and Clay have quick lines. The climax of *Dutchman* gives Clay a long speech of perhaps eight-hundred words with no interruptions. As with *Zoo Story*, had *Dutchman* been written with many long speeches throughout, the ending would have just been long. But because it follows the short speeches, the long monologue is effective.

A play should not be just a series of short phrases tossed back and forth; that can become dull. Nor should a play consist of long passages; that can be dull, too, and perhaps worse. The playwright will carefully mix the ingredients as necessary. Tennessee Williams shows such care in *The Glass Menagerie*, Scene Three:

TOM

What in Christ's name am I—

AMANDA

(Shrilly.)
Don't you use that—

TOM

Supposed to do!

AMANDA

Expression! Not in my—

TOM

Ohhh!

AMANDA

Presence! Have you gone out of your senses?

TOM

I have, that's true, *driven* out?

AMANDA

What is the matter with you, you—big—big—IDIOT!

TOM

Look!—I've got *no thing*, no single thing—

AMANDA

Lower your voice!

TOM

In my life here that I can call my OWN! Everything is—

AMANDA

Stop that shouting!

A few moments later, as the scene is ending, Williams gives Tom a marvelously constructed speech. Amanda asks Tom where he's going.

TOM

I'm going to the *movies!*

AMANDA

I don't believe that lie!

TOM

(Crouching toward her, overtowering her tiny figure. She backs away, gasping.)

I'm going to opium dens! Yes, opium dens, dens of vice and criminals' hang-outs, Mother. I've joined the Hogan gang, I'm a hired assassin, I carry a tommy-gun in a violin case! I run a string of cat-houses in the Valley! They call me Killer, Killer Wingfield, I'm leading a double-life: a simple, honest warehouse worker by day, by night a dynamic *czar* of the *underworld, Mother.* I go to gambling casinos, I spin away fortunes on the roulette table! I wear a patch over one eye and a false mustache; sometimes they call me—*El Diablo!* Oh, I could tell you things to make you sleepless! My enemies plan to dynamite this place. They're going to blow us all sky-high some night! I'll be glad, very happy, and so will you! You'll go up, up on a broomstick, over Blue Mountain with seventeen gentlemen callers! You ugly—babbling old—*witch.* . . .

Tom struggles to put on his overcoat but his haste makes him get wrapped up in the sleeves. He tears it off and throws it across the room. It strikes against Laura's glass collection. There is the sound of shattering glass. Laura is wounded.

LAURA

(Shrilly.)

My *glass!*—menagerie. . . .

> She covers her face and turns away. But AMANDA is still stunned and stupefied by the "ugly witch" so that she barely notices this occurrence. Now she recovers her voice.

AMANDA

(In an awful voice.)

I won't speak to you—until you apologize!

Tom drops on his knees to pick up the broken glass, while Laura clings to the mantel. And the scene ends.

The effectiveness of that scene's diction stems from the short speeches that begin the sequence, followed by Tom's fantasy—a speech constructed of building images—and then the silence of broken glass. Neither all short speeches nor all long speeches would have been as potent. Williams orchestrates the scene neatly.

In summation, the playwright must consciously decide whether long speeches or short ones will best suit the play's needs. The following guidelines are significant:

1. No play should consist totally of short or long speeches. The lack of variety would be deadly.

2. Short speeches increase the play's pace.

3. Long speeches are more effective when used just for special moments.

4. A speech is too long if it contains more than one significant idea; if it stops other characters from responding; if it presents stimuli to other characters but does not let them react; or if it changes the character's outlook from one attitude to another.

5. The playwright uses long and short speeches carefully, intending more of the latter and saving the former for special moments. The playwright seeks to orchestrate effects.

6. When long speeches are used, the author will be sure they are carefully structured with attention to tempo and a sense of building.

One final word of caution is appropriate. There is here a focus upon the question of long and short speeches because producers and directors will glance through a script by an unknown and if the pages are filled with long speeches they are likely to put it aside unread. It is true that Shaw, O'Neill, and Wilson have written plays that are characterized by longish speeches and that have been staged well, but a new writer must establish credibility. Many long speeches throughout the play tend to stop the reader from tackling the new script.

Naming Names: The "Rule of Three"

Professional playwrights often refer to a "rule of three." If the writer wishes to be quite sure that the audience receives a certain piece of information, the writer will see that it is mentioned at least three times. The logic here has it that a detail might be missed the first or second time that it is mentioned—a sneeze or a cough or momentary distraction might obscure the detail—but three times is safe.

Of the details to communicate, the most important are the characters' names. If the audience cannot grasp the identifications, the characters will seem pale. Almost equally important is the significant quality of each character—the employment or relationship—that nails each character to place.

Ibsen's identification technique in *Ghosts* is quite effective. Notice how easily the playwright identifies the characters. The following is taken from the first act. Engstrand and Regine have been talking briefly. This is the Eva Le-Gallienne translation:

REGINE

You must be out of your head—you fool! Go on now—get out this minute. No—not that way—here comes Pastor Manders; the back stairs for you!

ENGSTRAND

(Goes toward door right.)

All right—I'll go. But listen—you have a talk with him—he'll tell you what you owe your father—for I am your father after all, you know; I can prove that by the Church Register.

(Engstrand exits; in a moment Manders enters:)

MANDERS

Good-day, Miss Engstrand.

REGINE

(Turning in glad surprise.)

Well! Good-day, Pastor Manders! Fancy! So the steamer's in, is it?

MANDERS

(He comes into the room.)

Yes—just docked. Dreadful weather we've had these last few days

REGINE

(Following him.)

It's a blessing for the farmers, Pastor Manders.

MANDERS

Quite right, Miss Engstrand! We city-folk never think of that.

Just before this exchange the "rule of three" already established the relationship of Engstrand and Regine, and their names. Here Ibsen uses the "rule of three" to identify names—"Miss Engstrand" twice so far and "Pastor Manders" three times—and relationships.

Specific details, not concepts or thematic materials, are dealt with in this so-called rule of three. Ibsen in the above scene works on names quickly. Other writers may space the three identifications further apart. Certainly Ibsen does: Manders, above, changes his mind easily. It is a small matter here. But he will continue shifting back and forth as the play progresses. In that sense, the rule of three also establishes character: One shift is not significant, but repeated changes take on added meaning.

The Speech: Beginning, Middle, and End

A given speech can be viewed in three parts: its beginning, its middle, and its end. Assuming that the speech is of sufficient length for those three parts to exist, we can identify which piece is likely to have the most impact and which will have the least. Armed with that knowledge, the playwright can then construct speeches to take advantage of the soft spot or the strength.

Generally the middle of the speech is apt to be soft, although there can be exceptions caused by word choice, special actors' instructions (underlinings and exclamation points), and other devices. The beginning will be stronger, and the ending will be strongest. For example, in *The Glass Menagerie* Laura explains she went to the park, even in winter's cold, rather than return to the upstairs business college:

LAURA
It was the lesser of two evils, Mother. I couldn't go back up.
I—threw up—on the floor!

The middle of the speech does not have the impact that is carried by the end. The speech would have been less effective if Williams had written:

I threw up on the floor! I couldn't go back up, Mother. It was
the lesser of two evils.

Constructed that way it is all downhill. Speeches should *build*. Even one word out of place can prevent the build:

It was the lesser of two evils. I couldn't go back up. I threw up
on the floor, Mother!

Because the beginning of the speech has "second place" in impact, it would be a waste to expend that strength in meaningless sounds. For example, how weak the beginning would be if Williams had written:

Oh, well. I mean, it was the lesser of two evils, Mother. I
couldn't go back up. I—threw up—on the floor! You know?

Beginning playwrights in particular must be warned away from these sounds: Oh; Gee; Jeez, man; I dunno; You know what I mean? They may have a place in a play that contains a character who must speak that way, but even so the playwright cannot expend the strength of the line upon such hollow noises. The writer should vigorously eliminate all worthless words, beginning with those so often found floating aimlessly at the beginning of speeches.

The middle of the speech provides a convenient place to "hide" exposition. It glares out less when in the middle than when in the end. For example, Eugene O'Neill has Rocky describe the expected visit of Theodore Hickman (Hicky) and his past visits in *The Iceman Cometh:*

ROCKY

Yeah, some kidder! Remember how he woiks up dat gag about his wife, when he's cockeyed, cryin' over her picture and den springin' it on yuh all of a sudden dat he left her in de hay wid de iceman?

(He laughs.)

I wonder what's happened to him. Yuh could set your watch by his periodicals before dis. Always got here a coupla days before Harry's birthday party, and now he's on'y got till tonight to make it. I hope he shows soon. Dis dump is like de morgue wid all dese bums passed out.

By crafting the exposition into the middle of the speech, O'Neill makes it sound acceptable. The end of the speech shifts from the exposition of the past into the present of the bar.

The ending of a speech should carry strength. It becomes awkward when it contains a phrase of only several words. The short phrase, tacked on like a caboose, defeats the otherwise strong ending. Read the following out loud and compare the first versus the second example:

That's right, isn't it?
against
Isn't that right?

Now shut up, will you?
against
Will you shut up?

Anyway, that's my paper, of course.
against
Of course that's my paper.

The playwright will seek to write the last words in such a way that the performer will automatically emphasize the final word or two. For instance, "That paper is mine" almost demands that the actor read it as, "That paper is *mine.*" In contrast, "Anyway, that's my paper, of course" likely will be read as, "Anyway, that's *my* paper, of course," and the last three words will drift away, weakening the effect of the line and speech.

Poetry in Prose

The playwright must not let his or her mind believe that prose demands dull diction. Even in prose, diction can create magical and uplifting moments in the theatre. No contemporary playwright illustrates the strength of poetic prose more than Tennessee Williams. He has an uncanny ability to lift the play with a moment of pure poetry, in the midst of commonalities. A good way to end this chapter on diction is with some of the powerful speeches Mr. Williams has given the theatre.

Tom's first lines to open *The Glass Menagerie:*

TOM

Yes, I have tricks in my pocket. I have things up my sleeve. But I am the opposite of a stage magician. He gives you the illusion that has the appearance of truth. I give you truth in the pleasant disguise of illusion.

Tom's last lines to conclude *The Glass Menagerie:*

TOM

Perhaps I am walking along a street at night, in some strange city, before I have found companions. I pass the lighted window of a shop where perfume is sold. The window is filled with pieces of colored glass, tiny transparent bottles in delicate colors, like bits of a shattered rainbow.

Then all at once my sister touches my shoulder. I turn around and look into her eyes . . .

Oh, Laura, Laura, I tried to leave you behind me, but I am more faithful than I intended to be!

I reach for a cigarette, I cross the street, I run into the movies or a bar, I buy a drink, I speak to the nearest stranger—anything that can blow your candles out!

(LAURA bends over the candles.)

—for nowadays the world is lit by lightning! Blow out your candles, Laura—and so good-bye. . . .

(She blows the candles out.)

(The scene dissolves.)

The Rules of Diction

1. Good diction must be clear and distinctive.
2. Poetic diction is used when prose will not suffice.
3. Realistic diction is *selective* and it *represents* contemporary speech.

4. Diction brings the characters to life; diction differentiates between characters.
5. Diction controls the tempo and rhythm of the play.
6. Diction should be clean and precise.
7. Diction must communicate all aspects of the play—from thought in its most sweeping concepts down to practical details.
8. Diction suggests the mood of the play, whether it be comic or tragic.
9. The language of the play gives the audience all the necessary information to understand the action, the characters, and the play's thought.

Chapter Twenty-One

Music and Spectacle

Introduction

Music and spectacle, the last two of the six elements that Aristotle observed in drama, are dealt with in one chapter because they share significant similarities. In comparison with the preceding chapters on the first four elements, these discussions will be relatively brief. Do not conclude, however, that these elements are unimportant. On the contrary, each element contributes a great deal to the audience's perception of the stage event.

In our modern theatre, music and spectacle have evolved to become less the playwrights' concern and more the province of the production personnel who interpret the play—that is, the directors and choreographers; the designers of scenery, costumes, lighting, sound effects, and makeup; the musicians, vocal or instrumental, who provide incidental music; and the theatre technicians. As technology improves, bringing a concomitant interest in finding uses for technological bits and pieces, production personnel become "black box" experts who give to themselves yet more control over aspects of music and spectacle. Therefore, today's playwrights tend to feel an erosion of their control of music and spectacle; they may, as a result, focus more upon plot, character, and thought. But the writer should not abandon music and spectacle. They belong to drama.

Music and Spectacle in Greek Drama

We remember that in the early theatre, rich combinations of all six elements could be found in one package. Western theatre stems from the song and dance spectacles that were extremely popular in ancient Greece. Those events, created by and for general tastes, were religious exclamations of joy and discovery. The activities, which were at first loosely organized and with few aspects of formal theatre as we think of it today, involved almost all of the population regardless of wealth or stature. Today we have difficulty understanding that total involvement because we have nothing in our culture comparable to those events. Perhaps modern America's closest approximation would be the Mardi Gras celebrations, and in particular the elaborate street parades, in New Orleans before Lenten season.

From those ancient song and dance ceremonies, for and by the public, evolved the formal Greek theatre. *Those spectacles gave theatre its life and nourishment; the rituals gave theatre its form and purpose.* Theatre continued to aim at the entire population, not at a mere select few of certain social or intellectual standing. It used all possible means at its disposal to communicate fully to the large audience, and these means were later defined to be plot, character, thought, diction, music, and spectacle. Theatre began as a total theatrical experience.

Greek theatre's *purpose* was tightly interwoven with the religious rituals. The theatre sought to illuminate the mysteries surrounding humankind, to find order in the universe or to understand the lack of order disturbing an uncertain world. Theatre looked at the relationship of humans and the gods, at the meaning of life, and at the questions that could not be answered. There was a celebration of life. The theatre continued the traditions established by the ritualistic ceremonies.

Theater's *form* reflected the song and dance spectacles. Greek playwrights demanded music and spectacle. For example, the Greek playwright would carefully write a choral ode that would not only be rich in meaning but that would also create dance movements for the chorus. A meter for one verse would suggest a certain rhythm, and to that verse the chorus would dance-move to one side of the stage, or toward the audience. The next verse would control the movement back to the starting side of the stage, or away from the audience. At significant moments a leading character might express a deep emotion by singing, perhaps a bright hymn of joy or a somber lament. Others might softly echo the emotion.

Often modern-day productions of Greek plays will cast a dozen performers into the chorus and have them "group-chant" all lines. The people responsible for the resultant mess have no sensitivity to the power of the written line. The Greek playwrights never intended the chorus to speak together: The Greeks were canny showmen and would never have allowed the muddy noises that will result from having twelve people speak in unison. Instead, chorus dialogue would be divided into lines, and each line would then be assigned to a certain member of the group. The first line might be spoken by a member of the chorus with a commanding bass voice, the second line could be assigned a tenor, the third line to a gentle baritone, and the fourth to a harmonic quartet.

The following example from the Euripides *Medea* will illustrate music and spectacle in the Greek theatre. Imagine a gigantic outdoor amphitheater built into a hillside. There are several thousand people watching. The stage—the Greeks called the stage floor an "orchestra"—juts out in a large semicircle. In the middle of the stage is an altar. Behind the stage are simple structures to provide what we would call wings. From the wings enter the Chorus of Corinthian Women. Assume that there are a dozen members of this particular chorus. Six will enter from each side.

The numbers preceding each line are mine and refer to the cast member who speaks the line. Arbitrarily for the sake of this example we have cast a gentle soprano voice as number 1, a husky alto as number 2, a heavy alto as number 3, a high soprano as number 4, and so on.

CHORUS

#1:
I heard the voice,
#2:
I heard the loud lament
#1 and 2:
Of the pitiful lady from Colchis.
#4:
Oh tell me, mother, is she still Unquiet?
#3:
As I stood
By the house with the double gates
I heard the sound of weeping from within.
#1:
(Repeats last three words musically.)
#2:
(Repeats last three words musically.)
All:
I grieve for the sorrow of this family
#4:
(Repeats line musically.)
All:
Which I have come to love.

There is a distinct rhythm to these lines: "I *heard* the *voice*, I *heard* the *loud lament.*" If you read the speeches stressing those accents heavily while you walk across the floor you will note that the lines dictate to you a movement pattern.

Greek theatre emphasized other aspects of spectacle. Costumes and masks contributed satisfying ritualistic tones. Careful physical arrangements of leading performers and chorus members would stress visual compositional factors for aesthetic appeal; these were the "pictures" that are derided by some of today's theatre practitioners who are blind to the powers such visual qualities have.

In Greek theatre, plot and character would be enhanced by song and movement. These combined to communicate the play's thought. The result of the rich combination was total theatre. And just how effective can total theatre become? "Strong men fainted and women miscarried," we are told about the audience's response to one particularly effective moment in a Greek tragedy, which is grisly evidence of the strength that comes with effective use of plot, character, thought, diction, music, and spectacle.

Aristotle observed theatrical events that sought that totality, and his empirical observations of the Greek theatre led him to conclude there were six elements of drama. We must understand that his reference points are to that total theatre experience, because we might otherwise be confused about his inclusion of music and spectacle. We are not prepared to accept the thrust of Aristotle's observations, because our modern drama makes little significant use of these two elements. With awareness of the nature of Greek productions, however, we better understand the impact of music and spectacle.

Music and Spectacle in Modern Theatre

Music and spectacle today are crucial to opera, musical theatre, dance, and outdoor pageant. These art forms are dependent upon the strong contributions of music and spectacle, and often they soar to heights of achievement that drama must struggle to match. In them are essences similar to Greek theatre: Today's opera, for example, resembles Greek tragedy in production qualities and story; and our musical comedy is akin to Greek comedy.

It is appropriate here to single out the musical—the musical comedy or musical play—because it makes full use of all the six elements and therefore often has a remarkable effect upon audiences. No doubt one reason the musical comedy is so popular is that it avoids the elitism sometimes found infecting theatre; the musical tends to communicate to a large audience, and it does not seek to remain within a tightly inbred elite group who present plays to each other. The musical comedy makes rich use of spectacle and diction; characters tend to be relatively narrow and plot often is simple and predictable; thought typically is positive, uplifting; and of course music is powerful. Musicals combine all aspects of theatrical art and at their best succeed in meeting artistic challenges that the legitimate stage often misses. Given all of its strengths, then, how strange it is to encounter the self-proclaimed expert who proclaims loudly that the musical "just isn't art." One smiles to think what the Greek playwrights would have said to such an expert. Indeed, one Greek playwright did address such people: *The Clouds,* a comedy by Aristophanes, satirizes the Sophists who, jibes Aristophanes, believe argument is at its best when it ignores truth.

Music and spectacle are not limited to opera and musical comedy. Some modern playwrights such as Bertolt Brecht have brought those two elements into plays to emphasize didactic messages. In Brecht's parable, *The Good Woman of Setzuan,* for example, he calls for projections of images and captions, which is a use of spectacle. Songs comment on the action to bring the audience to an awareness of the play's thematic statements. Fragmentary scenery, another quality of spectacle, makes the audience hold a critical view of reality; fully representational scenery would not be as effective for Brecht's purposes because audiences would accept the false as true without pausing to challenge intellectually all premises.

Brecht uses music and spectacle to enhance thought. Other playwrights bring music and spectacle to the drama to ensure communications of emotion. For example, Tennessee Williams calls for a "fiddle in the wings" and other music, plus a large assortment of projections of legends and images, in *The Glass Menagerie.* Emotions grow in such atmosphere. For *A Streetcar Named Desire,* Williams wants a "blues piano" which is important throughout the play to convey location and mood, and a particular polka is a symbol for plot materials; in addition, for one scene in particular in which the men play poker, Williams specifies a "picture of Van Gogh's of a billiard-parlor at night" and describes the colors for the spectacle. Arthur Miller's instructions for *Death of a Salesman* include music that is "small and fine, telling of grass and trees and the horizon," and he calls for a set that will permit free and easy movements through time and space.

Definitions and Principles
of Music and Spectacle

- *Music is to the ear as spectacle is to the eye.*
- *All that can be heard is music.*
- *All that can be seen is spectacle.*

From the above operational premises will follow a number of principles regarding music and spectacle. Certainly, actors' voices create music. The *sound of the words* also is music. For that reason, poetic diction has added appeal. Song can be used to control inflection, emphasis, and accent.

It is helpful to think of music in two categories: incidental and integral. *Incidental music,* often described as "background music," is not an actual part of the play's action. Incidental music more often is used before the play begins, or during breaks in the action, and it is less often used during the action. The exception is found in films and television productions. Incidental music often underlines the action, and television soap operas are extraordinarily fond of using incidental music to provide a sense of climax—a "stinger"—where the playwright does not seem able to write one. But in films and television productions there are electronic mixing devices for volume control of words and music. On stage there are no such devices, and music playing while actors attempt to speak is often merely noise.

The second category of music can be called *integral* music. It is part of the dramatic flow of action. Operas and musicals—the musical comedy and the musical play—make use of integral music. Here the music has dramatic value. Here the action is paced around the music, and when the songs begin the spoken dialogue will end, preventing conflicts of sound.

Integral music, as in the song "I've Grown Accustomed to Her Face" from *My Fair Lady*, will be part of plot and character, often adding to the play's thought as well. *Incidental* music, as in the "fiddle in the wings" for *The Glass Menagerie*, does not.

If it is carefully used, *integral or incidental music can add emotional impact to the play.* Music allows a flow of emotions, a relaxation of inhibiting barriers that may delay the reception of feelings.

Music should not interfere with the forward motion of plot and character. Music should not overpower the spoken words.

Music, as Aristotle says, is pleasurable regardless of the dramatic values. Music, correctly employed, can help satisfy the hunger for the beautiful that brings audiences to theatre.

Spectacle, as noted earlier in this chapter, is often controlled by designers of scenery, costumes, and lighting. Playwrights may suggest spectacle for environmental communication: What the audience sees will tell much about the social, financial, and geographic surroundings of the play's universe. Time and place are stated by spectacle, by the settings and costumes.

The visual elements create the universe in which the play lives. Modern playwrights therefore are quite specific about matters pertaining to spectacle, in contrast to writers of the past who worked in theatres with little awareness of visual communications. In today's scripts one finds carefully written instructions concerning the stage environment, and our writers, aware of the importance of environmental factors upon character, will describe visual qualities in detail. Often there are clear influences of cinematic techniques. Our theatre tends toward strong use of production values, and in your play you will be wise to give full descriptions of all that you "see" while creating the world of the play.

Summary

Music and spectacle are two of the arrows that belong in the playwright's quiver. They cannot substitute for plot, character, and thought—the playwright must be sure those essential three elements are sufficiently strong—but they can enhance all aspects of the play, and when they are richly created they can enlarge the play to greater dimensions. Music and spectacle contribute a great deal of beauty and emotion. You must develop skills with these elements in order to use them freely.

Exercises

1.   Obtain a copy of Anton Chekhov's play *The Cherry Orchard.* Carefully read stage directions that describe the visual aspects of the stage. Within the dialogue, too, you will find implications of the way the people move and their environment. Write down all pieces of spectacle: What do they contribute to the communication of the play?

2.   Read *Desire Under the Elms* by Eugene O'Neill, and note the way spectacle creates the atmosphere for this genuine tragedy. List the qualities of spectacle that O'Neill uses: How do they contribute to the communication of the play?

3.   Read *The Importance of Being Earnest* by Oscar Wilde, and note the contributions of spectacle. List the specific visual qualities of the play. How do they contribute to the play? What in particular do they suggest that is markedly different from the qualities you noted in *Desire Under the Elms?*

4.   Note the way music is part of *The Glass Menagerie* and *A Streetcar Named Desire,* both by Tennessee Williams. Make a list of each play's music. How do these communicate the playwright's intentions?

The Playwright
in the
Writing Class

———————————————————

There are literally hundreds of writing classes available to you. Some are short summer workshops, others are available in local adult education classes, and still more are found in colleges and universities. Correspondence classes, easily available, may attract your attention. You will make your selections based upon reasons that are valid for your own needs. My recommendation, not totally unbiased because I teach college-level playwriting, is that most playwrights benefit more from college instruction than from other courses that are available. Taking a course at college is not the same thing as enrolling in a degree program; most colleges will permit you to take playwriting class without officially meeting all entrance requirements. You may wish to inquire about that possibility at the college of your choice.

A playwriting class will involve give-and-take criticism. You will read your play aloud in class, and then receive comments from the instructor and your peers. The chapter "Giving and Accepting Criticism in the Playwriting Class" is partially a tongue-in-cheek recommendation about the critical process. For you to benefit from the class, you must be determined to learn how to participate in the critical process.

Chapter Twenty-Two

Giving and Accepting Criticism in the Writing Class

Introduction

"*Criticism?* What, of *my* stuff? You gotta be kidding!"

We are not kidding. Let us understand clearly that an integral part of any good playwriting course must be criticism that is carefully designed and constructed. There is no substitute for criticism, and the playwright has to learn to give and receive intelligent and sensitive criticism if he or she is to grow with and learn the arts and crafts of playwriting. The playwright unwilling to participate in the process shouldn't be in the writing class at all.

"But . . . But . . . But! Listen to those people speak so disrespectfully of my magnificent baby. Why, that's flesh of my flesh, part of my heart, product of my genius! If they don't love my play, they are saying they hate me. Fools. I bet they'd really feel dumb if I surprised them by telling them this is Sam Beckett's play. Hey, that's it! Next time I'll sneak in a new script by Beckett and read it to 'em, then sit back and listen to them make their foolish comments about *that* play!"

"Criticism" does not mean "finding faults." In the playwriting class the word means a highly-tuned response to the student writer's work, an educated evaluation of the play, an attempt to perceive the script as would an audience at a production. Critical comments seek to identify the play's strengths, so the playwright will feel encouraged and so he or she will not lose those points during revisions. Criticism also points at the play's weaknesses, so the author will avoid such holes in the future and will, for this particular play, better target the next revisions. The goal is to help the writer improve.

All of this sounds fine in theoretical terms, but it becomes sticky in actual practice. Accepting criticism in the playwriting class is akin to being captured in the dentist's chair. No matter how much one may be told that the drilling and probing is meant kindly, there is every reason to want to escape the pains.

The playwriting class intends to help the writer. For most playwrights, that intention is clear. For them, the educational experience becomes extremely valuable. For some, however, the process is just too painful. Why are there such different responses within the same class? The answer is that the latter writers have not learned how to give and accept criticism.

If you are to benefit from a playwriting class—from any writing class or any class dealing with creativity—you will have to come to grips with the critical process. What is equally important, one must also come to an understanding of oneself and the reasons one finds criticism so difficult to accept or to give.

Understand that the playwright has justification for hypersensitive reactions to criticism. The actor, for example, has less time and self invested in a role than the author has in the script. Much of the criticism an actor receives concerns merely mechanical aspects of acting (audibility, posture, gesture, diction, and business) that are quite distant from the performer's inner being; in contrast, the playwright is criticized for a work into which he has invested his soul. The director gives less of the self than does the author. The novelist or poet should not worry about a piece failing in front of an auditorium of people responding all together. The playwright, however, is there in front of the crowd.

The playwright has no others out there on the limb. It is a solitary business, playwriting; the script succeeds or fails due to the writer alone (at least it does as a script, but in production the creative efforts of many others will be significant factors). The script in a very real sense is an extension of the inner being of its author, a giving of the self. The playwright has reason to think of the play as "flesh of my flesh, part of my heart." Often the script is the product of an extensive writing period, sometimes many years, and so the criticism strikes at the playwright's dedication not for just a short rehearsal time of the play but also for a great deal of his or her actual life. No wonder, then, that the playwright is so sensitive to criticism; no one can be surprised that the playwright is wounded more deeply than the others in the production.

One would expect that the playwright would be more at ease with others of his kind in a playwriting class. Indeed, one would expect that because the author enrolled in the writing class, that individual would not only tolerate but actually would want full critical treatment.

Unfortunately, into the playwriting class will often come the writer who refuses to open to the educational process. Because of that individual's irritable ill-will, others in the class become distracted. In a short time the entire class process becomes adversely affected by the one writer's hostility to criticism.

These playwrights who refuse to accept criticism fall into types. Below are descriptions of some of them. Of course *you* are not here, but perhaps you will recognize some of your peers.

Types of Closed-Door Writers

1. *The Negatively Deaf.* A spittin' cousin of the Positively Deaf (who nods and smiles at all suggestions that the script be trashed, saying, "Thank you, thank you kindly for loving my play"), the Negatively Deaf manages to hear only the negative but never the positive comments. "He hates everything I write," says the Negative Deaf about the class instructor. "They all hate me and therefore won't say anything nice about my writing" is the Negative Deaf's view of the class. The Negative Deaf wears selective ears. He or she would wear out except for refreshing him/herself with paranoia pills for breakfast.

2. *Who, Li'l Ol' Me?* Break out the Kleenex because this one will become a rain cloud at the faintest hint of a discouraging word. No one in class dares injure the soft little feelings.

3. *The Wall.* It used to be human. Here's a shield that hides the tender self from comments. Unfortunately, the rest of the class is unable to see the person behind all of that structure. Contact is lost except for notes sometimes tossed over the barbed wire and broken glass that lines the wall top. Probably there's a good guy in there. We'll never know.

4. *I Come From Mount Olympus.* The playwright who thinks he is a visitor from the Mountain would describe the situation in this way: "There is always a superior smile gently playing over the lips of that extraordinary human who is regrettably (and one hopes, temporarily) placed in proximity of inferiors. Poor things, they can never understand the Gods." But members of class would speak of the irritating manner, the arrogance of a person with no perceivable reason to be so proud, and the stifling pseudo-intellectual manner of making simple things into complex mysteries. The visitor from Mount Olympus smiles at each comment. It is difficult to speak through that condescending smile. Gods work in mysterious ways their wonders, and all that.

5. *The Porcupine.* Porky, a surly brute, responds by tossing barbs for every barb received, real or imaginary. He is such a grump that the class will leave him to sit in solitary discomfort atop his flawed, never to be corrected, playscript.

6. *Duh, I Hoid D'Bell, I Hoid D'Bell!* She comes out swinging, too. Any sentence begun by the critic is stopped halfway by the warrior's wild swings.

7. *Hey, Boss, It's Up to You to Get Me Motivated to Write Good Stuff!* There's not much to be said about this oh-so-good-spirited vessel just waiting to be filled. The writer abandons all responsibility and waits for someone to create magic.

8. *Bug Off, Buddy. This Here's One of Them Creative Arts and I Ain't Listening to Nobody Tell Me How to Do It!* Here's a vessel quite full, thank you—primarily full of itself. Not much can be said to this one, and certainly no one wants to suggest that there are "rules" that deserve attention, because that so obviously inhibits the flow of creative juices. You can guess what the plays will look like.

9. *(Wide-eyed and with an oh-so-meek tone) But Mother Liked My Play. And My*

Friends. Just Everyone. You feel like a cad to disagree with mother. Such a poor, sensitive little soul.

10.   *(Spoken in a hiss) You'll Get Yours!* Speak a single word against the work of this writer and revenge will be swift when you read *your* play. Muggers are more pleasant.

Every writing class has the potential to contain one or more of these closed-door personalities. Just one can affect the group so negatively that the class begins to suffer. Usually the whole group will lose cohesiveness and instead the class will become random individuals who no longer contribute support and care to each other. The truth of the "bad apple" bromide is seen. The list above is tongue-in-cheek, but only partially.

The point here is clear: *There simply is no point in enrolling in a writing class if one does not wish criticism.* If one wishes to hear nothing but limp praise, let that writer seek it elsewhere.

Rules for Criticism in Class

There are some devices to help learn how to handle criticism in the playwriting class. There is one overall secret to the process: *A positive attitude toward criticism is essential.*

We ought to repeat that concept for emphasis. No better advice can be given to those who give or receive criticism.

Some other concepts follow:

1.   *Criticism always refers to the work and never to the person.*

Comments are aimed directly at the play but not at the playwright. If fault is found, that fault lies within the script and not its author. "This play is weak" is acceptable; "You write weak plays" is never acceptable.

2.   *All comments are intended to help the author revise the script to improve it.*

Ways of revising the weak spots should be suggested: "Here are the play's strengths—*keep them*—and here are weaknesses—try to get rid of them."

3.   *Criticism must be honest.*

Some critics attempt to pull punches by saying a series of sweet nothings. This helps the playwright not at all. Positive and negative statements must be honest and true.

4.   *The playwright listens attentively but silently to criticism.*

The author must show receptivity to criticism by attentiveness; equally, the author must avoid all possible signs of negative responses by remaining silent while criticism is being given. Interruptions, explanations, and protests are outlawed while others speak.

5. *The playwright takes notes of critical comments.*

The author ought to write down the gist of every critical comment given. It is part of the way the author shows receptivity to the critic, and it is also necessary to record comments rather than trust the memory.

6. *To the degree possible, criticism does not rest upon subjectivity alone.*

"I like it" and "I don't like it" are valid responses to a play, but the author needs to know *why* the critic likes or doesn't like the script or its components. The critic needs to list a series of objective responses to help the author better perceive the subjective attitude.

7. *The critic should attempt to organize comments into a readily understood set of priorities.*

The critic ought to clearly state what comment is important and what comment is minor. They should be addressed to the play's plot, its diction, its characters, and its thought.

8. *The playwright should accept all comments when they are given. Later, after due reflection, some comments will be discarded and others saved.*

In the emotion-packed situation of hearing one's "baby" criticized, most playwrights mentally erase many of the comments. That may be understandable, but it is poor use of critical values. It is better to record all comments and study them later when less emotional involvement is present.

Not all comments will be valuable. Those studied carefully and then found wanting can be discarded. But they need to be examined first, not thrown out instantly.

9. *The critic should watch his or her tone of voice and word selection.*

The critic should be aware that the author may respond to a tone or a poorly selected word and conclude that the critic intends quite a different meaning. The critic ought to attempt to speak in a measured and friendly tone of voice, with precisely chosen words.

10. *The playwright is not to infer more than what is meant.*

The playwright needs to keep emotions firmly in check and focus upon the ideas expressed by the critic. It is all too easy to infer a meaning when nothing of the sort was intended.

11. *After all the criticism is over, the playwright can ask questions.*

The author remains silent while criticism is in progress. When it is completed, the author can ask questions to clarify points or to obtain information about new areas. Such questions can guide the critic toward concepts important to the playwright.

Writing classes encourage those in the course to evaluate the work of classmates. One must learn how to give criticism and how to receive it. Both are vital ingredients in the process of learning how to write. The writer who refuses to learn either of the two is limiting personal growth.

For students enrolled in academic classes, there is a heady freedom in the playwriting class; sometimes that freedom is also distressingly open-ended, making the class appear unstructured. For other students, the fact that the class deals with creative work seems to suggest freedom to go off following any tangent; thus, when the instructor attempts to pull the writer's attention to more profitable explorations there is resentment. The instructor may become baffled by beginning playwrights who, within a week or so, seem to have so much knowledge that they object to any suggestions or statements that would attempt to redirect the writer's freedom.

Some students may feel that the classes stress the negatives. Undoubtedly that may be true, although it may also be true that there is need to discover the problems that are characterizing the scripts. The student should remind himself, from time to time, that the instructor indeed *does* want to help the individuals in the class (if that were not true, surely the instructor would have been discovered for the fraud he or she is, and dismissed); the instructor may sometimes appear to be doing something else, but the students should assume that the reasons are valid. It is also true that in many cases the instructor of a playwriting class is also an experienced play director, and there is something about that breed that focuses upon negative aspects of what is happening in order to eliminate them, apparently often without perceiving the positive.

There is little that anyone else can do to ensure that the individual writer will participate wholeheartedly in both portions of the criticism process. The responsibility rests with the individual. The alert writer will use critique sessions to learn how to improve. Ultimately, the student writer will find that his or her ability to evaluate personal writing will be enhanced; learning to search for the strengths and weaknesses of others' scripts will help the writer examine personal writing more carefully. This circular action and reaction is highly valuable. The author who refuses to learn the method of criticism is refusing to learn how to judge her own work. The author who ignores her responsibility to self and to the class will ultimately receive little benefit from the experience; worse, such a person may well injure the overall class experience for others.

The playwriting class can be exciting and even fun. The very idea of such a class vibrates with positive shock waves: Here will be brought together a group of people overflowing with creative energies and hungry to express ideas and concepts, ranging from the farcical to the tragic, eager to learn and willing to give deeply of the self, and led by someone who has been able to make such classes successful in the past and who has helped student authors achieve their potentials. There is a magic suggested here. Here can be a group that will be the embodiment of Shaw's Life Force. With such potentials and with the scope of personal benefits that one can receive from the fulfillment of these potentials, the individuals in the class obviously have reason to try to contribute toward the overall experience.

Now That You've Finished Your Play

Chapter Twenty-Three

Production
and Publication

The Cardinal Rule: Your Play Must Be Ready

Rule number one in connection with the production and publication of your play is simple. *You must never submit your play for production or publication until you are quite certain the script is absolutely stageworthy.* Do not send your play to producers or editors unless you are convinced it is in absolutely first-class condition and cannot be improved. You must understand that you have a natural inclination to try to hurry along the process: Dreams of production have sustained you during those long hours of labor on the play and it is only natural that you are eager to see it presented to an audience. But you must not let that desire overcome your sense of perspective about the script's Quality. No one should see your play until it has been made perfect.

"*Well, maybe my play does have a couple of problems here and there, but it sure is better than most of the plays I've seen on stage.*" Who declared this to be a competition? And are you the best judge? There is something unsavory about the idea of a playwright promoting his or her work by commenting negatively about the plays of other writers. At any rate, if you admit your play does have a problem, why not exert your efforts toward solving the weaknesses instead of wasting energy worrying about other playwrights' flaws?

"*But my mother [boyfriend/wife/roommate/neighbor] likes my play a lot.*" That can be a significant opinion if your mother is a play producer. Relatives and friends, however, tend to be loyal and supportive; and while that is quite proper, it does not make their opinions objective.

"I'm going to send my play to that playwright [this agent/critic/director] and ask for suggestions. They can help me." Perhaps they can, but why should they? The blunt truth is that they have no obligation to read and comment on scripts that come to them unsolicited. Commenting takes a great deal of time and patience, something these people do not owe to strangers, and their time is very valuable. They likely will return the play to you unopened so there can be no possibility of a later lawsuit claiming that someone stole your play.

"I think it is worth the gamble. Maybe they'll like it." Maybe they will not. Is it a worthwhile gamble? Do you think they will feel positively about the next piece you send them if this submission is badly flawed?

"Can't I expect helpful comments from this publisher or that producer?" No. The top publishers and producers receive hundreds of scripts. Imagine how many hours would be expended if they attempted to comment meaningfully on each play. Bear in mind, too, that the large offices employ preliminary readers who are assigned to pass along only the very best few scripts. You need comments from experts, not preliminary readers.

You do yourself no favor by sending your play out too soon. If you do, you will build up dreams and hopes during those months you wait to hear, thereby putting yourself into a vulnerable position of being made depressed when the script is returned to you with a curt note or, worse, merely a form rejection slip. Rule number two, then, is no less dogmatic than rule one: Do not search for exceptions to rule one. You don't need the frustration.

"But aren't there publishers who won't look at a play until it has had production?" Yes.

"Or unless the play is submitted by an agent?" Not quite true, but an agent is extremely helpful.

"And agents pay little attention to writers who have not been published or produced?" Generally the agent prefers to deal with established playwrights.

"It begins to sound like a Catch-22 situation." Yes. But there are a number of avenues you should explore. You have other choices—unless, of course, you already have had professional productions or are represented by an agent. There are other ways you can find help leading to production.

Look at Home First

Instead of the full-scale New York Broadway production, think of other options you can find. Your goals are to perceive what you can do to improve your play and to achieve production. Both will greatly help you improve your writing skills. Given that, perhaps the major professional production is not as essential to begin with after all. You should investigate the possibilities of production within your locality. You may be surprised to discover that getting a production is not so difficult after all.

Five "Sizes" of Production.   There are five sizes or levels of production, ranging from simple to complex, inexpensive to costly, and private to public. Each one can help you to better perceive weaknesses and strengths of your play. Armed with that insight, you can then revise it.

For these productions, the playwright is neither performer nor director. Your job is to observe your play and audience responses. You cannot do that if you are involved in production details.

The following are the different types of productions:

1. *Informal reading of a work-in-progress.* This is often done in someone's living room; it consists of having people rehearse together once or twice before they read it aloud to invited friends and guests. A discussion follows. The reading is ideal for a play not yet in final shape, and the playwright can learn a great deal about the play's plot and characterization from observing the performers and audiences; the discussions can point up some other areas of strength and weakness.

2. *The staged reading.* One moves from a home to a more public location for this, and the performers are rehearsed more before they read the play to the audience. They will carry scripts and have minimal stage movement—often the performers are put on tall stools behind music stands holding scripts. There is no attempt to achieve production values with setting, costuming, or lighting. Nonetheless, a properly prepared stage reading can be gripping entertainment.

3. *A studio production.* This can be called a "studio" or a "lab" or a "second season" show—the three terms are relatively interchangeable—and it refers to a smaller-scaled production than a theatre can present on its formal main stage. For this production, the room will be smaller and the stage less well equipped; audience facilities will be spartan; and the production will have had little design work in setting, costumes, or lighting. But for you, the playwright, there are distinct advantages to the studio production because it places full emphasis upon script and performance. For this type of production, unlike for the first two types, actors will be well rehearsed and will have memorized lines. Audiences at studio productions are trained to the values of new plays and experimental work. A studio production offers the playwright excellent opportunities to see how the script plays in a production without having the tensions associated with the major stage; there the atmosphere is more of a "make or break" kind.

4. *A showcase production.* The showcase intends to focus attention upon one part of the whole. Think of it as a "here I am, hire me" effort: A given performer, or perhaps a director, showcases his or her talents, hoping that critics who were invited will attend and write positive reviews, and hoping that scouts, agents, or producers will also come to offer employment to the performer or director. The showcase may focus upon the script. These productions most often are found in New York. They may run two or three nights. For the playwright, a showcase production demands a well-polished script because anything less would deny the showcase's advantages.

5. *Full production.* Whether it is seen in a small town's theatre or on Broadway, the full-scale production is an extremely exciting venture. Here you will find top talents working on all aspects of your play, and a spirit of dedication and commitment prevails that is contagious. In comparison with the previous four levels of production, the full-scale effort appears to be well-financed and there may be a feeling of opulence. So much money and time is invested that tensions of course run high.

These five levels of production can be stepping stones for you. The benefits are obvious. For you and your play, improvements can be expected. And these may serve as introductions to help you attract the attention of the New York producer or agent.

Before you think of New York, however, you must understand that you have alternative theatrical organizations to consider. Let us mention good organizations worthy of your attention.

Some Theatres Away from New York

There are theatres, some well-known and respected, outside of New York City. Others, perhaps not as well known, nonetheless do quality work. Instead of aiming for a New York production, perhaps you might consider other organizations.

1. *Your own group.* Do not make the mistake of thinking you cannot form a group for the production of your play. The cost may well be little to rent a theatre for a few nights, and you may be surprised at the willingness of theatre people who volunteer their knowledge and talent to help you present an original play. You and some key advisors should not experience major difficulties in mounting, say, a staged reading, presented with a sense of style and pride. Local organizations appear to be ready-made naturals for such efforts—a senior citizens group for plays by their members, or a summer teenage workshop for a play about young people, or a college women's club for children's drama.

Even though this idea may suggest to you a type of "vanity theater" or even a movie scenario about Judy Garland and Mickey Rooney with an old barn for a show, it is worth serious consideration on your part. If it is properly approached, the new organization can make significant contributions for theatre in your area. You must remember, too, that in the past this approach has given birth to some of the world's foremost new theatre movements such as André Antoine's Théâtre Libre in France or the Provincetown Players in America. The latter was largely responsible for giving Eugene O'Neill his start, and the former presented many new playwrights of the emerging realistic-naturalistic movement.

2. *Church drama.* Theatre and religion are intricately interwoven. A theatre historian will tell you of the close ties between the two in ancient Egypt several thousand years before the birth of Christ, of the linkage of religious festivals with theatre in Greece, and of the rebirth of theatre in the Church during the medieval period. Modern playwrights have written strong plays with deeply religious qualities such as *Godspell, A Sleep of Prisoners, J.B.,* or *Jesus Christ, Superstar.* Plays with such themes often are well-set within churches, and many churches may even sponsor secular productions. You may explore the possibility of having your play presented within a local church. Usually rents or fees are quite inexpensive. Of course not all plays are suitable for a church presentation, but modern church practice is open-minded to new ideas.

3. *The community theatre.* In their beginnings, community dramatic organizations were designed to produce a type of theatre that was an alternative to Broadway's slickness and commercialism; they were prompted by a spirit of experimentalism. The "little theatre" groups started in order to present new plays. There was a desire to give patrons theatrical experiences other than those of New York.

The exciting noncommercial spirit has left most community theatres today—they now tend to present Broadway plays almost exclusively—but there yet remain some exceptional theatres dedicated to the cause of new plays, such as the Waterloo (Iowa) Community Playhouse. You certainly should consider submitting your play to community theatres in your area. Almost all of them have the personnel and the free time in their production schedule to give your play at least a staged reading, and their costs will be minimal. A full-scale production is also a possibility.

4. *Children's theatres.* Organized children's theatres exist on various levels, and if you are interested in writing for young audiences you will find producers for your work. Perhaps they may be groups under the guidance of a larger theatre or perhaps they may be groups working independently, such as the highly-respected Honolulu Theatre for Youth.

5. *The educational theatre.* College and university theatres, plus a few forward-looking high school drama groups, deserve your attention. There is a commonly-accepted belief within educational theatre leadership that colleges and universities must become more actively involved in production of new plays, and certainly you may want to talk with the theatre faculty at the nearest college or university theatre. You are not limited just to those within your own area, of course. Do not ignore the high school theatres; if you have a viable one-act play, you will find that high school "play festivals" provide a ready market.

6. *The regional theatre.* This blanket term refers to the professional theatres that exist in all parts of the country. Some are well-known for their interest in new plays. The Mark Taper Forum (in Los Angeles), The Actors' Theatre of Louisville (in Kentucky), and the Arena Stage (in Washington) are leaders in the presentation of new plays. Some of them accept freelance submissions, although a query in advance is often advisable, and most will attempt to bring the playwright to the theatre for casting, rehearsals, and production. The regional theatres have often given premieres of plays that have subsequently gone to Broadway. Regional theatres typically have excellent theatre facilities, and the personnel maintain standards no lower than those of New York.

These options indicate that you have a number of avenues to explore. Broadway, attractive though it may be, is not the only place for your play. It may not be the best place. The above list is suggestive; as you consider the possibilities, think of other theatrical opportunities.

Selected Play Producers

I refer you again to rule one. Do not send your play to any of the following professional theatres unless you are sure that it is totally stageworthy.

When you mail your play, include a SASE—self-addressed stamped envelope—for its return. Your failure to enclose the SASE may mark you as a nonprofessional. The theatre may not return your play.

I urge you to enclose, too, a self-addressed stamped postcard. Clip it to the cover of your script. On it, write a simple sentence such as, "We received your play today (date: ———) and we hope to let you know of our decision around (date: ———). Signed: ———" This will let you know your play arrived there safely.

Multiple submissions are not popular with some producers, but when one notes that there are producers who say that they do not report sooner than five to eight months, the playwright must be permitted to send copies of the script to more than one organization. Of course you must always keep copies for yourself. Scripts can be lost.

Some producers prefer a query letter before you send them your play. Because theatre policies often change, and because the list below can easily grow out of date, I suggest you write a query letter before submitting your play to the following producers.

The list below is not complete. For additional producers of new plays, ask for assistance at your city library. The reference librarian can guide you to additional listings.

Play Producers: Addresses and Details. *Academy Festival Theatre.* Box 88, Lake Forest, Illinois. 60045. Professional company. Will consider full-length plays or one-act plays on a unified theme. Reports in two to four months.

Actors' Theatre of Louisville. 316 West Main Street, Louisville, Kentucky. 40202. Artistic Director: Jon Jory. Literary Manager: Julie Crutcher. Address plays to New Play Program. Professional company. Two theatres, one a proscenium with 635 seats; the other, a thrust with 181 seats. Freelance submissions are acceptable; a query is not required before submission. Reports in three to six months. ATL presents approximately thirty new plays each season. It also sponsors a major playwriting contest that typically closes by mid-April. They generally prefer a cast to number under fifteen.

The American Repertory Theatre of Cincinnati. 2319 Clifton Avenue, Cincinnati, Ohio. 45219. Professional. Children's theatre. Cast is to be no more than four; sets and costumes should be minimal. There are two companies, one a touring company (scripts with educational thrust are welcome to take audiences into new and different experiences) and the other in residence.

The American Stage Company. P.O. Box 1560, St. Petersburg, Florida. 33731. Artistic Director: Dennis Krausnick. Address scripts to: John Berglund. A professional theatre of 175 seats in operation from October to May. Presents one original play plus staged readings each year. Freelance submissions are acceptable; a query is required before you submit your play. Reports in six to eight weeks. Maximum number of characters: six to eight.

American Stage Festival. P.O. Box 225, Milford, New Hampshire. 03055. Address scripts to Larry Carpenter, Artistic Director. Professional theatre of 480 seats presenting two to three original plays annually. Seasonal operation, summer. Freelance submissions are not acceptable; submit through agent only. Wants full-length plays with a cast size of two to eight.

Arena Stage. 6th and Maine Avenue, S.W., Washington, D.C. 20024. Artistic Director: Zelda Fichandler. Address scripts to Literary Manager (John Glore). Professional theatre; three stage areas—an 800-seat arena, a 500-seat thrust, and a 180-seat cabaret. Average one or two premieres per season. A query is required before submission of a script (include a synopsis) unless it is submitted by an agent. Reports in eight to sixteen weeks.

Barter Theatre. P.O. Box 867, Abingdon, Virginia. 24210. Allow up to eight months for report. Levels of productions range from full-production, to workshop, to staged readings. Wants the full script, not an outline.

Casa Mañana Theatre. P.O. Box 9054, Fort Worth, Texas. 76102. Professional; children's theatre; presents theatre-in-the-round children's plays and musicals. Address scripts to Bud Franks, Artistic Director. The general public season is June through August; Children's Theatre season is September through May.

Cleveland Playhouse. Box 1989, Cleveland, Ohio. 44106. Professional theatre. Wishes material between September and May; presents musicals and nonmusicals. Allow four to six weeks for report. Presents originals suited for general public.

Creede Repertory Theatre. Box 269, Creede, Colorado. 81130. Professional theatre. Interested in a wide range of plays with little restriction regarding genre or length; not interested in required nudity or plays requiring difficult technical work or large casts. Reports in three months.

Contemporary Arts Center. 900 Camp Street, New Orleans, Louisiana. 70130. Community theatre of 132 seats presenting eight shows annually and one or two originals each year. Artistic Director: Don Marshall. Address scripts to Emily Carey Cronin. Freelance submissions are acceptable; a query before submission is preferable. Cast size should not be excessively large. Playwright is brought to the theatre for rehearsals and production; playwright receives a $1000 fellowship.

The Cricket Theatre. 528 Hennepin Avenue South, Minneapolis, Minnesota. 55403. A professional theatre annually presenting six mainseason plays and five to eight originals. "The Cricket is dedicated to the living American playwright. Any style script is welcome." Freelance submissions are acceptable; reports in six months maximum. Funds available for works-in-progress presentations. Artistic Director: Lou Salerni. Address scripts to Sean Michael Dowse, Associate Artistic Director.

Dallas Theatre Center. 3636 Turtle Creek Blvd., Dallas, Texas. 75219. Maximum cast size: ten. Interested in full-length dramas and comedies.

Hampton Playhouse. Winnacunnet Road, Hampton, New Hampshire. 03842. Address scripts to Alfred Christie, Artistic Director. Professional 500-seat proscenium theatre operating from June 15 to September 3. Prefer small cast shows with one set. Freelance submissions are acceptable; a query before submission is a good idea. Reports "quickly," in one week usually.

Honolulu Theatre for Youth. Box 3257, Honolulu, Hawaii. 96734. Address scripts to John Kauffman, Artistic Director. Professional theatre operating all year; two theatre spaces, one a proscenium with 650 seats and the other a 350-seat flexible space. Scripts should run sixty to ninety minutes, have not more than ten in the cast (less is better), and not be fairytales. No technical extravaganzas. Seeks plays treating contemporary concerns of young people; myths and legends especially of Pacific and lands bordering the Pacific. "Most stuff submitted for children's productions is awful. There is a need and market for good plays," says Jane Campbell, Managing Director. Freelance submissions are acceptable; query before submission helps but is not necessary. Reports in four to ten weeks.

Lake George Dinner Theatre. P.O. Box 266, Lake George, New York. 12845. Address scripts to David P. Eastwood, producer. This is a professional theatre operating from late June to mid-October. Wants small casts, limited sets, no nudity, and minimal profanity. Freelance submissions are acceptable; query first.

Long Wharf Theatre. 222 Sargent Drive, New Haven, Connecticut. 06511. Accepts many genres; accepts full-length and one-act plays. Presents staged readings and full productions.

The Mac-Haydn Theatre, Inc. P.O. Box 204, Chatham, New York. 12037. Professional theatre-in-the-round with 348 seats; operates in summer. Musical summer stock. Interested in full-length legitimate musicals, two hours long, cast size of twenty to twenty-five. Freelance submissions are acceptable; no query required; reports in six to eight months. Address scripts to Lynne Haydn or Linda MacNish, co-producers. "We are most interested in legitimate music for trained voices, no rock or fad music. We will not consider obscenity, nudity, or bad writing."

New Playwrights' Theatre. 1742 Church Street, N.W., Washington, D.C. 20036. Artistic Director: Harry M. Bagdasian. Address scripts to Ms. Lloyd Rose. Each script submitted is carefully read by at least two members of the team of script evaluators; scripts are returned to the playwright with two critiques. Accepted scripts may receive invitation-only readings up to full-scale production. Restrictions: "Please, no more than fourteen cast members." Freelance submissions are accepted; query is preferable first. All styles are acceptable. NPT is one of the few theatres in the country exclusively producing works by new playwrights.

Old Log Theatre. Box 250, Excelsior, Minnesota. 55331. Artistic Director: Don Stolz. Old Log, a professional theatre, operates fifty-two weeks a year. It is interested in small-cast full-length plays with one set or a simple multiple set. Freelance submissions are acceptable; no query is required; reports in four weeks.

O'Neill. The *Eugene O'Neill Theatre Center.* Summer address: 305 Great Neck Road, Waterford, Connecticut. 06385. Plays accepted between September 15 and December 1 at New York address: Suite 601, 1860 Broadway, New York, New York. 10023. The summer conference gives selected playwrights professional attention. Submit a script (one only) with two self-addressed, stamped envelopes, one large enough for the return of the script and the other an ordinary business size. With the script include a short biography. Selected playwrights will have expenses paid to attend the O'Neill Conference.

The Repertory Theatre of St. Louis. 130 Edgar Road, St. Louis, Missouri. 63119. Address scripts to Wallace Chappell, Artistic Director. Professional theatre presenting three to five original plays annually in a large (750-seat to 950-seat) thrust stage and a smaller (125-seat) flexible stage. Accepts works in progress or full-length plays; freelance submissions are acceptable; reports may be in several months.

Seattle Repertory Theatre. P.O. Box B, Seattle Center, Seattle, Washington. 98109. Artistic Director: Daniel Sullivan. Address scripts to Alison Harris, Literary Manager. Professional theatre; main stage is a proscenium with 860 seats; the second theatre seats 160. Presents four new plays in the work-in-progress season each year. Freelance submissions are acceptable; a query is required before submission, consisting of the author's professional resume, ten pages of dialogue, and a plot synopsis.

Syracuse Stage. 820 East Genesee Street, Syracuse, New York. 13210. Artistic Director: Arthur Storch. Address scripts to Tom Walsh, dramaturg. Professional theatre presenting six to nine productions annually, two to three originals. Main auditorium has proscenium stage and 499 seats; second stage has

199 seats; cabaret theatre seats 125. Cast size: fifteen or less; no restrictions as to content; Biblical adaptations are discouraged. Freelance submissions are not accepted: Scripts must be recommended by actor, director, designer, or agent known to Syracuse Stage.

Theatre Americana. Box 245, Altadena, California. 91001. Community theatre; annually presents four productions, two to four originals. Address scripts to Playreading Committee. Seeks full-length plays, dramas, musicals, and comedies. No nudity or pornography, limited profanity; cast should not be too large; number of scene changes should be limited. Available is a brochure and information for playwrights.

Virginia Museum Theatre. Boulevard and Grove Avenue, Richmond, Virginia. 23221. Address scripts to Tom Markus, Artistic Director. Professional theatre; annually presents eight productions, one to three originals. Interested in full-length plays and also in musicals. Has a proscenium stage with 500 seats. Freelance submissions are acceptable; reports in three months.

Waterloo Community Playhouse. Box 433, Waterloo, Iowa. 50704. Address scripts to Charles Stilwill, Managing Director. Professional community theatre operating all year, presenting seven adult plays and seven children/youth productions, one to four originals. Main auditorium has a proscenium stage and seats 368; second theatre is flexible staging and seats 173 to 225. "We are always looking for good plays with more women than men." No nudity, minimum profanity. Freelance submissions are acceptable; query not required; reports in twelve to twenty-six weeks. "We must find a way to convince more theatres to produce new plays," according to Mr. Stilwill.

Most of the above organizations will pay royalties on various scales; most will subsidize the playwright's transportation, room, and board during rehearsals and production. A number of comparable producers can be found by the astute playwright; for further lists, see your reference librarian.

Publishing Your Play

Play publishers can be divided into two basic groups: the book publishers and the magazine publishers. Generally, the former publishes acting editions and the latter includes a play within the scope of an edition; the former is in business to publish plays and the latter receives little income from plays. The book publisher works with you on a royalty basis; any production company presenting your play must pay your publisher, who in turn shares some of the funds with you. The degree of sharing is worked out in contracts. If you receive 50 percent of royalties, and if your play is presented three times for $35.00 the first showing and for $25.00 on the following nights, your take of the royalties will be $42.50. In addition you receive a percent of income from the sale of books, usually 10 percent.

Play publishers accept freelance submissions—you do not need an agent in order to submit your play—and believe that it is best if your play has been produced one or more times before you send it to them. The production should have given you additional insight into the play and the revisions would have made it better, they believe. Note, by the way, that productions directed by the playwright are not desired.

Some publishers will send you a brochure or other materials describing the materials they seek. Before you send your play to them you can ask for that information.

As it was noted earlier regarding sending scripts to play producers, when you send your play to a publisher you must include a SASE. Also helpful is the postcard that the publisher can return to you to indicate receiving the play. Of course your play must be typed neatly. Samuel French will send you a script format if you ask.

Selected Play Publishers: Addresses and Details. *Anchorage Press, Inc.* Box 8067, New Orleans, Louisiana. 70182. Mr. Orlin Corey, Editor. Ms. Anne Gowdy, Associate Editor. Scripts should have had three or four different productions playwright's direction of the work does not count; prefers the productions be in different regions and by various levels of theatre practice. Anchorage Press has specialized in publishing plays for children for nearly half a century—one-act plays, full-length plays, musicals, and adaptations. Publishes approximately eight to ten plays a year. Payment: 50 percent of royalties, 10 percent of retail price of books sold. Reports to author between 30 and 120 days; longer period suggests serious consideration.

Baker's Play Publishing Company. 100 Chauncy Street, Boston, Massachusetts. 02111. John B. Welch, Editor. Publishes primarily for the amateur market—high schools, community theatres, and children's plays for university touring productions. Also the largest publisher of chancel drama in the world. Has placed manuscripts in regional and off-Broadway production. Publishes one-act plays, full-length plays, infrequent musicals, adaptations if suitable, and chancel drama. Payment: Royalty splits. Reports to author in three to four months. Accepts freelance submissions; prior production helpful but not essential.

Contemporary Drama Service. Meriwether Publishing, Ltd. P.O. Box 7710, Elkton Drive, Colorado Springs, Colorado. 80933. Arthur L. Zapel, Editor. Publishes approximately twenty-five to fifty one-act plays and fifteen full-length plays; directs offerings to junior high and high schools, colleges, and churches. Will not publish materials that would be unsuitable for those groups—those including extensive profanity or adult situations. Accepts freelance submissions; prior production not mandatory but preferred; reports in thirty days. Offers a free brochure describing types of materials desired. Royalty payments by arrangement.

The Dramatic Publishing Company. 4150 N. Milwaukee Avenue, Chicago, Illinois. 60641. Kit Sergel, Executive Editor; Sara Clark, Manuscript Editor. Publishes one-act plays, full-length plays, musicals, children's plays, adaptations, and chancel drama; approximately forty new titles per year. Will not accept scripts shorter than thirty minutes playing time; language unacceptable to general public is discouraged. Accepts freelance submissions; scripts need not have had prior production; reports in forty to sixty days. Payment by royalty arrangement; some scripts are purchased outright.

Dramatics Magazine. 3368 Central Parkway, Cincinnati, Ohio. 45225. Ezra Goldstein, Editor. Publishes articles regarding theatre; aimed at theatre art students and teachers; publishes one-act plays. See a copy of this magazine at your local library before you send your plays to it: this is an alert and lively publication.

Eldridge Publishing Company. Hill Avenue (P.O. Drawer 216), Franklin, Ohio. 45005. Kay Myerly, Editor/Manager. Aims at smaller high schools and church groups; publishes one-act plays, full-length plays, musicals, children's plays, adaptations, and some chancel drama. Publishes approximately three to five one-act plays and two full-length plays annually. Prefers casts of sixteen to twenty, primarily female instead of male, and uses no suggestive material. Wants good comedies. Freelance submissions acceptable; prior production not essential but it is better to have the play test-performed; reports in sixty days. Payment: Royalty contracts for well-known authors, cash for lesser-known authors.

Heuer Publishing Company. 233 Dows Building, Cedar Rapids, Iowa. 52406. J. Vincent Heuer, Editor-in-Chief; C. Emmett McMullen, Editor. Publishes for junior and senior high school markets; one-act plays, full-length plays, some musicals, no children's plays or chancel drama, seldom adaptations. Prefers noncostume plays; all plays must be suitable for school production. Accepts freelance submissions; reports in three weeks. Purchases amateur rights, cash payment.

Lillenas Publishing Co. Box 526, Kansas City, Missouri. 64141. Paul M. Miller, Editor. Aims at church productions; publishes one-act plays, musicals, children's plays, and chancel drama, not full-length plays or adaptations. Accepts freelance submissions; reports in sixty days. Payment: Negotiable. Offers a free "Contributor's Guideline" brochure.

New Plays, Incorporated. Box 273, Rowayton, Connecticut. 06853. Patricia Whitton, Editor and Publisher. Publishes plays for adults and teenagers to perform for young audiences; in-school touring productions and college theatres are the main customers. Looks for material that is original in content and/or style; tries to avoid children's theatre stereotypes such as cute dragons and premarital problems of princesses. Publishes approximately four new plays annually. Accepts freelance submissions; plays should have had prior production, preferably directed by someone other than the author. Purchase: Percentage of royalties.

Performance Publishing Co. 978 North McLean Boulevard, Elgin, Illinois. 60120. Virginia Butler, Editor. Publishes one-act plays, full-length plays, musicals, children's plays, adaptations, and chancel drama; annually publishes ten one-act plays, ten full-length plays, five children's plays, and three musicals. Sends yearly catalog to 36,000 junior high schools, high schools, and colleges; customers include all producing groups in country. Accepts freelance submissions; plays need not have had prior production—all scripts are considered, but no X-rated material is wanted. Reports in two to three months. Payment: Royalty.

Pioneer Drama Service. 2172 South Colorado Blvd., P.O. Box 22555, Denver, Colorado. 80222. Shubert Fendrich, Editor-Publisher. Anne Fendrich, Managing Editor. Scott Smolensky, Music Editor. Publishes approximately ten titles a year; aims for junior and senior high schools, community theatres, children's theatres, melodrama theatres, youth groups, and park and recreation theatres. Simplicity of production is important; customers are conservative and therefore there are strict limitations regarding subject matter and language. Accepts freelance submissions; prefers scripts to have had prior production; reports within a month. Payment: 50 percent of performance royalties, 10 percent of copy sales. Sponsors contest: write for details; contest closes March 1 annually.

Plays, The Drama Magazine for Young People. 8 Arlington Street, Boston, Massachusetts. 02116. Elizabeth Preston, Managing Editor. Publishes seventy-five to eighty plays annually. Subscribers are public schools and libraries. Material must be appropriate for young audiences—no suggestive materials, no incorrect grammar or characters with speech or physical defects. Playwrights are urged to send SASE for specification sheet before submitting a play. Accepts freelance submissions; reports within two weeks. Payment: Cash; it varies.

Samuel French, Inc. 25 West 45th Street, New York, New York. 10036-4982. William Talbot, Senior Editor. Lawrence Harbison, Editor. Publishes one-act plays, full-length plays, musicals, children's plays, and adaptations; no longer publishes chancel drama; perhaps 60 percent of yearly output are plays that have recently been produced in Manhattan professionally, and perhaps three one-act plays are from freelancers. Aims at all theatrical groups. Accepts freelance submissions; scripts need not have had prior production; reports to playwright in six weeks to eight months. Insists playwrights should use standard professional play manuscript format; playwrights should put script into two-ring or three-ring binder. Suggests playwrights send $2.00 to Lawrence Harbinson for a copy of "Guidelines" that specifies what he wants in manuscript typing format and also gives details about markets. Payment: 10 percent of book royalties, 80 percent of amateur production royalties; 90 percent of professional production royalties.

Aids for Playwrights

A number of books and organizations deserve your close attention. You may find some of these materials in your local library or bookstore. Other materials you may wish to order; prices are given for some you are not likely to find in your library:

Dramatists Sourcebook, available from Samuel French, Inc. (address above) for $8.58, including postage. Lawrence Harbison says it is "the most comprehensive source of marketing information for playwrights there is."

Writer's Market, annual hardcover publication from Writer's Digest Books, listing literally thousands of markets for all sorts of writing, with chapters regarding theatre producers and publishers, marketing scripts for TV and radio, and the like.

The Writer's Handbook, annual hardcover publication from The Writer, Inc., containing a hundred chapters of techniques and advice from world-famous writers, along with lists of thousands of markets for all sorts of writing.

Literary Market Place, annual directory that includes theatre magazines, producers, and publishers.

Grants and Awards Available to American Writers, from PEN American Center, 47 Fifth Avenue, New York, New York, 10003. A list of prizes, awards, fellowships, and grants. Order by mail: $3.00 plus 50¢ postage.

The Dramatists Guild, at 234 West 44th Street, New York, New York, 10036, publishes a *Quarterly* and a *Newsletter* with vital information for playwrights.

Information for Playwrights, from Publications Department, Theatre Communications Group, 355 Lexington Avenue, New York, New York, 10017, for $4.00. An important organization, TCG intends to help playwrights discover markets for their scripts; the TCG newsletter for playwrights contains information regarding contests, meetings, and producers.

A Writer's Guide to Copyright, one of several available books discussing author's rights. The new regulations are defined. This publication is from Poets and Writers, Inc., 201 West 54th Street, New York, New York, 10019. It costs $4.95. When you write for it, ask them to send you information on their other services.

The Playwright and Copyright

The copyright is akin to a patent on an invention: Its goal is to protect the creator of a new work.

Must all works have a copyright? No.

Won't my play be stolen if it doesn't have a copyright? There is a possibility, I suppose, but it happens so seldom that the danger is invented more than real. I have difficulty accepting the premise that a producer or publisher intends to "steal" plays. What happens, however, is that some small theatre groups will present plays without paying royalties; whether or not your play is covered by a copyright, that may happen, and your recourse is the same with or without a copyright.

What happens if my play is published but not covered by a copyright? That makes a difficult situation; technically, your play will be in the "public domain"—anyone can use it without asking you for permission—if it is published without being protected by the copyright. That might happen with the publication in a so-called little literary magazine that is not copyrighted, but most publications have automatic copyright protection for all contents.

How do I copyright my play? Obtain form "PA" from the United States Copyright Office, by writing them at Library of Congress, Washington, D.C., 20559, or telephoning (202) 287-9100 and leaving your name and address on the recording device. Class PA includes published and unpublished "performing arts" materials. You fill out the simple form and return it with a copy of the play and a $10.00 check or money order. If you wish additional information you can write to Information and Publications Section of the office above, or telephone (202) 287-8700.

Should I copyright my play? If you have finished revising it and are preparing to make a number of copies to send to producers and the like, yes. Once you have done so, you inform readers of the copyright details by putting a notice on the cover. The copyright office information sheet tells you how to do that.

Chapter Twenty-Four

Your Play Is Produced!

Introduction: Your Play is Selected

It is the best of all worlds: Your play has been selected for production! Dates are set, auditions have been announced, a rehearsal schedule exists, and production personnel meet to talk about your play on stage. The director and all those other strangers hold your "baby," and as you listen to their discussions about interpretation you grow vaguely disturbed. You hope that they understand the tender infant's needs, but these people find aspects of the script to support dramatic concepts that you aren't sure you wrote. The best of all worlds begins to have dark corners. You discover with a shock that these strangers seem to think they own your offspring.

Is the playwright excess baggage when the play goes into production? What is the author's role? What does the playwright owe the director and performers, and what is their responsibility to his play? Should the playwright be present for auditions and rehearsals? Who is in charge of what? Does the playwright discuss characterization with the cast? Do you revise the play during rehearsals? What revisions are necessary?

Professional or Amateur?

If this production is to be a professional one, all questions will be answered by your agent, by various guilds, by traditions and understandings, and by contracts. The professionals you contact most often—the producers and the directors—are veterans with experience in handling original plays and the anxieties of the playwright. If, on the other hand, this will be an amateur production, there will be no contract. There are few original plays presented in the amateur theatre, which may mean that you will be working with people who have no knowledge of the needs of the playwright. The lack of experience can create trying moments.

The following comments intend to help the playwright establish amiable working relationships with producers and directors. The goal is to be sure that the new script receives the best possible production and that the process is exciting and enjoyable. The comments, addressed primarily to the amateur theatre, should smooth the ruffled feathers that are a customary part of the new play experience.

Who's in Charge Here?

More confusion, and resultant ill-will, stems from a lack of understanding of roles than from any other single aspect of producing an original play. The issue can be made complex, with many confusing subdivisions that are wasteful of collective time and creative energy, or it can be solved with a simple guiding principle applicable for all cases:

The playwright is in charge of all matters pertaining to the script, and the director is in charge of all aspects of production.

No one makes a change in the script except the playwright. Directors and performers can became casual in their treatment of the script, and offhand changes may have far-reaching effects, all to the playwright's anguish.

The director is solely responsible for all aspects of production. No matter how strongly the writer believes he or she has a better sense of the play's goals than anyone else, only the director can give instructions or comments to casts, designers, or crews.

Do these two guidelines prohibit either party from making comments and suggestions? No. If the director finds problems within the script, the playwright should be told—tactfully. If the playwright hopes for different qualities in the production, the director should be told—tactfully, and at the right moment.

Establish Communication Lines Early

If both the director and playwright think of the production period as a marriage, with each accepting a 75 percent responsibility for maintaining good communications, the working relationship has a good chance of being strongly positive. Before the play goes into rehearsals, the director and playwright should meet for nonpressured discussions away from the harried atmosphere of the theatre. They need to free-wheel in these talks, each letting the other know the inner workings of his or her personality. Their goal is to establish working communications early, when there is no pressure, so they can more easily talk when the tensions mount.

Auditions

Should the playwright attend auditions? Certainly.

Should the playwright tell the director who to cast in what role? Never. The playwright should understand that the director is better trained to recognize performance capabilities; you may see some surface aspects, but you are not the best judge of acting talent.

Should the playwright give opinions if the director asks? Of course.

Do you have the right to veto a given performer? Only if you and the director have previously discussed this specific issue and come to a common agreement. Veto powers are quite strong and you ought not use them casually. If you believe that a performer is totally wrong, at the proper time tell the director you have an opinion you'd like to express before the play is cast. Talk in a private corner and explain your reasons.

Physical qualities. Often the playwright has a vision of how the character looks. "She is red-headed, the cute-as-a-bug's-ear-sort, with a radiant smile." But the director is thinking of a rather stocky blonde whose smile is at best of a low wattage. There is a red-head at the audition, but you can tell that the director does not intend to cast her. What do you do? Shrug it off: Acting ability is more important than physical appearance. Trust the director's evaluation. You will always have a twinge of sorrow, but imagine how badly you could feel with an inept performer who only looks right.

If someone auditioning asks questions, should you reply? No. Let the performer get all information from the director. You do not want to run the risk of adversely affecting that performer's auditions.

Casting. It is a complex process. If the director asks your opinion, give your best response. Express your opinions, but let the directorial staff make decisions.

The Playwright at Rehearsals

Should the playwright revise the script during rehearsals? Yes, emphatically! The idea of having the playwright present during the production period is so that the author will be able to revise the play in order to improve its stageworthiness. You will need to attend rehearsals frequently to see what may need revision. Most plays need a great deal of reworking, and the playwright can best see the weaknesses by attending rehearsals.

While at rehearsals, should the playwright discuss characterization with individual members of the cast? Never discuss characterization behind the director's back: It is poor form or worse to draw a performer aside and suggest how to play the character. That will confuse the performer, and when those suggestions begin to take effect during rehearsals the director will not understand their source. Talking to cast members without the director's knowledge is a challenge of directorial authority. Don't do it, and don't do even innocent activities that might be misunderstood in the rumor mills. You ought to tell the director, before the play gets into production, that you will not talk to the performers unless the director specially requests you address particular topics.

How many revisions will the playwright make? As many as are needed to obtain a Quality script.

When does the playwright begin taking notes for revisions? At the first read-through.

How often are the revisions given the cast? The playwright and director will work out a schedule. The playwright should not delay giving changes that affect characterization.

When does the playwright stop giving revisions to the cast? The director and playwright will have decided upon certain cut-off dates. You must bear in mind that the cast has to have time to settle in with the final version. If they are dealing with a full-length play and a six-week rehearsal schedule, perhaps director and playwright will draft a schedule that says no revisions in Act One will be permitted after week two, no revisions in Act Two will be accepted after week three, and no revisions for Act Three after the beginning of week four. An inexperienced cast, or a play that has special technical demands, could need more rehearsal time without changes.

Revisions at Rehearsals: Priorities and Techniques

The operational premise of revisions is that the play can be improved. The author is free to make both major and minor changes, but the author also is free to avoid making changes regardless of the desires of the director.

Areas to Consider for Revisions

Listed below are a number of subjects that the playwright should consider when beginning to examine the script during rehearsals. To the degree possible when dealing with generalities, the subjects are listed in order by priority. In all cases, the playwright should attend rehearsals in order to search for weak spots that need corrective revision.

1. Clarity of Thought.

Questions.
Is the play *clear?* Does it all add up to make sense? Is the play all part of a complete unit?

Does the play's thought surface adequately? Is thought implied by the totality of the action?

Is the play's subject set forth? Does the play's theme follow the subject? Should the subject be made clear earlier? Do all actions add up to the subject and theme?

Does the playwright fall into the trap of didactic writing to express thought? Look toward the ending portions of the play in particular: Does the author's message leap forward here? If so, can this direct statement be eliminated without damaging the communication of thought? If not, does that mean the play's action does not adequately project the play's thought?

Possible techniques. How does the playwright discover if the play's thought is clear? Obviously, the opinions of others can be valuable: After all, the playwright already knows what the play "means" and can see clarity with ease. Others, less familiar with the author's specific intent in this play, may see only cobwebs.

Ask for advice from a trusted mentor or critic: "Come to my rehearsals, please, and afterwards tell me what you perceive as the underlying intellectual cohesive quality of my play." You can ask careful questions to help find out what the play communicated: Ask for definitions of the play's subject and theme. Do not coach the answers by the way you phrase the question or by facial reactions to indicate if the answers are "right" or "wrong."

Your goal is for the *script* to communicate the whole. Never should the author "explain what it means." Playwrights must resist the temptation to lecture on the play's thought: The play itself must communicate fully, with no aid from the author.

If the play's basic thought is not communicating, the playwright will go through the entire play with a colored pencil and put small checks by every action and reaction or speech that carries some of the overall meaning of the play. Then at rehearsal the writer will listen to those areas in particular to see if they are being properly stressed. If they are not, a revision may be necessary to bring out the area more strongly.

The writer especially will look to see if the protagonist's goal is clear and if the protagonist's plan is communicated. Also the writer will look at the point of attack: Is it clear? Does it help indicate the basic thrust of the play? Finally, the author looks at the play's foreshadowing: Does this help pull attention to the theme?

2. Conflict.

Drama depends upon conflict. Drama is the art of the showdown. It is the clash of wills, sparking actions and reactions. A play with no conflict is a play with no dramatic tensions, full of words but somehow empty of action. Conflict must be sufficiently elaborated for the play, and it must be adequately sustained.

Questions.

Does the play contain genuine conflict? Or do the areas you intend for conflict instead become mere bickering when the performers go through the action? Bickering, debates, minor disagreements: these are not the ingredients of conflict. Are your conflicts adequate?

Do the conflicts sustain? Or are they defused? Do the characters begin confrontations only to have those conflicts weakened by the exit of one or the other? Do the characters too easily pull out of the conflicts, in effect giving up? Do the areas of conflict last long enough for them to become significant factors in the play?

Does the play seem to be all one tempo, one volume level? Don't blame the performers and director: They more than likely are responding to the stimuli presented by the script. The playwright must engineer the "mountains and valleys" into the script, not expect the director to force the cast to create them. Conflict and complications will change these important production levels.

Do the characters tend to remain unchanged during the course of the play? Possibly the problem is that they do not become involved in conflicts that would stimulate them into different attitudes and emotional ranges.

Possible techniques.   During rehearsals the playwright should listen carefully to the specific scenes or beats intended to present the basic conflict. Perhaps the writer will prepare before rehearsals by going through the script and checking the scenes that seem awkward. If those scenes are flat in rehearsals, the writer must decide if the fault lies in script or production; if it is in the former, the writer should be sure that a revision will contain the necessary dynamite. If, however, the writer is quite convinced that the script is not being played to its potential, a quiet talk with the director is necessary.

The writer might also check to be sure the play's point of attack is early enough and strongly presented. Usually a late or weak point of attack will prevent conflict from growing in production.

3. Characterization.

Questions.

Do the characters demand attention, or are they too colorless? Are they human? Are the performers finding the characters unique and unusual, perhaps even eccentric, or are the performers all playing the characters as if there is but one character?

Are the characters motivated for their actions and inactions? Do the performers seem just to jump from one stance to another without reason? Do the performers show that they find reason for the character's behaviors and emotions? Are the performers making those reasons adequately clear?

Does the play need to make the audience like one or more of the characters? If so, does the play succeed? Do the performers seem to find in their characters those positive attributes of personality that you intended?

Watch the actors' movements when they are not being blocked by the director: Do they seem to sit or stand idly while reading lines? If so, perhaps they are indicating a quality of the way the character has been written. On the other hand, if the actors instinctively move toward each other, or circle warily, or retreat, then the playwright can assume the script is prompting them to emotions.

Does the play seek a protagnoist-antagonist structure? If so, does it show? Do the performers react as protagonists or antagonists? Do the protagonist's goals seem clear? Does the protagonist's plan seem emphasized? Are there sparks during protagonist-antagonist conflicts?

Possible techniques. During the rehearsal period the performers will grow to know and understand the characters with a depth that will amaze the playwright. Some performers will know the character better than the author, and will be able to speak feelingly about the character's background and memories even though the playwright did not build those qualities into the character. For the writer there can be no better source of information about the characters than the performers. They can answer questions directly; they will indirectly communicate even more to the playwright who is sensitive enough to observe.

Often directors ask performers to describe characters with metaphors. This character, the performer might say, is like a bear prowling for dinner. Or he might be like a gentle morning breeze off the ocean—or a rough sea. Or he might be like a Beethoven finale. The playwright who is present during these discussions will gather quick insight into the character.

Directors also ask performers to describe how the characters feel during the course of the play, how they feel toward others, how they change, and what motivates those changes. Again, the playwright should be present, taking notes.

The playwright should work with performers and director to establish strong characterizations. When requested to change lines or actions in order to enhance characterization, the writer should be cooperative if the change helps the overall script.

A trusted mentor or critic can also help the playwright. When such people come to rehearsals, the playwright can ask questions that speak to specific problems. "Did you like the way the character in the first scene shouted at the wind?" "Did you believe he actually was going to slap her?" "Do you like the protagonist?" The most significant question is, "Do you believe the character and do you *care* about him?" Objective responses from a sensitive critic will help the writer overcome subjective evaluation of characters.

A word of warning is appropriate here, however. The insensitive critic will only confuse the writer. What is worse, the ignorant critic will attempt to hide his lack of knowledge beneath a smoke screen of terminology. I have seen a sharp young playwright badly misled by an insensitive and ignorant critic—a college professor of theatre whose position suggests at least some fundamental knowledge—and I doubt that the writer has ever regained clarity of expression since that event. The playwright must not allow the play to be touched by those sorts of hands.

4. Emotions.
Effective drama is communicated with *emotions*.

During rehearsals the playwright should carefully observe the whole of the play. Do the performers seem to find emotions to play? Does the play create emotional responses in the characters? Can the people in the rehearsal hall recognize the emotions?

Revisions during rehearsals can enhance emotional attitudes and reactions, and the playwright is wise to find ways of emphasizing the rich, full range of emotions. If the performers appear to be having difficulty finding playable emotions, the playwright should examine the script to see if emotions are both large enough and adequately sustained to carry the drama.

5. The Plot.
Rehearsals provide the playwright with a somewhat restricted view of the play's plot. In early rehearsals, the director and the performers will not yet have found how to stress plot elements—they will likely be working harder on characterization—and therefore the author has difficulty judging the play's structure. Usually, the plot's impact will increase while performers are beginning to polish for production. Unfortunately, while the playwright can then judge plot more easily, there may not be time for revisions.

The following list includes areas of plot that the author should observe during rehearsals. Even though the director and the performers may ignore plot details, the astute playwright should attend rehearsals prepared to look just at the following qualities. The careful observer will be able to judge effects, even though rehearsals do not focus upon plot.

a. Exposition.   Exposition all too easily can become dull and talky. The play tends to drag during prolonged exposition, and the more exposition there is, the sharper become the tempo problems. To take corrective action, the playwright who finds exposition to be too strong should consider:

1. revisions to imply, rather than state directly, the background information;
2. revisions to eliminate as many phrases and sentences from expositional passages as possible;
3. recasting of sentences so exposition will appear in the middle, rather than standing alone;
4. placing of expositional passages to appear later in the play.

b. Foreshadowing. Foreshadowing can increase suspense and thereby build audience interest. If it is done with a heavy hand, however, it can make the play appear to be melodramatic. In these cases the playwright may wish to diminish the thrust of the foreshadowing units. Often it is simply a matter of using less powerful words or recasting the sentence so that the foreshadowing does not jump out.

Removal of foreshadowing should be the last resort. Foreshadowing has some intrinsic values that warrants its inclusion in plays, but I suspect it is even more significant because of its influence upon the playwright. It seems that the more foreshadowing, the more the playwright adds complications and reversals that make a stronger plot, almost as if to justify the foreshadowing. Eliminating the warning notes, then, would seem less advisable.

c. Point of Attack. This crucial part of the plot must be sharp and clear. It is, after all, the moment that shapes all that follows. In rehearsals the performers may not be conscious of the point of attack, and too often directors ignore the moment, which means that the playwright will have difficulty judging if it is script or performance that clouds the plot's first unit.

If the script is to be revised to increase impact of the point of attack, the following techniques can be considered:

1. Delete as much as possible immediately before and after the point of attack so it can stand higher.
2. Build meaningful pauses before and after the point of attack.
3. Increase the emotion in the lines that contain the point of attack.
4. Increase the reactions of the characters to the point of attack.
5. Aim foreshadowing at the point of attack.

d. Complications. These twists and turns are the heartbeat of the play's action. A complication not only changes the direction of the play—which creates action—but it also stimulates characters to respond into greater dimensions. If the play seems to grow talky, most likely the problem will be a lack of complications. Certainly a play that becomes static is one with too few complications.

If complications appear to be short-lived, the fault most likely rests with the script that does not sustain the moment. If complications appear too large, almost certainly the director is letting those moments be overplayed.

e. Climax. The climax is the highest moment of all the play. The playwright cannot judge from ordinary stop-and-go rehearsals if the climax is appropriately sized. Only a nonstop continuity rehearsal will show the climax in relation to the rest of the action, and unfortunately many directors hold that particular rehearsal late in the overall schedule and the author is not able to make substantial revisions. A request to the director for a nonstop run-through of the play early in rehearsals certainly is in order.

6. Entrances and Exits.

Do major characters seem to ooze on and off the stage? Do they enter with little impact, creating merely small change in the ongoing action? Do they exit casually with no special reason? Are entrances and exits ignored by others on the stage?

These suggest a low-key play, perhaps a dull one. The playwright can observe entrances and exits during rehearsals. If these moments fail to contribute a sense of purpose and motion, the author is well-advised to rethink the moments. Often a few careful changes will spark a new dimension both to character and to scene. Minor characters can drift in and out, but major people should enter and exit with vitality and fire.

7. "Words, Words, Words."

Note the verb contemporary audiences use to describe attending a play: They will "go *see* a play." Seldom will people "go to *hear* a play." The distinction is important. Twentieth-century audiences are less enraptured by a playwright's verbal skill than were audiences several centuries ago. We properly think of Shakespeare's audiences as assemblages of *ears*—they would go "hear" a play— but in this era of motion pictures and television images the concern is for the visual and less on the aural. Hamlet, asked what he is reading, could reply, "Words, words, words." Willie Commonman today silently holds up the magazine by way of answer.

The playwright should have accomplished all small changes in wording before rehearsals begin. If the small changes are necessary, they should be taken care of quite early in the rehearsal process. The little changes tend to seem to be nit-picking to directors and actors, and if the author thus communicates attention to such minor elements they may well respond by suggesting a host of other comparable changes. The playwright does not want that.

More significant cuts and changes can be made later in rehearsals. Can the performers communicate, with a facial expression or a shrug, the essence of a two-dozen-word sentence? If so, cut the sentence and insert a simple stage direction. Can the actor nod to express agreement as effectively as saying, "Yes, indeed, I agree with you?" If so, cut. Can a touch express concern and sympathy where the words tend to get awkward and heavy? Cut. Does the play have passages that will easily be identified as "undoubtedly greatly loved by the playwright"? *Cut!* Does it have speeches that come from the playwright, not the character? Does it also have long rambling passages, musings, or idle contemplations? Cut, cut, cut!

A few words too many can weaken a scene; a long speech can ruin a moment; a burdensome passage that the author just could not bear to eliminate will press heavily upon an act. No play will collapse simply because it has too many words, but the burden is a heavy one that creates cracks and weakens the whole.

The play's words should consist of active verbs, not passive ones. The references should be concrete, not abstract. Proper nouns instead of pronouns usually are less confusing. The words must fall easily from the actor's mouth, not twist the tongue.

The playwright should use the rehearsal process to make revisions that will improve the play. By working quietly and never distracting the performers and director, the writer will be able to change the play in both minor and major areas. Even after production, the wise playwright will judge audience response and revise yet again, thinking of the *next* production of the script.

The writer should think of rehearsals as a laboratory in which experiments are being conducted. Often the director and performers will be trying a number of different approaches to discover how to present the play, and the writer should not make the mistake of concluding that these experiments are intended to be staged in the production. The writer, too, should experiment during rehearsals to find the best way for the play to come to life.

Epilogue

The Playwright's Medium:
The Mind of the Audience

A "how to" book is permitted one last piece of advice: I hope you will find writing plays enjoyable and I wish you all good fortune. May the process be personally enriching and the product publicly acclaimed. Let this be a guide:

> *The playwright's medium is the mind of the*
> *individual members of the audience.*
> *Your goal is to evoke images.*
> *The best tool possible is not one that you own*
> *but instead one that is waiting there, in the mind of that*
> *person in the audience:* the imagination. *Aim there.*

Index